Dear Tom

Dear Tom

L E T T E R S   F R O M   H O M E

TOM COURTENAY

Doubleday

LONDON · NEW YORK · TORONTO · SYDNEY · AUCKLAND

TRANSWORLD PUBLISHERS
61–63 Uxbridge Road, London W5 5SA
a division of The Random House Group Ltd

RANDOM HOUSE AUSTRALIA (PTY) LTD
20 Alfred Street, Milsons Point, Sydney,
New South Wales 2061, Australia

RANDOM HOUSE NEW ZEALAND
18 Poland Road, Glenfield, Auckland 10, New Zealand

RANDOM HOUSE SOUTH AFRICA (PTY) LTD
Endulini, 5a Jubilee Road, Parktown 2193, South Africa

Published 2000 by Doubleday
a division of Transworld Publishers

Extract from 'Pistol Packin' Mama' words and music by Al Dexter © 1943 Vogue Music
Corp/Edwin H. Morris & Co. Inc., USA, Warner/Chappell Music Ltd, London WC2H 0EA for
the world (excluding USA/Canada). Lyrics reproduced by permission of IMP Ltd. Extract from
'The Old Vicarage, Granchester' by Rupert Brooke, *The Poetical Works*, ed. Geoffrey Keynes,
Faber & Faber, 1946. Extracts from *Billy Liar* by Keith Waterhouse, published by Michael
Joseph reproduced by permission. Extract from *Shut Up and Sing* by Caryl Brahms and Ned
Sherrin reproduced by kind permission of Ned Sherrin.

A catalogue record for this book is available from the British Library
ISBN 0385 60095 X

Typeset in 11½/15pt Granjon by Falcon Oast Graphic Art

Printed in Great Britain
by Clays Ltd, Bungay, Suffolk

1 3 5 7 9 10 8 6 4 2

For Mam, Dad
and Ann

CONTENTS

ACKNOWLEDGEMENTS

Jane Bradish-Ellames, whom I describe as 'my literary agent, I suppose', got the ball rolling. She was never in any doubt that Mother's letters could be shaped into a book and kept encouraging me to write. She also said that I would benefit from the editorial skills of James Rogers, and she was right. Then, quite by chance, I met Ursula Mackenzie, who became 'my publisher, I suppose', at a party and got her interested in Mother's story. When Jane assured me I could not possibly have found a better guardian angel for my project she was even more right. Ursula lavished a huge amount of feeling, affection and know-how on Mother and me and I shall always be grateful to her. She also made sure that my copy editor would be Katrina Whone, who has been helpful beyond the call of duty.

My friend Polly James' delight in Mother's letters was inspiring to me. Isabel, my wife, was very forbearing and supportive and made her contribution, too. My sister Ann told me lots of details I had either forgotten or not realized. She stayed in Hull with Mother and Dad after I had flown the nest and her contribution to these recollections has been immense.

PREFACE

*'Its just something that makes a moment stay and
you don't forget that time that's all.'*
Annie Eliza Courtenay, on her letter-writing

When I was a student in London, between 1955 and 1960, my mother wrote to me every week from our home near the Fish Dock in Hull. The first three of those years I spent at University College London, reading English. I really wanted to be a student at the Royal Academy of Dramatic Art just a few hundred yards further along Gower Street, and that's where I spent the last two of my five years as a student.

During my final year at UCL, I started to keep Mother's letters. After her death the cardboard box containing them became my most treasured possession. I have always wanted to publish these letters. That is something she would have loved, though she wouldn't have thought it possible. My letters to her no longer exist, but I was a reluctant correspondent in my youth, so we are not missing much.

The best way I can help Mother, who is the *raison d'être* of this book, is to describe our world, hers and mine, up until I went to London, and then to punctuate her letters with some account of what was happening to me while she was writing them. I will introduce the people who inhabit the letters: my sister Ann, Grandma Quest, Mother and Dad's sisters and brothers and in-laws. There were plenty who used to pop into our little house in Harrow Street.

Dad, after whom I was named Tom, used to send me the green

Saturday version of the *Hull Daily Mail*, the *Sports Mail* as it was known, and also wrote me the occasional letter. He loved Mother more than he loved himself, and this book is intended as a tribute to him, too.

VISIT
April 1997

Uncle Pat and Aunt Dorrie were living in a small, new block of flats in a pleasant close off Hessle Square. I announced myself on the intercom and walked up the stairs to the first floor. Aunt Dorrie met me at the front door and showed me into their tidy little living room. Uncle Pat didn't get up when he saw me. He couldn't. He could scarcely get his breath. His luxuriant silver hair, of which he had always been so proud, was still neatly combed, but his teeth kept slipping down as he spoke, and the top of his underpants was showing above the waistband of his trousers. He had always seemed so strong and vigorous – more so than Dad, his brother. But not now.

The last time I had seen him, about three years before, he had been much more like the Uncle Pat of my childhood. Always a passionate socialist, he had had a novel idea: 'Why can't some of the Queen's money be given out to young couples who've just got married? She wouldn't miss it and it would help them get started. I've had my life. Your Aunt Dorrie and me have got all we need. But for newly marrieds these days it's very difficult.' I hadn't liked to point out that it might be a tricky scheme to manage fairly. Who would do the sharing out? And to whom? It had seemed to him to be a more equitable way of allocating resources, and he hadn't wanted anything for himself.

Weak as he now was, he seemed excited that I had come to see him. 'You've made my day, Tom. You've made my day.' My presence took him back to the days when Mam and Dad were still alive, and he wanted to say far more than his lungs would let him. He reminded me how poor he had been before the war when they were first married.

'We're like kings and queens now,' said Aunt Dorrie. Uncle Pat recalled the two weeks during his working life when he had made really good money. Post-war. 'The years after the war were the best time for the working man.' At the end of his first big week he had returned home laden with presents for Dorrie: dresses, chocolates, and 'some novels'. He didn't say what the novels were. 'I told him I didn't read novels,' said Aunt Dorrie. Anyway, he had got them for her. His second big week was after he had retired. A pal had got him a week's work with a lot of overtime, painting a ship in Hessle dockyard. Ninety-seven pounds, he had earned. He still couldn't believe it.

'Reach me wallet off sideboard, will you, please, Dorrie?' She did so, and he got out of it an old clipping from the *Hull Daily Mail*. It was a photograph of a huge warehouse he and Dad had once worked on. They had painted the company's name on the side of it, in large letters, very high up. Uncle Pat had always been proud of his reputation as a bit of a daredevil. 'Nobody had more accidents than I did.' And he laughed.

'One weekend he took me to see where he was working,' said Aunt Dorrie. 'These two great tall buildings with just a plank of wood between them, and he told me he used to run over it. It was really frightening. I told him I didn't want to see anything like that again.'

Mostly, though, he had worked on the Fish Dock with Dad. 'I know I was supposed to be the strongest, but your father could climb anything I could.'

Like Dad, Uncle Pat had been a chipper and painter. They got the trawlers ready for sea, chipping down to the steel plates and then repainting them. The climbing came in when they had to paint the masts and the funnels. 'Your father and me were always together. We worked together. We drank together. When he died part of me died with him.'

'Do you remember when we both went to see Dad in hospital, Uncle Pat, and you told me what a tough little bugger he had been when he was a kid?'

'Oh yes, nobody ever got the better of him. He'd never back down.'

I remember being surprised when I heard that. I had never known it. I couldn't help feeling proud to hear that Dad was brave, and it helped me to understand why he had been so hard on me when I wasn't.

When I was six or seven, after we had moved to the Hessle Road end of Harrow Street, I managed to worm my way into the Hessle Road end gang. There had been some rough lads at the Fish Dock end but I had survived them, and it didn't take me long to find my place at the Hessle Road end. The leader was called Johnnie Ellerington. His younger brother Ronnie, who was my age, came next in the pecking order. Then me. Then their cousin Colin Ellerington, then Harry Graves. The order was loosely based on ability in street games: football, cricket and rugby touch. Rugby was played with rolled-up newspaper tied with string; football and cricket with whatever small ball we could lay our hands on. In fact I thought myself a superior player to Ronnie E., though I knew better than to say so. His game was aggressive but I thought it lacked my vision. Last in the pecking order was little Gordon E., though perhaps it would be fairer to think of him as *hors de* pecking order because he had a hump on his back and it was said he would never get any taller. When I first saw him he'd just come out of hospital. His entire upper body, what there was of it, was encased in plaster. I liked little Gordon. He bore his infirmity with patience and good humour. And I felt safe with him.

Having no doubt about my all-round superiority over Colin E., I wasn't afraid to let it be known: 'You don't know how to play football,' I announced, which was unwise of me. His cousins Johnnie, Ronnie and even little Gordon egged him on to dispute the matter. 'He's a big 'ead, Col. You can tek care of 'im.' I didn't like being surrounded by a gang of lads one of whom was being encouraged to punch me. I retreated, weeping.

'What the hell's up with you?' asked Dad when I got in. I tried to explain. His scorn was boundless. 'You soft little sod.'

Having accepted a place below Colin E., at least in his eyes, I had no doubts regarding my superiority in general athleticism over Harry

Graves. Nor should I have had. He was hopeless. When I said so, however, there was no-one to back me up. I was forever telling them I wanted to do a lot better in life than work on Fish Dock, and their nickname for me was 'professor'. Harry was encouraged to teach me a lesson, and once more I was no match for naked aggression. 'Oh, 'ell, I'm crying. Me Dad'll play 'ell with me. 'e can't stand it when I cry.' This heartfelt admission turned the tide in my favour, and the lads were suddenly on my side. They had fathers too. So together we looked for a suitable puddle of rain and I did my best to wash away the offending tearstains. I don't think the rainwater can have mixed unnoticed with the day's grime.

'Does it look as though I've been crying?' 'Nah,' they assured me. Sympathetic but not accurate.

Once home, for a short while all seemed well. I thought I'd got away with it. Then his gaze settled on my face. That awful, stern look. And the strange word he used that I don't know how to spell. 'Have you been ruerring?' I hated that word. I've never heard it from anyone else. Was it to do with 'rue'? I can't find it in *Chambers* under any spelling. The stem of the word sounds like the part of Germany we used to bomb during the war. The Ruhr. When he said it, it seemed to imply a particularly spineless form of crying, and distressed me far more than the lads in Harrow Street ever could. 'Have you been ruerring?' Horrible. Mother was very comforting when she put me to bed, sniffing, and I remember wondering how it could be that one of my parents was so loving when the other was so hard on me.

But, then, he wanted me to be able to cope with life. Although he longed for me to be educated and not to have to work on Fish Dock, there was no guarantee then that I wouldn't work there, and if I did I would be no use to myself if I were a cissy.

I was thinking of all this while Uncle Pat had his thoughts, too. Then he looked sadly into my eyes for several seconds and said quietly, 'You were his god, you know, Tom.'

My first memory of Dad: I'm sitting on the toe of his boot when he has just got home from work. He's sitting with his legs crossed, so we can ride on the topmost boot, which he lolls up and down. He's laughing. Little Ann and I take turns. He has to hold Ann's hands to keep her on board, but I can ride like a jockey. Such a big black boot, covered in paint. And such a handsome man, my mind's eye tells me.

He carried me all the way to Hull Royal Infirmary once. He had his big coat on. He had that coat for years and it made him seem very powerful. I felt secure perched high on his left arm, near his shoulder. I had got a pea up my nose. I used to love playing with Sunday dinner's dried peas before Mother steeped them. I liked the way they rattled in the pan. I was trying them for size in my nostrils, and one pea fitted one nostril so perfectly it could not be budged. The more I tried to retrieve it, the further up it went. All that way he carried me, on what must have been a Saturday afternoon (the peas not having been steeped). But he didn't complain, they got it out, and back at home I proudly showed it to Mother.

Dad always wanted me to excel. 'Our Tom could walk three months before that,' he would say of some aspiring toddler. And as for talking, well, you'd have thought I held the world record. 'Very quick to start talking, our Tom, wasn't he, Annie? Oh yes, you were talking in no time.' I didn't mind. I liked being praised.

Not that I had it all my own way. 'You're a cheeky little sod, I know that much,' I can hear him saying. But if it delighted him that I was quick to start talking, he could hardly expect me to stop the flow as I got into my stride.

'Wait till your father gets home,' was Mother's last resort when either Ann or I or both were unmanageable, and it would help to calm us down. He only ever hit me once, and not particularly hard, but that glancing blow had the weight of the world on it. There were no such things as babysitters and Ann and I would be put to bed so that Mam and Dad could go in Club. It was safe to leave us. And Mrs Hinchcliffe, next door, had Pat, Linda and Charlie to look after and didn't have many nights out because her husband was at sea. But we wouldn't be tired and would lark about noisily, spoiling the neatness of their scheme. Up he came one night in thunderous mood and gave me a clip. That did the trick. Not a peep more out of us.

We had a bit of a do one night at Grandma and Grandad Quest's. I gave them a song, even though they had no piano for Mother to play, after pretending to be reluctant. 'What about Ann? She'll give us a song.' I didn't want that. I was the performer. So I quickly obliged. That same evening I pulled Dad's chair from under him and he hit the floor. He had had a few pints, so he was laughing. I don't know why I did it. I regretted it immediately, though there was no reprisal. I don't think it was very good for his back. I sometimes wondered whether my stupid deed hadn't contributed to his later lack of mobility as much as his two accidents.

He had one fearsome outburst against me, some years after I pulled the chair from under him. It was a Saturday night, after he and Mam had been in Club with Grandma Quest. He was no drunkard, nor was he irresponsible. The beer usually made him mellow, but not on this occasion. I would have been fourteen or fifteen. He started out: 'You're a cheeky little sod,' which I had often heard before, but this time he was full of venom. I don't know what I'd said. Nothing particular. Perhaps confidently explaining how well I had just done my homework. It was probably fuelled by his life, with its lack of opportunity, and the austerity of his upbringing. He made me out to be a selfish, ungrateful, disrespectful little worm. 'You don't know you're born, and nothing's good enough for you. We've all got to dance attendance on you. If I'd carried on like you when I was your age I'd have had seven sorts of shit knocked out of me.' His tirade was all the more shocking for coming from nowhere. Mother and Ann were silent, Grandma kept muttering quietly, 'No, no,' and I just sat there sniffling. It took days for the atmosphere to lighten. Nothing was ever said about his attack, but he did eventually put his arm round my shoulder. For all he wanted me to be something, perhaps he sometimes thought that I was so much more fortunate than he had been. Which was true enough. Mother was the best thing that he did have. And he had to share her with Ann and me.

Perhaps he was trying to hold on to the mastery for a while longer. A year or so after his outburst he was hit by a car, and his broken leg took ages to mend. He was never the same again. His arthritis grew much worse. He could no longer climb masts, so they gave him a job as paint-store keeper. He was lucky to get that – it was physically much easier, though the hours were longer.

After his second accident a wry, philosophical acceptance of his lot became more the rule. He was very fond of the expression 'the average working man', among whose numbers he included himself and Uncle Pat. I didn't much care for it, having inherited Mother's awareness of a way of living away from Fish Dock. As she wrote, 'I don't think one should have to be thankful for a piece of bread and wear second hand shoes and like pawn shops.'

'Dad,' I said quietly, 'you're not the average working man, you're below average.' We were miles past the 'you're a cheeky little sod' stage, so he just thought about it for a moment and contented himself with a smile and, 'Yes, I suppose you're not wrong there.'

Perhaps he knew I was just trying to get things straight. He told me that when I could first talk he had loved it when I asked him, 'Why do we have five fingers?' 'I don't know, Tommy, we just do.' He used to like explaining our bellybuttons to Ann and me. They were made by God's thumb when He said, 'You're done.' He made a fart-like raspberry sound as he pressed our bellybuttons and we'd shriek with delight.

Aunt Dorrie brought me a cup of tea. Until meeting her, the three great loves of Uncle Pat's life had been Dad, who was two years older than him, his Roman Catholicism, and his beer. I remember him telling me that he had warned Dorrie before they married that he loved his beer. I am sure she can't have failed to notice, but he, being honest, wouldn't have wanted her to think he'd give it up for her. They had two lovely daughters, Cath and Marie. Their son lived for only three days. Mam and Dad went to see the little thing one Sunday. Mother told me it looked for all the world as though it were asleep. It meant that I was the only male Courtenay produced by the two brothers, and this intensified Uncle Pat's interest in me.

He had a small tot of whisky on the table by his armchair. He put it to his lips only once. 'I hardly touch it these days,' he muttered, with only a trace of regret.

He fell silent for a while. Then his face lit up. 'Show Tom your ring, Dorrie!' Their diamond wedding was just a few months off. Thinking perhaps that he might not make it in person, he had already bought her a ring. She held out her hand to show it to me. It was elegant and sparkling. 'Isn't it beautiful!' she said. 'That wasn't cheap,' said Uncle Pat. It probably cost his life's savings. 'Worth it, though, for a good 'un.' He meant a good wife, not a good ring. Though it was a good ring.

In those last few days of his life, goodness held sway. He told me how beautiful Aunt Dorrie was. He told me that the nurse who came three days a week to look after him was an angel. And then he started to talk about my mother, his dear brother's wife, who had been dead for thirty-five years.

'I remember going to see them when they'd only been married a week. She was beautiful, Tom. She had a black dress on and her hair came down to her shoulders. She was a queen, Tom, a queen. A queen among shit.' I had never heard him say that before. It took my breath away.

'Do you mean, Uncle Pat, that Hessle Road was a bit rough for her?' I eventually managed.

'Rough? They were shit compared to her—'

'There were some good sorts there,' interrupted Aunt Dorrie.

'Of course there were,' said Uncle Pat. 'But they were shit when you think of what she was. She was the most honest person in the world.' I took hold of his hand.

'I think it was very hard for her on Hessle Road, bless her,' said Aunt Dorrie.

When I was a boy I used to think Uncle Pat was quite a bit more exotic than Dad. More dashing. When he came back from the war he brought a photo of himself in an army rugby team. I was very impressed. Rugby Union, too. Not common everyday Rugby League. And he had a bit of a scar on his nose. Though he got it not from fighting Germans but because he fell over some barbed wire one night when he was drunk. He used to laugh about that. Still, a scar none the less. And in the army he had worked with mules. That also impressed me. You didn't get mules on Fish Dock. 'Did they kick you?' I asked hopefully. 'You know, Tommy, when people tell you something has got a kick like a mule, well, they're talking bullshit. Mules don't kick.'

When I was older and he'd had a pint or two we would have a religious discussion. Of his Catholic family he was by far the most devout. He would have loved me to be as ardent a worshipper as he was, but my denominational position was unclear. According to Mother, who wasn't a Catholic and didn't care for any organized religion, I was first christened into the Church of England. Mother simply wanted me to be given my names, Thomas Daniel. She wasn't interested in the religious aspect. This had greatly upset Uncle Pat, who appealed to Dad during the week, while they were at work, so the following weekend I was christened again, as a Roman Catholic.

Our religious discussions always began with the same sentence: 'You know I'm your godfather, Tommy?' 'I do, Uncle Dan.' He was always Uncle Dan when Mother was alive. She thought the name Patrick was Irish, therefore Catholic, and somehow decadent: 'He's Daniel Patrick Courtenay, not Patrick Daniel. He only ever goes on about religion when he's full up. It's the beer talking.' Mother had deeply resented being indoctrinated by a Catholic priest in order that she could marry her sweetheart Thomas Henry Courtenay. 'When the priest was giving me my instructions, do you know, Tommy, his trouser buttons were undone.'

When Mam and Dad were first stepping out together they bumped into Uncle Pat in front of the Presbyterian Hall on Anlaby Road. On being introduced to his brother's girlfriend, Uncle Pat immediately asked her, 'What religion are you?' Mother neither knew nor cared, though it certainly wasn't Roman Catholic, and she answered, quick as a flash, 'Presbyterian. What religion are you?' Mother told me this with a smile and the glint of battle in her eye. She easily won the war against Uncle Pat over Ann's and my religious upbringing. Dad had never been as keen a worshipper as his brother. He had been an excellent boy soprano and had had to sing in church all day Sunday till he was sick of it. Whatever religious feelings he did have must have been greatly tempered by Mother's hard line. Only once can I remember Dad taking us to a Catholic church. She stayed resolutely outside.

Uncle Pat would usually try to win me back into the fold when we were out together. In a whisper, if Mother was at hand.

'As your godfather, Tommy, you know that I'm responsible for your spiritual welfare. Have you been giving any thought to your religion?'

'Uncle Dan, if we behave honestly and treat people decently; if we're as good as we can be, why do we have to be religious? Isn't life beautiful without religion? When you come home from work and see Aunt Dorrie standing on the step to greet you, isn't that wonderful enough for you?' (I think I must have had some beer, too.) Uncle Pat/Dan was taken aback by my idyllic vision of his home life. 'Oh yes, oh yes,' he said, but without much attack. He had great need of a world beyond this one that he could contemplate and aspire to.

It wasn't unreasonable for him to feel Irish. The Courtenays had come from Killaloe, a little place near Limerick, two or three generations earlier. Dad's sister, my Aunt Agnes, told me she had been to Killaloe with her husband, Uncle Wilf Spaven. They had enquired at the pub if there were Courtenays in the area, and indeed there were. But Uncle Wilf, perhaps wisely, although he loved his brothers-in-law, hadn't fancied calling on them. 'You don't know what we might find.'

For all she didn't share Uncle Pat/Dan's religious views, Mother knew well enough what a good heart he had. It made him easier to tease. She used to anticipate the first thing he might say. One evening Dad looked quite smart in his best suit. 'Dan will ask you if it's a new one,' said Mother, knowing his socialist concern that any worker should be doing better than his fellows. And sure enough when he arrived in Rayner's saloon bar with Aunt Dorrie: 'How are you, Annie? Is that a new suit you've got there, Tom?'

'I'm buggered, I'm buggered,' sighed Uncle Pat.

'I think he ought to have a rest now,' said Aunt Dorrie. So I hugged him, kissed him and left.

Aunt Dorrie saw me to their front door. 'It was good of you to come all this way, chuck.'

'Oh, Aunt Dorrie, it was beautiful to see you both.'

Four days later he died.

At his funeral my cousin, big, outgoing Michael Spaven, told me he had been to see Uncle Pat in hospital, two days after my trip to Hull. 'I want to die, I want to die,' Uncle Pat had moaned. 'Nobody's stopping you,' said Michael with typical candour. And Uncle Pat had laughed.

ANNIE ELIZA

Mother was born in 1914. Her father, Grandad Quest, was an army cook during the Great War. He once showed me an old photo of a huge tent with trestle tables outside it where the men were being fed.

Mother told Ann and me only snippets about her childhood. And always wistfully. As though she wished it had been more beautiful, with more flowers and less poverty. Being poor meant being too much taken up with drudgery, with helping her mother to look after her younger brothers and sisters, and with net-braiding (making the nets for the trawlers) when she left school aged fourteen. It didn't leave enough time for imagination, for self-expression, for storytelling – what she thought of as 'poetry'. Most of all, it meant not being properly educated.

She was never satisfied with her lot, which made her different from the rest of her family. She didn't have the Hessle Road attitude of making the best of a bad job. Aunt Dorrie was quite right when she said Hessle Road was a bit rough for Mother. I don't think she could quite figure out how she came to be there. She had been posted to the wrong address. And she had two ghostly precursors, her mother's first-born twins who died at birth. I can imagine Grandma Quest telling her all about them even before she was old enough fully to understand. And how heavily that would weigh on her. More than on Grandma who'd lost them. Not one, but two who had died before her and whose illnesses she irrationally felt she'd inherited. There must have been some reason for her being so consistently ill, and the death of those twins was as good as any. Her poor health and other people's illness and hardship had a lot to do with Mother's antipathy towards organized religion. I sometimes feel that God might have had quite a bit of explaining to do when she stood before Him.

She didn't love either of her parents the way my sister Ann and I loved her and Dad. I don't think they quite understood her. I remember Grandad Quest calling her 'Moanalot' after a character in *ITMA*. 'Questionherlot' would have been more accurate. And she hated Grandma's fecklessness with money. It made them seem even poorer than they were. A big family needed good housekeeping, and theirs didn't always get it. She writes in one of her letters that she had fantasized with a girlfriend about being married to rich husbands, on the way back from taking payments to a money-lender on Grandad's behalf. 'Romancing', she called it. She also suggested that they imagine being married to poor husbands, but that was no fun and didn't last. She was always determined to get the most out of the housekeeping money she got from Dad. No money-lenders for us.

One of the snippets she did tell us was that, aged eleven or twelve, she had bought herself a red penny notebook from Woolworth's to write stories in. She had always wanted to write stories. And though she never felt the world she was born into was entirely her world, she liked observing it. It was rough and ready, but also lively, funny and human. She would have loved more education than she was allotted. It would have helped her to describe the world around her. And it would have helped her to express her longing for a more beautiful world.

She also told us about the piano. It was bought, doubtless on the never-never, so that her younger brother Tommy, who died aged nineteen of diphtheria, could have lessons. Mother found to her delight that she could get tunes out of it just by sitting down in front of it and fooling around. She could pick out a tune with her right hand and accompany it with chords from her left hand. Vamping, she called the accompaniment. Her brother, in spite of or because of his lessons, couldn't do that and was put out. Mother wasn't at all interested in having piano lessons. She didn't want to play scales. Melodies were what she liked and she could find them herself.

One of Grandad Quest's sisters, Great-aunt Jane, had married into money, which, in Grandma Quest's opinion, she was inclined to keep to herself. I can recall visiting her one Sunday but don't remember any cakes or biscuits, so maybe Grandma had a point. But Mother must have touched her heart because she offered to set her up in some kind of dress shop. Aunt Jane, rightly, didn't think Mother's fragile physique was cut out for net-braiding. I can remember regretting that she didn't take up the shop offer – it would have been so much more ladylike than net-braiding. But Mother didn't want to be alone in a shop, nor be indebted, I suspect. She was used in her big family to having people around her, and she liked the company of the girls at the net factory, tough though the work was. They would have loved telling her about themselves. Her soulful eyes would draw anybody in, and she was a wonderful listener. 'They pick me out and I'm glued.' Ann told me she ran a savings scheme for the girls, to help them buy their underwear.

I think Mother said so little about her childhood because she didn't think it was up to much. It wasn't till she found Dad and had Ann and me that her life made sense to her. 'I suppose my luck is You, Ann and Dad, and more so if I could really write.'

Aunt Agnes said that when she first met Mother at a dance she had seemed such a fragile little thing. 'There was nothing of her. But she said straight away, "You're Tom's sister, aren't you? I love your Tom."' As ever, getting to the heart of the matter. After Dad had introduced her to his own mother (who died just after I was born), she had told him ominously: 'She won't make old bones.' Dad was six years older than Mother and he liked to joke that on his way home from work he'd seen this skinny little schoolgirl playing in the street and had thought nothing of her. He didn't mean it. She used to tell us how handsome she thought him as he strode along from Fish Dock, his overalls covered in paint. Then would come her little joke: 'You wouldn't think so now, to see him sat there in his singlet, blowin' off.' And we'd all laugh.

There was never anyone but him, though she once told me about a tailor named Hyme who was sweet on her. I quite fancied the idea of a father who was a tailor. I would have got regular pocket money from a tailor. But would I have been different, I wondered. Would I have been at all? And having asked myself such an unanswerable question I concluded that it had probably worked out for the best.

In Dad Mother found a true partner, someone as intelligent as she was, to love and cherish her. Thomas Henry Courtenay and Annie Eliza Quest married on the Saturday before Christmas in 1935. She was twenty-one, he was twenty-seven. After I was born in 1937, and Ann in 1938, she was able to start her childhood all over again. And give it a better outcome.

I have no definite first memory of her. A beautiful head, the soft brown hair falling around it, bends over me and kisses me. It's my mother. How can I describe her? Her image fills my head. It's as though a huge expanse of my brain were impregnated with it. It's something sweet that makes me happier than it makes me sad. Yet she died in 1962, when I was twenty-five.

She was slightly built. Not busty at all. She comes up to Dad's ear in a photograph I have and he was of average height. It's a strange thing when you realize how much bigger you have grown than your mother. 'You wouldn't leave go of my pinny,' she once wrote. Yet all of a sudden my arm could go right round her shoulders and give her a squeeze.

She wore a wraparound pinny for housework. With usually just a blouse and skirt and cardigan. And a grey overcoat. That's what I preferred. She once got a horrible garish blue coat cheaply from Jack Stather's sister. I didn't like the way it went in and out and I told her it was ugly. That was during my last year at UCL when I was very bad-tempered. I never saw her wearing it again. I liked her to look ladylike.

She had pretty legs. The bottom half, anyway – that's all she showed. She would sometimes lift her skirt *just* above her knee. 'You can't say I've got a bad pair of legs, can you, Tommy?' She would place her hands on her knees, half bending, and move her knees together and back while crossing her hands over. It looked as though her knees were melting one through the other. Very Twenties and girlish.

She had large blue-green eyes, the most soulful I have ever seen, with high cheekbones and a radiant smile. She was pleased that she had high cheekbones. She had once read in *Woman's Own* that they were the distinguishing feature of some great beauty.

When I was a child I felt much closer to her than I did to Dad. It was easier to talk to her. She was such a wonderful listener. The dictum that children should be seen and not heard was never in her book. She would have missed too many laughs. Except of course when she was tired and I was overreacting and she sent me off to get sympathy from Grandma, who was tougher than she was. 'Ma, Mr Brabbs showed my composition to Mr Beeken,' would delight her. She didn't think it was showing off, as Dad thought it was, or said he did. She thought it was being happy. And besides, she had helped me with my composition, joining excitedly in the process of putting a bit of life into it. She loved my being able to express myself. It's what she had always wanted to do.

The first song I remember Mother teaching me was a funny one. It's how I came to learn the words 'turned up'.

> Mary Ellen at the church turned up.
> Her Ma turned up
> And her Pa turned up.
> Her Auntie Gert,
> Her rich Uncle Bert,
> And the parson in his long white shirt turned up.
> But no bridegroom with a ring turned up,
> But a telegraph boy with his nose turned up
> Brought a telegram to say
> That he couldn't wed today
> And they found him in the river with his toes turned up.

She loved it when I did the 'turned ups'. But it didn't take me too long to learn the rest of it, and she did the 'turned ups' and her smile lit up Hessle Road.

'Mary Ellen' came from her memory, but most of the songs we sang together we heard on the radio – a huge assortment of British and American popular numbers, which drift unaccountably into my head to this day. Without warning or apparent reason I find myself quietly singing wartime American hits.

> Lay that pistol down, Babe
> Lay that pistol down
> Pistol packin' Mama,
> Lay that pistol down.

Sometimes there are words missing, though the tune still haunts:

> South of the border, down Mexico way
> Dee di di daa di dum
> Di daa di dum
> Come out to play . . .

Sometimes the songs I sing make no more sense now than they did fifty years ago: 'I'm an old cow hand/From the Rio Grand.'

They drift into my head anyway and demand an airing.

We would listen together, I would learn the words and Mother would pick out the tunes on the piano we got when we moved to number 29 and had a front room. Singing songs and writing something extra special at school were the things we did together, for fun. They're what we had in common. I can't imagine contemplating any sort of life in the arts without her having been there. The yearning to express myself and the instinct for doing it I got directly from my mother, gift-wrapped.

29 HARROW STREET, HESSLE ROAD, HULL
1941–59

The Hessle Road runs west, more or less parallel to the Humber, from the centre of Hull to the little town of Hessle. It is three or four miles long and most of the streets on the south side of it lead down to the docks. At least they did in the Forties and Fifties when I grew up there. A mile and a half from the city centre, going west, Boulevard, Eton Street, Harrow Street, West Dock Avenue, Subway Street, Rugby Street and Flinton Street ran south towards St Andrew's Dock, the Fish Dock. It was the most westerly of Hull's docks, built at the end of the nineteenth century to accommodate Hull's growing deep-sea fishing industry.

While I was in Hull visiting Uncle Pat I drove down the Hessle Road to see what remained of the place I grew up in. I parked my car in what is left of Harrow Street, near where I guessed number 29 had been.

The fishermen's pub, the Star and Garter, so named but never so called, had stood on the corner of Hessle Road and West Dock Avenue. It had always been Rayner's, after a legendary pre-war owner who had been known to tell fishermen when he thought they'd had enough to drink. When I lived in Harrow Street that was unthinkable. Deckhands, the biggest drinkers, had only forty-eight hours to get their beer down before going back to sea for another three weeks, and they were allowed to do so without let or hindrance. The floor of the long fishermen's bar was covered in sawdust – very effective against spillage and overflow. On the north side of Hessle Road, across from West Dock Avenue, Division Road boasted a cemetery, and a tiled, free-standing lavatory inside which a metal plaque read, 'Would gentlemen please adjust their clothing before leaving this urinal.' It was aimed at the fishermen who had been disgorged from Rayner's opposite, but it had little effect. In my mind's eye I can see one now, full as could be, in a pale blue suit with flared trousers, and square-toed shoes, staggering out, clumsily doing up his flies. The square-toed shoes were all the rage. The deckhands joked that wearing them you could stand nearer the bar.

After Rayner's, the leading attraction was the Langham Cinema, just round the corner from Harrow Street, where Mother, Ann and I used to watch Tyrone Power and Linda Darnell. Its car park, near the end of Harrow Street, made an excellent football pitch because there were hardly ever any cars in it. If sometimes there was one, the cinema organist, Mr Donald, shooed us away. The Langham Cinema had a huge foyer between the ticket booth and the auditorium. When I was little, standing by the wooden rail in the sixpenny queue on the left, I used to think the people far across the foyer in the tenpenny queue on the right were going to see another, altogether more beautiful film.

In my first years in Harrow Street the stables opposite the Langham car park still functioned. The horses pulled the huge carts, called rullies, which transported the wooden kits, or gigantic buckets, of fish. The stable yard made an excellent place for hide and seek. We used to climb into the empty kits and disappear completely. Inside they were covered with dried fishscales. I liked picking them off as I waited to be discovered or give myself up.

The south side of Hessle Road around Harrow Street now resembles the set of a Wild West film: fronts, with almost nothing behind. The street entrances with their old nameplates are still there in between the shops, but there are no streets now, only boards, warehouses and wasteland. An industrial estate. All the houses, shops, West Dock Avenue School, and the various working men's clubs have been pulled down. On Hessle Road the Langham Cinema is now a supermarket. Rayner's is still there but the sign no longer says the Star and Garter, but Rayner's, to commemorate Fish Dock days, presumably.

The Division Road cemetery, where Grandma and Grandad Quest lie, has been made into a park. All the headstones have gone except those beside the low wall running along Division Road. It looks pleasant, but I wouldn't want to cross it at night. The once proud urinal is no more, though you couldn't say it has left no trace because it has – in tarmac, there on the pavement where it used to stand. It wasn't as big as I remember.

I was keen to see if our old fish and chip shop, the Regal, was still there, so I crossed back over Hessle Road and walked to the end of the remains of Harrow Street. There it was, though shuttered up and no longer called the Regal, but Curtis's – 'for Courtesy'. Surely not the Mr Curtis of my day? I strolled on and soon arrived at a fish and chip shop unknown to me. I went in. 'Patty and chips, please. Is Curtis's closed now?'

'No, they're away on holiday,' said a pleasant lady. 'Aren't you an actor?'

'That's right. I used to live down Harrow Street. The Mr Curtis I remember can't still be on the go?'

'No, it's his son.'

'My name is Tom Courtenay. Would you tell them in Curtis's that I asked after them, please?'

Fifty-odd years since my last penn'uth of chips from the Regal. The actual, final penn'uth I don't recall. Etched in my memory is Mr Curtis's dreadful announcement: 'No more penn'uths. Two penn'uths only from now on.' No more penn'uths! I couldn't believe my ears. I looked at my poor penny in disbelief. It wasn't that easy to come by a penny. Even an errand for generous Grandma couldn't entirely be relied on. A biscuit or two, certainly – several if they'd already gone soft. But a penny very much depended on how her week was going. And as for tuppence – dear, oh dear! So, aged seven, I already knew that life was no longer what it used to be.

Nineteen ninety-seven, and the patty and chips were excellent, eaten out of the paper, strolling along Hessle Road.

I wasn't born in Harrow Street. I think it was Subway Street, so called because it ran down to the tunnel that led under the railway lines to Fish Dock. Mother told me that the evening before I was born she heard

'Pennies From Heaven' on the radio. As I was expected any minute she thought of it as my signature tune. I didn't arrive till around seven the following morning and even then somewhat reluctantly. Perhaps I didn't fancy the idea of Hessle Road. The midwife had to resort to the use of forceps to help get me out, so my head got squashed. I didn't look quite human. Dad just had time to see me before he went off to work, and he was worried by the shape of my head. He couldn't receive his workmates' congratulations as wholeheartedly as he would have liked. Where had I come from? By the time he got back home, however, my head had recovered and I looked like a human baby. He was thrilled. 'I had always wanted a son, Tom,' he told me much later. 'To try and give him the chances I never had.'

I was their first child, and Mother had a hard time with the pregnancy. It made her even more sensitive than usual. For weeks she thought there was a funny smell in the kitchen. Dad finally had to take up the floorboards. 'I couldn't find anything. Could I buggery.'

Ann arrived fourteen months after me. She was no trouble at all. No funny smells, no forceps. She wasn't expected to be a girl. 'It'll be another boy, Annie,' they all said. When she was nineteen Mother had had an operation to remove one of her ovaries. (One of her three *big* operations, she called them.) According to the experienced ladies of the neighbourhood, this meant that she wouldn't be able to have children of both sexes. Either boys or girls – not one of each. Dad was delighted when they were proved wrong. He never forgot what his mother had told him about his sweetheart's physical fragility, and he believed a daughter would one day help him to look after her.

I don't remember living in Subway Street, but I can remember living in Eton Street for a time. Next door to a little girl. I found her fascinating and got into trouble once for lifting up her skirt. I was keen to know whether she had the same curious arrangement as my little sister. After we had flitted to Harrow Street, Mother used to send me to get butter from Eton Street, because it was a penny a pound cheaper there. I liked to watch the woman in the Eton Street shop hacking at the huge mound of butter with a wooden pat.

We lived at the Fish Dock end of Harrow Street at first, when Ann and I were still very little, in Fern Grove, a small terrace at right angles to the street, in what was known as a sham four – two rooms upstairs and two downstairs. It backed on to Mother's parents Grandma and Grandad Quest's house, and I used to like using their lavvy because it was much less be-cobwebbed than ours, and the newspaper hung in neatly torn sections on a piece of string. Their house was a shop. At least it had been a shop. They hadn't done very well. Grandma Quest, so the story went, had mistaken the takings, which she kept in a large pocket on the front of her apron, for profit. There were three shops in Harrow Street, not counting Grandma's defunct one. Mr Lacey's was opposite Grandma's at the Fish Dock end. His efficiency may well have contributed to Grandma's lack of success. Mr Duke's off licence-cum-grocery store was halfway along Harrow Street. It was taken over by Mrs Hales shortly before I left for London. Mr Duke was a bit of a misery and never said much. Mother had much more scope for gossip and stories with Mrs Hales. Mr Brooks' shop was near the Hessle Road end of Harrow Street. Mother used other shops in the neighbourhood in search of the best prices, and they were all great sources of news and chit-chat. Who was getting married, who *had* to get married, who was expecting, who had just had another one, who had shown himself up in Club the other night, who was in hospital and who was no more.

We flitted to the Hessle Road end of Harrow Street, to number 29, when I was still very young. It was opposite West Dock Avenue Juniors schoolyard and next to Brooks' shop (where eventually I got my *Wizard*, and even more eventually my *Punch*). I had scarlet fever when I was four, and I think the ambulance came to pick me up from number 29. I was very disappointed not to be carried out on a stretcher. When anyone was taken ill I used to love seeing them being carried on a stretcher from their front door and into the ambulance, and when the doctor said I had to go to hospital, ill as I felt I relished the thought of being stretcher-borne. I would be able to dangle one arm down. But no. The ambulanceman carried me in his arms in a blanket, so I didn't look nearly so ill, nor nearly so impressive, to the curious young Harrovians who always gathered round a waiting ambulance. The nurses in the hospital more than made up for the omission of the ambulanceman. Memory tells me those few weeks were an idyll, spent mostly on the nurses' knees. A dark one and a fair one. My very own Scylla and Charybdis, comforting and delightful.

Number 29 boasted three bedrooms instead of two, so the rent must have gone up. It was paid to a Mr Dufton. Downstairs there was the front room, where Mother had her piano; the living room, or kitchen as we called it; and the scullery, or kitchen as it would now be called. The scullery had a gas cooker and a sink, a pantry, and later on an iron bath which Dad somehow managed to install. He painted the inside of it, and the paint used to come off on us. For most of my childhood, though, we used a zinc bath in front of the fire. In the back yard: a lavatory and a coalhouse, a small, ugly plot of earth, and, near the scullery back door, an outside tap and drain where on a cold dark night I used to pee as quickly as I could manage, standing on the doorstep. The scullery also housed our washday requisites: washtub, gas-fired copper (for heating the water) and the mangle, or wringer as it was known. In between engagements the copper rested in the pantry bottom, the washtub in the back yard. Upstairs, we had Mam and Dad's bedroom, the bedroom I shared with Ann, and the back bedroom for Ann when she got older.

The front door was on the right of the house, next to Brooks' shop. Our front passage ran past the front room on the left to the foot of the stairs. At the foot of the stairs was the door to our livingroom (kitchen, we said). Our passage never had a lightbulb in it. At night I'd ask one of my pals to hold the front door open till I got to the safety of our living quarters. Likewise I'd ask Ann to close our living-room door after me as I hurtled down the dark passage to the front door. I didn't like the dark. When at grammar school I heard about houses with halls, I used to think it would be nice if we had one. Then I realized we did have one but it was called a passage, which was much more accurate terminology considering the speed with which I moved along it.

The house was ill lit because electricity was considered an expensive item. When in later years I used to stay downstairs reading by our naked ceiling light, after they had all gone to bed, Mother would sometimes express concern about the electricity I was using. I would offer a bit of science: 'Five hours of electricity for a lightbulb costs a farthing, Ma.' She was never convinced.

On one side of our living-room fireplace, opposite the passage door, was a built-in cupboard, below which was a set of drawers, also built in. In the recess on the other side of the chimneybreast was the piece of furniture upon which sat the radio, hired from Rediffusion. There was a drawer in the top of it that contained among other things the photo of Uncle Pat's rugby team, and below the drawer were two doors hiding a single-shelfed interior. Tiddles once had her kittens in the bottom of it. I actually saw one being born. A ginger one. That went down very well at school next day.

At right-angles to the ginger kitten's birthplace was the window on to the back yard and, along a bit, the scullery door. The wall opposite the fireplace was home to the understairs area as well as the door from our passage. It contained the gas and electricity meters, a coat rack, old shoes and junk, and was curtained over by a blanket. I didn't like it under there. It was dusty and dark. Especially of course when the electricity ran out. 'Go and put a shilling in the meter, Tommy. There's one in me purse on mantelpiece.' Eager to instruct, I would point out that money in the meter wasn't wasted, that you'd still get two shillings' worth of electricity if you put in two shillings together rather than one at a time, and I wouldn't have to grope about among rubbish and spiders in the dark. But Mother had her system. Perhaps she fancied that if you put in more than one shilling at a time the shillings would somehow overlap and you'd get less value for money.

Our living room was a sort of dull mustard colour, though I wouldn't swear to it. Distempered, I think. The wall that separated our headquarters from the front room was just a wall – unembellished save for the chaise-longue against it. We called it the couch. It had had a long career, and the head end was worn through to its innards. It may well have started its days at number 29 in less than perfect condition. It was probably a bargain. Whenever we had visitors I used to find some way of covering it up. This once put me in a terrible quandary. I had just acquired a dressing-gown – a cast-off from my better-off cousin, Michael. He had outgrown it. I was off school for a day or so with something or other, which gave me a chance to wear my nearly new dressing-gown over my pyjamas. There was a knock at the door. Mother went to see who it was. She didn't let them in but came from the front door to report. 'It's Mac and Looey from school.' As they came down the passage I had to decide. Should my dressing-gown drape me or the couch? I chose the latter, and then had the problem of letting it be known I had a dressing-gown, without revealing the entrails of the couch.

'Warm, isn't it? I've had to take my dressing-gown off,' did the trick. Very important that my grammar school friends realized that though my father worked on Fish Dock I had a dressing-gown and we had a perfectly acceptable couch.

The table we ate our meals off stood against the wall between the back-yard window and the scullery door. The half we ate off was permanently unfurled, while the half nearer the wall was doubled over. Things were kept on that half, on a strip of lacy cloth. The Ornament, for one. The Ornament wasn't remotely ornamental. It was a metallic, copper-coloured vase used for putting things in. A pencil, a pen, a comb, the odd button and Dad's pools coupons waiting to be filled in. The half of the table we ate off usually had something on it, too. Cups and plates weren't cleared with any alacrity. I often had to make a space before starting my homework. Mother didn't like housework. For one thing she didn't always feel well enough to do it. I can recall coming home from school, going in back way, and seeing her through the living-room window: half asleep on the couch looking exhausted, hardly any colour in her cheeks, and in the foreground the unwashed breakfast pots still on the table. I always felt our house was untidier than anyone else's. Once when I came in she was having a natter with her friend Olive, of whom she was very fond. I thought the room looked a mess so I proceeded to tidy up, putting things in a drawer and demonstrating what could be done with a little application. They both laughed at me but I don't think Mother liked me doing it in front of her friend and now I wish I hadn't. Dad and I both sometimes wanted Mother to be a more efficient housewife. He once brought home from Fish Dock a huge stoker's shovel and a heavy deck-sweeping brush for use in the back yard. I found her gazing at them wryly. 'I'll tell you what – we'll never have burglars. They'll think giants live here.' They saved up to buy a hoover. To buy *her* a hoover, as Dad put it. He was very sanctimonious about it, as though he had bought her a passport to a life of ease. 'As though he had done something holy,' as Mother once wrote. But it was a heavy bloody thing for her to lug around, and she wept one day when it broke.

Our sideboard stood in between the passage door and the understairs area. It was where you looked when you couldn't find something. It was home to one of Mother and Dad's wedding presents, a glass biscuit-barrel that had retained its silver-plate lid but had lost its handle. It wasn't very useful because we never had any biscuits. Dad didn't like biscuits. He said they were eating for eating's sake. 'You can eat biscuits when you're not hungry.' When Uncle Bernard, Dad's kid brother, home from sea, bought Mother a box of Black Magic, she would keep them in the sideboard. We would all be offered one. I always had a montelimar because it was the biggest. Ann liked caramel. Dad wouldn't always have one. It depended on his mood. He made a great stand about not eating anything in the evening: 'I never eat anything after me tea.' He almost made a moral issue of it. Sometimes, though, he would relent and have a chocolate. It had to be a soft one, because of his teeth. Dad was very proud of his pre-war dentures. It was only very late in life that he needed a new upper set. Occasionally, when the week's money allowed, Mother would fancy a little bit of fish in the evening. Ann and I would have the chips. When Dad was feeling grumpy and took his moral stand against after-tea eating, she had a ready answer: 'You don't mind getting full of beer, though.'

On the wall above the sideboard hung an art deco mirror. In order to see in it, Ann and I used to stand on a wooden strut that ran between the sideboard's stubby little legs. Dad's easy chair was on the other side of the fireplace from the couch, and there were some upright chairs wherever they could find room. The couch eventually gave way to an old leather three-piece suite. Hide, Mam and Dad said it was. Thought of as being especially hard-wearing leather. Why some leather was 'hide' and some wasn't, I never knew.

The biggest change to our living room during my childhood was the installation of a modern fireplace. One of those square, tiled shiny beige monstrosities and all the rage. Unlike the old kitchen ranges, they didn't need much cleaning. It meant less work for Mother. No more black-leading on Friday mornings. We were among the last in the street to have one and even then it was a bargain, because one of the tiles was chipped. You could sit on the raised bits at either end of the hearth, and, as Mam and Dad said, it threw a lot of heat out. Its topmost tiles provided a new home for the Ornament. I was of course glad that we were now in fashion, but it wasn't as homely as the range it replaced. I had been fond of fiddling with the wire on the old fireguard. It had stayed in place long after Ann and I ceased toddling. Like an old pal. And it was handy for drying things on. It never occurred to me that it had been put there to protect us from the fire. With either fireplace, ancient or modern, we could be very cosy and warm in our living room, if nowhere else in the house. Most Fish Dock housewives had red-mottled shins from sitting in front of the fire.

Monday teatime, Mother would bake bread. When I got back from school she would still be kneading the dough in an earthenware pancheon, glazed on the inside. It was round, and about twice as wide at the top as at the bottom. I sometimes see them nowadays in antiques shops. The solid lump of dough would sit in the bottom of the pancheon, by the fireplace, and miraculously rise, spreading itself luxuriantly to the pancheon's brim. I could never resist giving it a poke, and sometimes I would pull a little bit off to chew. It was much better cooked. The operation was timed so that the first batch of hot cakes, made flat and round from the risen dough, would be emerging from the oven as Dad got home from Fish Dock, at about twenty past five. We had them piping hot with fried bacon. 'Beautiful,' as Dad used to say. Then, 'Mind you, a hot cake with butter is a meal in itself.' The bread would last a couple of days or more. Even cold the rounds were known as hot cakes. Cold hot cakes were very good toasted.

The smell of the baking bread was the most attractive of our household aromas. Dad's wind the least. It was a family joke. When I learnt that the German for father was pronounced 'farter', I couldn't wait to get home and tell the three of them. Even more powerful was the smell of his cigarette smoke. He rolled his own and the tobacco had an odd name: Bird's Eye Shag. I often went to get it for him. 'If they don't have Bird's Eye Shag get me half an ounce of Old Friend.' And did it smell! Years later when he used to visit me in London that smell would hang around for days after he'd gone back to Hull, as though it were keeping an eye on me.

My least favourite day for coming home from school was Wednesday. Washday. We had to share the fire with the clothes horse. The house seemed dank and cold, and Mother would be tired after her day's struggle with the wet clothes and the heavy washtub and wringer, and not so sunny as she could be. After her third operation she couldn't put the wet things through the wringer or clear the washtub out of the scullery without Ann's help. Though Mother hated housework and was limited by her strength in what she could do, she cleaned very thoroughly, scrubbing upstairs floorboards white and polishing the lino on calloused knees.

She did the ironing on Friday evenings after tea. We would have a small cake each with our tea on Fridays, to celebrate pay day. They were called maids of honour, and I used to go and get them from Betty's baker's shop on Hessle Road. Dad used to go for a drink with Uncle Pat on Friday, with Mother's approval. That's what they had agreed. I would sometimes get her a bottle of Guinness from Mr Duke's beer off-shop. I liked to run errands for her. My favourite was to Mr Tuton's in Subway Street. The secret was not to go along Harrow Street, Hessle Road and Subway Street, but through West Dock Avenue schoolyards Junior and Senior, down an alley in West Dock Avenue, over a wall, and along an alley in Subway Street that came out opposite Mr Tuton's. Back the same way. I loved to amaze her with the speed of my return. 'I go, I go, look how I go!' as Puck says.

Mother didn't seem to mind the ironing, and I liked watching her do it, on a cloth on the table. I would put spit on my finger and test the hot iron. I don't remember when electricity and steel took over from fire and iron. I loved Friday evenings when everything was clean and dry and warm. Sometimes I would dream on Saturday mornings that the weekend was over and it was back to school again. It was lovely to wake up and realize I was wrong. When I was playing for West Dock Avenue Juniors' soccer team, aged ten, my newly ironed shirt, with its black 'W' stitched on the chest, hung proudly on the line above the couch with the rest of the clean things, and my head would spin with excitement.

A few years ago I took Isabel, my wife, for a drive along Hessle Road. West Dock Avenue was still there then. It was on the other side of the school from Harrow Street and the houses were built in much the same way. I couldn't believe how small they were, how closely packed. Our living room must have been small too, but it was a hive of activity nevertheless.

In the days when she still had the strength, Mother used to take in netting. Though she no longer worked full time, after getting married she and some of the girls who had been net-braiders used to make lengths of net from home to earn a bit of extra money. A rod was hung from a couple of hooks fixed to the cupboard door and Mother started the netting on that. The twine came on large bobbins and had to be transferred onto wooden needles from which it was knotted into the net. The size of the squares of twine was determined by a wooden spool held in the left hand. A hard pulling motion was needed to knot the twine round the spool. It was tough work, and the twine was very rough on the hands. Ann and I used to help with loading the needles. I liked to think I was helping with the good work – until my patience ran out. ('It's all right, Tommy, you can go and play now.') After a week or so the room would be awash with netting. Working as many hours as her strength and the housework would allow, she would make several yards of net. Her section of net would be collected in an old pram by Aunt Alice and taken to the factory to be joined up with other contributions and made into one of the nets dragged by the trawlers along the fishing grounds. She would make a few shillings out of it. She wasn't able to do as much as her sister Alice, because she wasn't strong enough, and she did no more after her last operation.

Sometimes Mam and Dad would make us a carpet from strips of old cloth pulled into a piece of sacking. Rag rugs, they were known as. Mam and Dad seemed to enjoy the togetherness of the joint effort. Rag rugs in the making took up quite a bit of space. 'Don't sit there, Tommy, you're in the road.' They never made any in order to sell them, and the work seemed to me to take for ever, but when eventually a rug was completed there would be much proud discussion as to what it was worth. The value of things was always important. Mother would some-times ask, having put our meal before us, 'How much would that be in a restaurant?' She pronounced it 'reshchurront'.

Mother's cooking was homely and delicious and our meals went in weekly cycles. Neck of mutton with dumplings was usually on a

Thursday, corned beef hash earlier in the week, a piece of beef on Sunday, a bit of fish on Fridays. Puddings were the exception not the rule. Rice pudding sometimes, and on Sundays jelly and custard. I often went elsewhere in search of sweet things. Mother's Yorkshire pudding was very solid. When I came south I was amused to discover what a light and airy thing it could be. But, then, she wanted to be a writer not a chef.

Dad would often do some painting. He was very fond of 'graining', his aim being to make painted doors look as if they had grain like natural wood. He would cover them with a sort of brown varnish and then go over the still-wet varnish with his grainer, a narrow metal comb with long teeth. He would swirl it over and over the varnish in search of the grain effect. He was never satisfied with the result and would keep changing his patterns. The varnish stayed wet for ages, so he had all evening to experiment. He only ever did this at home, though he was not averse to showing his skill to a workmate who had called in for a demonstration. 'Young Gledhill's coming round tonight. He wants to have a look at me doors,' I remember him telling Mother. I was surprised when young Gledhill turned out to be the same age as Father. He seemed to like the doors, though. Dad also had a cobbler's last and he was very fond of trying to mend his working boots. Never easily. Bits of leather everywhere.

When Ann and I were little we had our baths in the zinc tub in front of the fire. The water would be heated in the gas copper in the scullery and the bath with the hot water in it carried onto the hearthrug. It was heavy and easy to spill, so there couldn't be too much water in it. The water soon got cold, and you were glad to be in front of the fire. Mam and Dad had theirs after Ann and I had gone to bed. I used to enjoy helping carry the bath and its cold, soapy contents safely through to the back yard to be emptied. When the bath was tipped up the water flooded our back yard before sliding down the drain. About the time that my sister started growing intriguing pointed things, Dad installed the iron bath in the scullery, for greater privacy, I imagine.

In our first years at number 29 Ann and I were washed ready for bed from a bowl on the table when the tea things had been (mostly) cleared away. I would sit on the table, next to the wash bowl, and maybe the teapot, Dad in his singlet reading the *Hull Daily Mail*, his ashtray on his chair arm, Ann and her patched-up doll awaiting their turn, Mother busy with soap and water and flannel.

I can see an old man sitting stiff and silent. The bald dome of his head is edged with long white strands, and his fingernails look very thick. Push White was his name. He was an old workmate of Grandad Courtenay's who couldn't reach his toes any more. He had called in on his way back from the public bath house so that Dad could cut his toe-nails. He used a pair of pliers. Old Push accepts Dad's help with great dignity, and Dad pulls his leg. 'There you are, old timer. That should last you for a day or two.'

Most elderly women on Hessle Road had at least one leg bandaged above the ankle. They got ulcers there from never being off their feet. Grandma Quest used to come to Dad to have her leg dressed. He was the only one who would look at it. I would sometimes dare myself to look at Grandma's ulcer, but never for very long. It looked to me like the pale yellow yolk of a fried egg after you have scooped up the runny part on your bread and butter.

Upstairs, Ann and I had only a bed in our rooms, but Mam and Dad had a 'utility' bedroom suite. I think that means it was made cheaply during the war. Bed, wardrobe and dressing table with mirror. The mirror could be swivelled up and down. You could see yourself either sitting down or standing up. Except that there was no mirror. Just the board on which the mirror had been mounted. The mirror had been broken when we moved from Fern Grove, making the art deco mirror in our living room even more in demand.

I have that mirror now. Isabel told me it was art deco. Mam and Dad with an art deco mirror. Who would have thought it? I wonder if they knew. It came to me when Dad died. And our sideboard clock. A Napoleon's hat clock, Isabel says. I recently bought a rose with that name: 'Chapeau de Napoléon.' It's an old rose with a sweet scent. Mother would have liked that.

I could have had our old sideboard, too. 'You're the heir,' said Ann. But I didn't keep it. Nor did she. I wish I had it now. I would like to hug it. I can still hear the click of the ball-bearing catches on its doors. I sometimes look in the art deco mirror. But its old reflections don't appear. Except in my mind's eye. In my mind's eye.

RELATIONS

I can remember thinking with considerable satisfaction, during a lesson at West Dock Avenue Mixed Infants – it must have been about members of the family – that I was very well supplied with grandparents, aunts and uncles. On Mother's side, Great-grandma Morrel, and Grandma and Grandad Quest; Aunts Alice, Phyllis and Barbara, and Uncles George and Jack. I couldn't fail to notice a lack of symmetry in the design, however. On the Courtenay side, I had only one grandparent – Grandad Courtenay. Grandma Courtenay had died just after I was born. Dad, like Mother, was the oldest surviving offspring of his family. Next to him came Uncle Pat/Dan, then, in chronological order, Aunts Agnes, Ivy and Marie, and Uncle Bernard, the baby of the family.

Like most of the Quests, Grandad Courtenay lived in Harrow Street. I can just about remember him walking home after a day's work on Fish Dock, but for most of my childhood he was retired. Wifeless and quite deaf, he had a crippled right hand. He had broken a tendon and it had not been well treated, causing his hand to splay out so that he couldn't grip with it. Uncle Bernard lived with him, when he wasn't at sea. Dad used to tell me what a great reader Grandad Courtenay had been. 'He even read *Paradise Lost*. He'd sit there with the house full, lost in a book, tears streaming down his face.' And Uncle Pat told me how tough he had been despite his size. Nobody could take advantage of him, one-handed or not. But the years of hard physical work, sometimes at sea, sometimes on Fish Dock, had taken their toll. When I knew him he seemed lost and lonely. Once Mam, Ann and I had to go into the scullery while Dad told him about an embarrassing hole in the front of his trousers.

Grandad Courtenay would call in fairly regularly, but in all truth Dad much preferred the company of Grandad Quest, who was a few years younger and livelier than Grandad Courtenay. It was Grandad Quest who seemed like the patriarch of the family. He was a foreman bobber. Bobbers unloaded the fish from the trawlers, swinging them in baskets onto the quayside. This was done from around two in the morning throughout the night, that being the coldest part of the day. On a sleepless night you would hear the clatter of the bobbers' metal-shod wooden clogs as they made their way towards Fish Dock. Bobbers would often sport a hugely bandaged finger – poisoned from getting fish bones stuck in it. Dad admired Grandad Quest. Not only had he done a great deal to help improve the working conditions of the men under him, he was generous, too. 'Nobody gets a round in quicker than your Grandad Quest.'

When I was little Grandma and Grandad Quest still lived behind the shop at the Fish Dock end of Harrow Street. Once trading had ceased, no attempt had been made to convert what had been the shop into a front room; it was simply abandoned and used as a passage to their living quarters. Again there was no light in it. When I went to see them at night I had to grope my way through the darkness as carefully as fear would allow, past the empty, dusty shelves, feeling for the sharp corner of the shop counter, before falling with relief into the warmth and safety of their living room. It was the Stygian area behind the counter that I feared the most. God alone knew what might be lurking there.

I always regretted the failure of the shop. What goodies might I have come by if Grandma had still run it! And what kudos among the lads in Harrow Street if she had had a proper shop instead of a defunct one.

'Go and show your grandma,' I can hear Mother saying when she wasn't feeling very well. Never one to hide my grief, I would burst in and present myself wounded and wailing before her, with a bump on the head or a scrape on the knee. 'Go and show your grandma.' So off

I would race along Harrow Street, wailing as I went. And Grandma, not so put out by my histrionics, would offer hugs and gummy kisses. Not to mention the odd biscuit. Grandma never had teeth when I knew her, which may help explain her fondness for Guinness. Not only was it full of iron, the Fish Dock wives' panacea, but it didn't need chewing.

I used to like going round to Grandma and Grandad Quest's. Besides the biscuits, there was Uncle Jack, Aunt Phyllis and Aunt Barbara, who lived at Grandma's too. They'd all make a fuss of me. Grandad laughed a lot. He thought I was a hoot. He had a long, sweet, beautiful face. It would have looked good on a concert pianist or a professor of anthropology. He would let me suck on one of his empty pipes, till such time as I felt sick – about four seconds.

I was always keen to 'go errands' for Grandma. For Mother I went errands for love. For Grandma, less careful with her week's money, it was for financial as well as biscuitory gain.

Grandma Quest used to help with the laying out when people died. It was a job she seemed to relish. Mother wouldn't have been able even to think of doing such a task. Grandma took Ann and me to see her own mother, Great-grandma Morrel, after she had helped lay her out in Mrs Robinson's front room. Great-grandma Morrel had lived with Mrs Robinson. I used to marvel at their hatpins. I would watch in amazement as the two old ladies plunged these hatpins deep into their skulls. I supposed this ability to stick pins in your head developed with age, but it seemed a risky business. When I tried sticking a safety pin into my own head it proved impossible, and it came as no surprise when I heard that Great-grandma Morrel was no more.

Ann and I were terrified of the white-clad figure lying in a coffin in Mrs Robinson's front room, and clung to one another for comfort. That front room had a white china doorknob, Ann says, at her eye level, and she can't see one to this day without feeling a chill. 'She's only asleep,' said Grandma. Mother was annoyed that she had frightened us with this needless visit. 'She would do it, though, wouldn't she, being Grandma?'

Grandma was much earthier than Mother, much more a typical Fish Dock worker's wife. She defended me stoutly when the little girl in Eton Street ratted on me for lifting up her skirt. 'He only wants to see what's there,' she said, and I was grateful for her support.

She once asked me if I knew the difference between little boys and little girls.

'What?' I asked, with a mixture of keen anticipation and acute embarrassment.

'Little boys have a tide mark just here,' said Grandma, and she pulled back the sleeve of my jersey. Sure enough, there it was: a ring of darkness just above my wrist. I was torn between pride in being so masculine and shame that my economic use of soap and water was now known to the world.

When Mother was pregnant with me, Granny still ran the shop. One of the services she offered was a savings scheme or 'club', as it was known. A shilling or so would go into the club each week, out of harm's way, and be collected at Christmas when extra money was required. A Mrs Wilkinson had been to collect her money from Granny, only to discover that Granny didn't have it. Mrs W. went to see Mother, and her rage, and the shame of Grandma's bad management, made Mother ill just when she wanted to feel strong. This particular bit of Grandma's fecklessness was never forgotten.

Grandad Quest died during my first term at university. I had been to say goodbye to him, and, not realizing how ill he was, I'd urged him to get up out of bed. He never did. Grandma was devastated but had the Hessle Road toughness to carry on without him. On the day he died he told her: 'I have always loved you and I always will.' It came from his heart, though it could well have come from one of the old songs they used to sing together. When I was home for Christmas after my first term at college, Grandma called in after visiting his grave. So powerful a ceremony was this for her, so much a part of her life without him, I felt prompted to ask her how he was. Then I remembered there was no point.

She made the best of her widowhood, and was very good at playing for sympathy. She would come round to our house in her black coat and sit meekly tapping her handbag. Like a little old parrot, its head cocked to one side, waiting to be offered a grape. Dad wasn't kidded, but he always had a soft spot for her: 'They don't make 'em like your Grandma Quest any more.' He admired her nerve and her resilience, and, of course, he dressed her leg for her. He never begrudged her a couple of bob for a Guinness or two.

Mother's brothers, George and Jack, were bobbers like their father. Successful bobbers were open to temptation. They had quite a lot of free time and there were plenty of Working Men's Clubs to while it away in. If Dad had a criticism of Grandad Quest, it was that he encouraged his offspring too much in the ways of the turf. Dad just liked the odd bet on a big race. His greatest success was Airborne, a grey that won the Derby at 50–1 just after the war. Uncle Jack was not at all bright but he could work out the most complicated odds. He loved a bet. As did Aunt Phyllis. For both of them a week wasn't a week without a bet or two. Which is why they often called on Mother on Tuesday or Wednesday. 'Can you lend us a shilling till Friday, Annie?' They knew she was a good manager.

Uncle Jack Quest was tall, dark and shambling with a sheepish grin, and you couldn't help liking him for all he was soft. He never married. Nobody would have him. When he came back from Burma after the war he bought me a tricycle. I never got anything else from him, not because he was mean but because the bookies usually got in first. He had been in the Eighth Army and had caught malaria. I saw him laid up with it, all feverish. Mam, Dad and I were home one night when he called in sobbing. He had thought he had a date but she hadn't turned up. 'Nobody wants me. Burma took my best years. Nobody will have me now.' We listened sympathetically and Mother made him a cup of tea. His great passion in life, apart from a bet on the horses, was sport, especially the Hull Rugby League team. When I went to see Hull with him I was astonished at how worked up he got. It was the first time I heard the referee called a shit house – though not the last.

Jack's brother George had the same long, sweet, humorous face as Grandad Quest. He wasn't hopeless like Jack and got married straight after the war. My pal Arthur and I once followed him and Aunt Joan along Harrow Street. We knew enough to appreciate the significance of his just having been wed. They had several children. My childhood was punctuated with the news that Joan was expecting another one. George used his hands a lot when he talked, like I tend to. He had a very expressive mime for being upset, flicking his forefinger from his eye down his cheek, to indicate tears. Once when he was in London on a rugby trip I was flattered and touched when he confided in me. 'Some of the lads have gone, you know, looking for women. I'm all right. I've got Joan.'

Mother's sister Alice's husband, Jack Stathers, worked on Dock as a fish-filleter. Mother didn't approve of him because she felt he didn't treat Aunt Alice well enough. He drank too much too early in the day. His small firm seemed to run out of fish to fillet quite early on. Either he started his filleting at the crack of dawn or was just very quick at the job, but he seemed to spend a lot of the afternoon in Langham Club in Harrow Street, and Aunt Alice was meant to dance attendance on him whenever and however he surfaced. 'I wouldn't stand for it, Alice, and neither should you.' But Aunt Alice loved him and was only too happy to stand for it, so Stathers, as Mother slightingly referred to him, was a bone of contention between the two of them.

An adopted uncle, Uncle Stan, who married Aunt Dorrie's cousin Teresa, was what was known as a ship's runner. He had the job of getting the deck hands on board whatever the tide time and whatever state they were in. It wasn't easy but he was very successful at it. He got a lot of tips. 'Back handers', they called them. Uncle Stan and Aunt Teresa had a modern fireplace long before we did, although the antisocial hours of his job, combined with its extremely social nature, put quite a strain on their relationship.

Dad's kid brother Bernard went to sea. He became a chief engineer on the trawlers. A chief, as they were simply known. These along with skippers and mates were the best paid of all the Fish Dock workers. Dad was occasionally in trouble with Mother for helping Uncle Bernard get his beer drunk in between trips. The brothers were very close, though there was an age gap of sixteen years or so between them. Dad used to hold mock fights when his brother was little, between Tom the Tiger and Bernard the Bull, and going out with his unmarried kid brother must have taken him back a few years. One night Dad sorted out a difference between Uncle Bernard and a ship mate when, full of beer, they started fighting in front of our house. He was on them in a flash. 'You'll cut that out, the pair of you, or I'll knock your fuckin' heads together.' That stopped them fighting. It was the only time I heard him use that word.

When Uncle Bernard's ship was due I would go and meet him in.

Visitors were allowed on board as the trawlers waited at the quayside to enter Fish Dock. Uncle Bernard used to take me down the ladder to his beloved engine room. It was very exciting when the customs officers came down after us, to search for duty-free cigarettes. You always knew when the fishermen had got their cigarettes through customs because they offered them round out of large, flat boxes of fifty or a hundred.

Dad was very pleased that his baby brother had such a good job. Uncle Bernard used to have his suits made. Hector Powe, the tailor was called. I remember Bernard sitting in one (we thought) extremely fine number with his dark hair sleeked back, navy style. 'Sixteen pound, this cost. Next trip it'll be one costing twenty pound.' We all marvelled. Uncle Bernard would sometimes give Ann and me a couple of bob, for which we were very grateful, and Mother got her Black Magic. Especially if he'd been leading Dad astray. He once gave me a whole lot of shirts with detached collars that had become too small for him. He had just had them severely laundered, and at first the starch in the collars almost cut my head off. It soon washed out. The shirts were a bit big, but as Dad was all too fond of saying: 'Anything fits a naked man.'

Dad's sister Agnes had married Wilf Spaven. Spav as he was known. A fish merchant, he was the most successful of all my uncles. He became chairman of Hull Kingston Rovers and also of the Rugby League. A big man and naturally more expansive than Dad, he had no airs or graces about his high standing in the family, and was very fond of his brothers-in-law. When he called in on his way from Dock he would never take his jacket off, which made me feel that he hadn't really settled. But how could a fish merchant settle when he had so much more on his mind than a mere dock worker?

A source of great pride to Aunt Agnes and Uncle Wilf was the considerable bulk of their firstborn, Michael, whose cast-off dressing-gown I had had the good fortune to acquire. Though slightly younger than me, he soon outstripped me in every direction. This was put down to halibut oil capsules. Now Mother was always very concerned that Ann and I be healthy. She didn't want us cursed like her. She wanted to feel she had produced good healthy stock, fragile though she was. Ann was less of a worry, from birth onwards, being physically more in the mould of Dad's sisters, but she was concerned that I was a bit scrawny –

especially the top half of me. ('I was always glad you had a good pair of legs on you, Tommy.') The outcome was that Mother tried the halibut oil capsules on Ann and me. They didn't do the trick and thankfully were soon abandoned, for they had a horrible aftertaste no matter what you had with them. Anyway, the significant difference between cousin Michael's diet and mine was perfectly clear to me. He had more cakes than I did.

I used to love going to cousin Michael's birthday parties. The lovely, gleaming, pink cloth covered a table piled high with cakes and tarts and custard and jelly. It needed enormous self restraint to stop from leaping at it before all the young guests were assembled, and getting a head start. 'You can't start on the lemon curds till you've had some sandwiches, Tommy,' I hear Aunt Agnes saying.

I went visiting one Sunday in between birthdays when they lived on Boothferry Road. Michael wasn't in and Aunt Agnes had to pop out for half an hour. Aunt Agnes said that Michael shouldn't be too long, and all too aware of the sweetness of my tooth she added on her way out, 'There's a cake you can have.' I had never been alone with a cake before. It was a sponge cake with a cream and jam filling. It looked very inviting. It was cut into four sections. The first section took me no time at all. I looked out of the window. No sign of Michael. I looked at the cake again. No harm in having another piece. So I was now alone with half a cake. I looked out of the window again. Still no sign of Michael. I looked at the half-cake. It was easier to see the middle of it, where the cream was at its thickest. I set myself to remember Aunt Agnes' exact words. 'Tommy, there's a cake you can have.' I was very good at grammar. '*A* cake.' Not some cake, not a piece of cake, not half nor yet three quarters of a cake, but *a* cake. I did what had to be done.

It was some time after her return that Aunt Agnes noticed the empty plate.

'Where's that cake gone?'

And from her tone I realized that I had overestimated her command of grammar.

'I've eaten it,' I hiccuped. Aunt Agnes said nothing but gave me a look. It confirmed what her tone had told me and I felt ashamed. And full.

WAR. AND HOLIDAYS

I was two when the war started and eight when it finished. Dad wasn't
called up. If he felt that cast aspersions on his manliness he never said so.
He was able bodied enough to have served. Uncle Pat said they went for
the army medical together, and Dad slipped through the net on a
clerical error. It would have been so much more romantic, I used to
think, if Dad had been called up, but what a blessing for Mother that he
wasn't. A woman in Harrow Street once pointed out to her that she had
been spoilt because she hadn't been without her mister during the war.
This enraged her. 'She said I didn't know what war was. Hell.' In fact
we were probably in more danger than some of my uncles in uniform.
On the easily discernible Humber, Hull provided a natural target for
the German bombers, and was then the third-largest port in the
country. On their way back from their raids on the Midlands or
Liverpool they used to empty any bombs they had left on us before they
crossed the North Sea. Hull people used to think they didn't get the
credit for the bombing they endured. Poor, soft Uncle Jack Quest had
by far the worst of it in the Eighth Army in Burma, but Uncle George,
home from Germany to marry Joan, assured me good humouredly that
he had never been in action. I might have been disappointed, but he was
thankful. And Uncle Pat got the scar on his nose from an intoxicated

encounter with some barbed wire, not from a German. I knew Uncle Jack Stathers was a Desert Rat, but I never heard what happened to him in North Africa. Maybe he didn't want to talk about it.

Our Air Raid Warden was a friendly, thin-faced man with a white tin hat and only one arm. I thought that made him a bit of a star. I imagined him shading his eyes with his extant hand as he searched the skies for enemy planes. But perhaps he just made sure we all got safely to the air-raid shelters, as lollipop men now help children across the road. Whatever he did he was entitled to wear that white tin hat.

It was terribly exciting when the air-raid sirens sounded, and I loved getting up in the night. We had to go as quickly as possible to the nearest shelter. Ours was in the schoolyard. They once let me give them a song in there. Unaccompanied. The nearest we got to a direct hit was when our windows were blown in. The German bombs made us quite a few playgrounds in the neighbourhood. 'Bomb buildin's' we used to call them. I would clamber about among the heaps of bricks, delighted when I found a piece of shrapnel. I had no idea what it meant.

Sometimes when Dad was on Home Guard duty Mother would take us under the stairs for safety. She didn't share my excitement that Germans were dropping bombs on us. After the All Clear sounded we would turn in with Mother, and when Dad got back from Home Guard he would sleep on the couch so as not to disturb us. When I got up he'd be lying in his uniform with his greatcoat on top of him. He didn't like me admiring his uniform and would go in the scullery and put on his working clothes. He must have known how much his being at home helped Mother. After the war one of his favourite pastimes was talking about when Ann and I were little. He would have missed all that in the army. Aunt Dorrie told me that Uncle Pat hated being in the army and fled home for the birth of his son – the one who died. Two Military Policemen came to get him. Aunt Dorrie was terrified that he would be shot for desertion, but the policemen thought his circumstances were extenuating and were happy enough just to round him up.

As part of the war effort we housed a petty officer cook called Bill Nicholls and his wife Hilda while Bill's ship was in dock in Hull. He used to sit me, aged four or so, in Mother's enamel pie dish and hoist me aloft, one-handed. 'We're going to have toasted Tommy.' Being a cook, he was well qualified to toast me, I thought, and he had a proper uniform with a jacket, which I found much more impressive than the bellbottoms Uncle Bernard sported. Mam and Dad were very fond of the Nichollses and kept in touch when the war was over. Ann and I adopted them: Aunt Hilda and Uncle Bill. Mother would talk wistfully of one day being able to afford to visit them in Portchester, Hampshire.

Her dream became a reality when Dad fell off a ladder while working temporarily on King George Dock, east of Fish Dock. The ladder had a rung missing, so his firm, Webster's, had to compensate him, and he got £750. I was about ten years old. They were very careful with their nest egg. Some of the family wouldn't have been. What partying and wagering there would have been in Harrow Street had Grandma or Aunt Phyllis come by such a windfall. But it did mean we could afford to travel to the dreamed-of south for our holidays.

Previously, we had always gone to Withernsea. 'Witherunsea', we called it, or 'With' for short. We used to stay in a caravan in a field. I once found a spider on my junior-sized bunk, and Dad's brother, Uncle Bernard, who was staying for a night before joining the navy, had to sleep on my bed all scrunched up because I wouldn't. I remember the spectacular though distant display of an air raid on Hull through the caravan's window. And the excitement of first seeing the sea. So 'With' had been delightful, but Portchester was much more sophisticated. I felt as enraptured at the prospect as Keats: 'O for a beaker full of the warm South.' We were northerners and we were going south!

The train journey from the Paragon Station, Hull, to King's Cross seemed interminable, Waterloo to Portsmouth less so. Uncle Bill had a little old Ford, and we crammed into it and tore all over the place: Brighton, Bognor, Lee-on-Solent, Arundel.

Uncle Bill worked on Portsmouth Docks. He was small, dark and chunky, and he used to take off his wide ex-navy belt and let me butt him in his very hard stomach. I could make no impression and he would pretend he didn't even know I was doing it. He would bowl at me in their back garden as long as I didn't try a cover drive and endanger his loganberries. He loved to tease me. In his vegetable garden, beyond the loganberries, he picked up a caterpillar and squashed it on my hand, to my great disgust. 'It's only cabbage,' he said. 'You could eat it.' His funny southern accent made him seem all the more humorous to me. He called Aunt Hilda 'Hild' for short and it sounded like 'Iwd'. My histrionic ambitions already forming, I once struck an attitude and asked him, 'Am I registering terror, Uncle Bill?' He made it into a catch phrase which he loved to deliver with arms raised against the approaching monster as mine had been. Aunt Hilda and Uncle Bill had no children and they loved having Ann and me around them. At the end of our first holiday with them, as they were seeing us off, Mother burst into tears in the railway carriage. We had had a week of sunshine and loganberries, sweetpeas and trees, Portchester Castle and laughter. She didn't want to go back to Harrow Street.

SCHOOL

' "Please may I leave the room?" You put your hand up and say, "Please may I leave the room?" ' I was five, and due to start school the following day. Grandad Quest was giving me guidance on how to cope with suddenly finding myself in the middle of a class of fifty mixed infants. I can remember them all laughing: Aunts Phyllis and Barbara, Grandma and Grandad and Mother. I wasn't the only one who was excited. School. That was the way out. That was the start of the journey away from the Fish Dock. It was never intended that I should work 'on Dock'. Not by Mam, not by Dad, and not by me. Ever since I can remember.

My early recollections of school are hazy. I wasn't that struck. I didn't get the attention that I got from Mother. There were various Misses. For a short period I was in a Catholic class at West Dock Avenue, because St Wilfrid's Catholic School had been bombed and its Infant Department had to be rehoused. Sometimes we were taught by Miss McGlaughlin, sometimes by a nun. Mother liked neither of them. She was convinced they had it in for me because they knew she wasn't a Catholic. 'That Miss McGlaughlin doesn't even like it if I bring two ha'pennies instead of a penny for your morning milk.' Fortunately for Mother's peace of mind, St Wilfrid's Mixed Infants was soon housed elsewhere and I stayed put at West Dock Avenue. Mother's influence, I am sure, and, besides, West Dock Avenue School was so near our house.

I still didn't like school. I can remember sitting at the top of our stairs wondering how I could painlessly throw myself down and incapacitate myself so I didn't have to attend. I could do the reflective bit at the top of the stairs, and could arrange myself into a sorry-looking pile at the bottom, whose discovery would have alarmed Mother, but I couldn't manage the falling bit in between.

Miss Davis, though a Protestant, was none the less very sharp and didn't think my mind was on the job in hand. 'Frame yourself, lad,' I remember her saying. More than once.

One day I arrived at school in a nearly new mac. It wasn't every day I got something nearly new, and I was very pleased with it. It was dark blue and made me feel like a naval officer. It was much admired as I hung it up in the cloakroom, and I couldn't wait till playtime so that I could put it on again. I sat in class dreaming I was on the bridge of a destroyer speeding towards the enemy.

Playtime arrived at long last and I went joyfully to be reunited with my mac. Imagine my horror when I found not it but a greatly inferior one hanging in its place. The same colour as mine, yes, but limp and jaded-looking. No naval officer would have been seen dead in it. I must have gloried in my mac too much that morning, and some jealous child had done a swap. I immediately took the changeling to Miss Davis and explained that it had been hung in place of my new one. There ensued a search of the cloakroom and an examination of macs of all hues and ages, but my beautiful mac did not come to light. The changeling fitted me, however, and at lunchtime I sadly put it on and Miss Davis escorted me across Harrow Street to our front door.

'I'm sorry, Mrs Courtenay, but Tommy's mac has disappeared and been replaced by the one he's got on. He says it's not nearly such a good one. We've looked high and low.'

'But this is his mac,' said Mother.

Miss Davis, who had really got stuck into the drama of the missing mac, was not pleased. Had I been a weevil she'd found in her self-raising flour, she couldn't have been more annoyed. Unable to attack me physically because Mother was so close, she gave me a withering look, let out a breathy gasp of frustration, turned on her heel and strode across Harrow Street back to school. Young Courtenay was even dozier than she had thought.

By the time I made it to the Juniors, aged seven or eight, I was enjoying school much more, though I regretted that as Juniors we were no longer mixed, but lads plain and simple. We had Misters then, not Misses, and in my last two years at West Dock Avenue with Mr Brabbs and finally Mr Nicholson I was beginning to do pretty well. Dad observed my schooling keenly. It meant a great deal to him that I did well. He was very good at figures, a gift I hadn't inherited. Ann and I used to call out sums for him to do. '117 times 93.' He always got the answer right, but he employed a cunning ruse to give himself extra time. He would always pretend he hadn't fully heard us the first time and ask for the sum to be repeated while he was working out the answer, and after another '117 times 93' he would come straight in with the answer and make it all the more impressive. We soon got wise to his method and changed the numbers the second time of asking.

English was my favourite subject, not arithmetic. It meant compositions, and that's where Mother loved getting involved. As though my education was hers too.

Mr Nicholson and his moustache had just left the RAF and he used to arrive at school on his motorbike in flying boots. Even though he may well not have been a pilot, he looked as though he had, and I was keen to impress him. He gave us a subject for the following day's composition: 'My favourite thing'. We didn't do homework at West Dock Avenue Juniors, but I couldn't resist thinking about my composition to be and discussed it excitedly with Mother. She liked my being good at writing. What thing should we choose? My favourite thing was an air rifle, the only trouble being that it wasn't mine but a lad's down the street – he let me handle it occasionally. So it didn't qualify. A shame, because it was beautiful. At home I used to play with one of Mother's plastic knitting needles. I pretended to conduct with it. But only recently it had snapped in the air as I reached a climax to the imaginary music. I was so startled that it made her laugh. I used to like to play with her kitchen knife, slapping it against my palm. I had recently used it to retrieve a threepenny bit from under the piano, banging my head on the underside of the keyboard as I did so. But a knitting needle and a kitchen knife didn't really seem the stuff of poetry. Then Mother had a wonderful idea. 'What about the football?'

I had always longed to own a football. They used to be the most glamorous of the prizes in the Housey Housey stalls at Hull Fair. Shiny new leather and infinitely desirable. We never managed to win one, but Dad did once acquire one for me – though it wasn't new. It wasn't even fairly new. That didn't matter. What did matter was that it had a hole in it. This somewhat tempered my excitement. Dad, however, was confident he could repair it. He got a piece of red leather and some thread and borrowed a special tool from work. He applied himself diligently to his patchwork, eventually declared himself satisfied, got a new bladder for it and blew it up. There it was, my very own football. The newness of the patch stood out rather, but there was no denying it was a football.

The next day at school I told Mr Nicholson I had a football and if any of the lads cared to come to field with me – the municipal playing fields near the Kingston High School – we could have a game. Several lads were keen. A semi-official party was organized and one evening after school off we went to field. We put our coats down to mark the goalposts and picked sides. As owner of the ball and author of the entire venture, I kicked off with some pride, stroking my treasured possession towards Ronnie Ellerington. He gave it an almighty thump. Now is not the time to question his motivation, and I cannot say whether my ball would have fared better had it been given gentler treatment so early on its comeback trail. As it was, Ronnie's aggression, coming when it did, proved too stern a test of Dad's cobbling skills. My beloved ball rose briefly into the air before dropping with a sigh.

The story of the football had everything. Longing, followed by an all-too-brief fulfilment. The stuff of life, the stuff of poetry. I couldn't wait to get back to school the next day and write it all down.

Mr Nicholson's response did not disappoint. To Mother's great delight I got nine out of ten. Two whole marks better than anyone else.

By now the Great Thing in my life, the way of one day escaping from the Fish Dock, was the forthcoming Eleven Plus examination. Should I not pass the Eleven Plus I would stay at West Dock Avenue, leave school at fifteen and work on the Fish Dock like everybody else in Harrow Street. Pass, and unbelievable horizons opened up. The Kingston High School, with its own playing fields and uniform. French, Latin, geometry. In short, a good education. That was the key. Then it wouldn't matter that we were poor.

'Kingy 'igh', as it was known in Harrow Street. The 'H' was silent. A mile and a half west along the Hessle Road, past the Dairycoates level crossing, in an altogether greener part of Hull near Pickering Park. Trees. Houses with bathrooms and inside lavatories. Houses not built for Fish Dock workers. Today Kingy High, tomorrow the world. Today West Dock Avenue Seniors, tomorrow the Fish Dock.

The 'Plus' in Eleven Plus meant that if you failed the first time you could have another go the following year. Failure! God help me.

My best pal at this time was Arthur, who lived in West Dock Avenue. He wasn't as rough as some of the lads in Harrow Street but he was more worldly than I was. He wasn't dreaming so much of what might be. We would go in fish shop. 'Patty and chips, please,' I would order. 'Two penn'uth of chips, please,' requested Arthur. But once his chips were in the bag he would add, as though coming out of a reverie, 'Oh, and could I have a patty as well, please?' He reckoned he got more chips that way. It did mean, however, that we had to travel the length and breadth of Hessle Road in search of fish and chip shops not alert to Arthur's method of ordering.

Unlike me, Arthur wasn't scared of being bad. We once went to Beverley races. Grandad Quest had given me a shilling to get in and a shilling to put on Admiral's Salute. Arthur said he knew how to sneak in and if I came with him I would have an extra shilling to bet with. I didn't dare follow him through the hole in the fence, but joined him a minute or so later having gone in through the proper entrance. Arthur, whose father was a bobber like Grandad Quest, also put his money on Admiral's Salute. The bobbers obviously knew something that day because it won. It was a grey horse. I can see it thundering past us. Needless to say, Arthur won twice as much as I did.

He used to love kidding me. 'Every time you play with yourself you get a spot under your dick.' I said I didn't believe him, but I couldn't wait to get home and check things out. To my horror there the spots were. I always reckoned every time I did it would be the last. Goodness was just around the corner. Sin would one day leave me never to return. But there they were. Recorded. Little white lumps gleaming through the thin scrotal skin. I glumly imagined the Day of Judgement. There I'd be on Hessle Road looking for all the world like a good person. 'Stop!' a loud voice would cry. 'We want to know who's good.' Everybody stopped. The Inquisitor walked along thoughtfully and pulled up sharply in front of me. 'Step forward, Courtenay, there's something I want to check.' He did so. 'Twenty-seven times! And how old are you?'

It was Arthur who told me that grown-ups did it. 'No,' I assured him, 'they only do it when they're married and they want to make a baby.' 'They're always doing it,' insisted Arthur. 'They like doing it.' We were in Harrow Street when he told me and I could see Mother standing on our doorstep in her clean pinny. I knew that what Arthur was telling me could not possibly be true.

Arthur and I went to take our Eleven Plus one Saturday morning at Askew Avenue school near Gypsyville. For such a special occasion I had been given a Mars Bar to eat when I had finished the exam. I found the tests straightforward enough, though I didn't quite finish the whole paper. Billy Spencer finished. Arthur pretended he'd finished and said it was a doddle. I gave him a bite of my Mars Bar.

A few weeks later I was in the school yard early one morning. I was usually the first there since it was just opposite our house. Mr Beeken, our headmaster, called me into the staffroom. He was looking very pleased. 'There's something I've got to tell you.' 'What, sir?' My heart was beating fast. 'You've passed your Eleven Plus. You'll be going to the Kingston High School.' How wonderful. 'What about Arthur?' 'No. You and Billy Spencer. Just you two.' Out of a class of fifty. I was beside myself with excitement.

The Eleven Plus exam, introduced after the war by the Labour Government, was thought by many to be unjust, to be a poor way of selecting children for higher education. My sister Ann was bright, yet she unexpectedly failed her Eleven Plus the following year. (It didn't stop her becoming a teacher later in life.) Two out of fifty seemed very long odds. Four per cent success rate was well below the national average. But two out of fifty was considerably more than none out of fifty. Without the Eleven Plus, imperfect though it was, I would have gone nowhere.

Billy, my fellow laureate, was my pal too. He and I were usually the top two in the class. His speciality was arithmetic, mine English. Billy could be pretty quick. I once noticed some white flecks on his fingernails. 'What are those white bits on your fingernails?' I enquired. 'Pureness of the nail,' he responded without blinking. I was impressed and hoped I had some pureness of my own. I checked my fingernails carefully. Not one single speck.

Mr Beeken was a tall thin good-humoured man with silver hair. He had taken our class for a week once when Mr Nicholson was ill. He liked to catch us out. 'What would be the first thing to happen if your fathers came into some money?' he asked us. My hand went up in a flash. 'Yes, Courtenay?' 'The first thing my dad would do is send me to a good school,' I said with great certainty. 'You mean this isn't a good school?' And he smiled. He'd got me there. He had known what I meant, however. And now I was going to a good school without Dad having to win the pools.

'You've passed your Eleven Plus.' 'Can I go and tell me mother, sir?' 'Of course you can.' And I ran the very short distance to our house as fast as my legs would carry me. Mother's face shone with delight when I told her, and we hugged and kissed. I had to go back to lessons, of course, though I could scarcely concentrate. Billy and I had been thought the most likely to pass. Three or four other lads had had hopes, however, and looked very disappointed. Arthur didn't seem fazed, but then he wouldn't have.

After school, my little sister was pleased for me and said she had known it all along. Mother and I could hardly wait to tell the news to Dad. As soon as I saw him coming down Harrow Street from Fish Dock I ran to greet him. 'I've passed, Dad, I've passed!' And he couldn't help but smile.

QUARTET

Like Mother, I had always felt I was supposed to be somewhere other than Hessle Road. On summer evenings I occasionally walked along the Humber towards Hessle. It wasn't a very beautiful walk. Along the tunnel under the railway lines to Fish Dock, and round the back of the warehouses on its dry south side where the trawlers were serviced by, among others, Dad's paint firm, Webster's. It was deserted in the evening. (The north side was known as the wet side – where the fish was unloaded.) There was a narrow walkway alongside the river behind the warehouses, which was strewn with old paint tins, bits of rope and empty crates. At the western end of Fish Dock there was Dry Dock. You could see the keel of a trawler when it was in Dry Dock, and it looked huge. Once beyond Dry Dock the path continued towards Hessle foreshore. I didn't know quite what a foreshore was, but it sounded a good thing to have near where one lived. And I liked to think I was walking along a riverbank. That's what children did in books. Except it wasn't beautiful. The Humber is very wide and brown, and the footpath skirted a corporation rubbish tip, so the air wasn't sweet either.

Whether I was inspired by the Christmas story, or by the song 'You Are My Lucky Star', I can't be sure, but either way it was My Star that kept me going. Up there late in the summer evening, alone and bright. It was a long way off, but definitely mine, and full of hope and promise. I saw it only a couple of times on that walk, but that was enough. I know now that it wasn't a star but a planet. But then it was a star and it was mine and it would lead me away from Fish Dock. I knew it, and it didn't matter about the smell. I don't remember telling Mother about my star, but she would have welcomed it. She was the living proof that Fish Dock wasn't where we really belonged. When I was young I had her to encourage me and understand my dreams. When she was young, who did she have?

I remember her asking her friend Olive, 'Who's he most like – me or his father?' It somehow mattered to her. I had just made her laugh, I forget how, so I was her 'little ray of sunshine'. That's what she some-times called me. Not always. My ill temper would affect her: 'Why do we all have to suffer 'cos you're in a bad mood? You've a face as long as a wet week. Straighten it.' But, the sun being out that day, 'Who's he most like?' 'He takes after you, Annie. He's the drawn image of you,' said Olive. She was no fool.

Physically I looked most like Dad. In parts I play nowadays I'm astonished by the way he turns up. I can see his smile in Harold Smith and I heard his anguish in Lear. But Olive was right in saying I took after Mother. If Dad is the ammunition I now use, it's from Mother I got the need to aim the gun and pull the trigger.

We didn't bottle our feelings up like Dad did. Sometimes the intensity of our reactions baffled him. Like when Mother cried because she'd broken the vacuum cleaner. She'd only broken the plastic around where it was plugged in, so it still worked, but she wept and wept. Perhaps it was a last straw because she hated housework and Dad had made such a big deal of getting it for her. He shook his head in disbelief at her tears. I remember him telling me years later that sometimes he'd got home from work and been completely unable to fathom what was eating her. 'I think sometimes, Tom, it was to do with, you know, women's cycles.' She once wrote to me, 'I am, like you say, tempera-mental.' So was I. And my excess of feeling, or at any rate the expression of it, baffled him too. Like when Tiddles was run over.

I loved Tiddles. She used to come upstairs and sleep on my bed. The first time she did so, she almost frightened me to death. We used to listen to Valentine Dyall, 'The Man In Black', on the radio, in a series of horror stories called, entirely accurately, *Appointment with Fear*. We had just had 'The Beast with Five Fingers', a story about a severed hand that went round strangling people, and that's what I thought I was hearing coming up the stairs and into my bedroom and jumping onto my bed. Thankfully it turned out to be Tiddles, not a severed hand, and I was purred at, not strangled. She was very clean, and used to try and go under the fire grate when she couldn't get out. She got run over by a van delivering to Brooks' shop next door. This happened on a Friday. Mother, knowing the deluge that would result, couldn't face telling me the truth when I got home from school. Tiddles was usually there to greet me, but not that evening. Mother just said she didn't know where Tiddles was, so I spent most of Saturday and Sunday looking for her. Eventually Mother grasped the nettle and told me Tiddles was dead. There was nothing, but nothing, she could do to console me. Time was the only healer. And we had no more cats after that.

But how I cried then was nothing compared to the torrent occasioned by the death of my black pigeon. I had four pigeons in a rough shed in the back yard in between the lavatory and the back wall. Two of them were the offspring of the first two I had, and my little hen was sitting on two more eggs. I had a batty friend in West Dock Avenue who had pigeons too. He was grown up, though you could only tell by his age. His house was of Dickensian squalor and his tiny back yard was full of his pigeon loft, so he seemed to be living with his charges. We both loved our pigeons. They weren't very good pigeons. We would occasionally take them somewhere by bike and let them loose. They would fly home, but we had no way of knowing which one got back first.

One day a racing bird came down to my friend's loft and laid two eggs. She was the real thing. My friend decided he would keep the smaller of the eggs, which would become a hen, and he let me have the larger one. I took it home carefully, removed the two eggs in my loft and put it in their place. Pigeons can't count, and I couldn't afford to have too many birds. The egg eventually hatched into a splendid cock bird. He soon outgrew his foster parents. He was very dark in colour – almost black, with a powerful chest and the intelligent red eye of a racing bird. I named him Blackie, and he was my pride and joy.

One Sunday morning (it would be a Sunday – so often the day for feeling sad) I got up and went into our back yard as usual to see my dear ones. The loft was strangely quiet. Had they got out? I looked up and saw four birds looking quizzically down at me, but no Blackie. I looked in the loft. Blackie was lying there motionless. I gently picked him up. His head hung limply. There were two small holes in his neck. A cat had got into my ramshackle shed, no longer worthy of being called a loft, and killed him. That was the longest I kept on crying in my life. I couldn't bear the heartbreak of the story's symbolism. The brave little hen (Mother), who had flown in from a better place to lay her eggs. And her offspring (me), so much more special than the Hessle Road birds around him. It was him the cat had got, not the wilier street pigeons. Later that week when I went round to Grandma's for comfort yet again, I heard Aunt Phyllis say with some amazement, 'He's still crying!'

Was Dad glad to have Ann! If Mother and I were the criers, Ann was the shoulder to cry on. Always has been for those around her.

Mother told me, sitting near the front-room window, that she cried one evening, holding me, still a baby, in her arms and worrying how on earth she was going to cope with another one on the way. 'I was out here, Tommy,' she said, indicating full breasts with her hands. Ann was born fourteen or so months after I was. 16 May, 1938. Mother told me that I didn't welcome my sister's arrival, and I can well believe it. I would have wanted Mother to myself. She told me (I thought) that I had once bitten my little sister, and Mother bit me to teach me a lesson. Ann assures me that it was she who bit me because I had hit her with an iron file Dad used for mending his shoes, and so Mother bit her. Either way, the biter got bit and we learnt that biting one another was wrong. We were their pride and joy when we were toddlers. Later Dad loved to recount, over and over, the simplest 'kinderscenen'. Usually me shitting myself and Ann eating coal.

Ann coped very well with my indifference towards her. She was more in the mould of Dad's sisters. She wasn't fragile like Mother. For much of our childhood she was taller than me. I remember once seeing a lad in Harrow Street squaring up to her with his fists. I slunk guiltily indoors, not delaying to defend her. There was always something very strong about her, and not just physically. She was a wonderful balance for Dad against over-emotional Mother and me, and she made us the quartet that we were. As complete as any string quartet. Annie and Tom, Tommy and Ann. As Mother wrote of Dad and Ann, 'they're a good pair'. Ann had the Courtenay intelligence, too. But I arrived home from Kingston High one day to find Ann in tears, being consoled by Mother for failing her Eleven Plus. I wasn't very sympathetic. I liked being Harrow Street's sole representative at the Kingston High School. Amazing to think that I could be so callous about my little sister. She seems not to bear me a grudge, seems somehow to have understood.

Ann and I were at our closest when Mam and Dad had a row. Dad went out with Uncle Bernard one Saturday afternoon and came home drunk. Mother threw a cup at him, quite a thing to do because we only had five. It missed him and hit the wall. I went, distressed, to pick it up. It featured a picture of the young Queen Elizabeth. The cup's handle had broken off, though Her Majesty was unscathed. Ann and I cried ourselves to sleep that night because they still weren't talking. We couldn't feel happy till there was harmony once more. I can remember how relieved we felt at seeing them walking together along Harrow Street towards Rayner's, Dad's sin of selfishness forgiven.

Two or three years after her Eleven Plus misfortune, Ann won a place at the Hull High School for Commerce, where she learnt shorthand, typing and book-keeping, so she, too, managed to slip Fish Dock's grasp. No net-braiding for Ann, and wasn't Mother glad. Ann was soon bringing in good money, which made life easier at number 29.

Mother had three major operations during her life. 'Big' operations, she always called them. 'So and so's got to have a big operation, poor bugger,' she would say, and go quiet. After the removal of an ovary at the age of nineteen because of a cyst, in her late twenties she had her second operation, which was for cancer. I was just old enough to read on the clipboard at the end of her bed that something 'the size of a pea' had been removed from . . . I couldn't make out the next word. It was in the region of her stomach, I believe.

Her last operation was around 1950, when she was only thirty-five or six. I loved helping to look after her. I'd take some tea and toast and lime marmalade upstairs before I went to school. The marmalade was a luxury. There were plenty of aunts to rally round during the day. I did one wicked thing while she was still in hospital. I helped myself to a piece of apple pie that Aunt Alice had made for us, thinking that Dad wouldn't have Mother's eagle eye for our rations. But he did. 'You wouldn't do that if your mother was here,' made me feel ashamed. I had let down the team effort of the three of us.

That last operation was for breast cancer. I told two school pals about it. They weren't very sensitive. I tried to explain that she'd never had much that stuck out so her appearance wouldn't be affected, but it's a difficult subject to share with your schoolmates. I moved my hand up and down in front of my chest to indicate flatness, and changed the subject.

She had radiation treatment for some weeks thereafter, and was then considered healed. But her surgeon, drat him, told her he couldn't guarantee she wouldn't get it again somewhere else. For the remaining dozen years of her life she was haunted by fear of cancer, and couldn't bear mention of the word. When Grandad Quest died from cancer during my first term at UCL, it was Dad who wrote to tell me. Not a word from Mother on the subject.

Delicate or not, when I was a child she was fearless on my behalf. She sent me off one day with a threepenny bit to get my hair cut. The barber's shop was just round the corner on Hessle Road. There were two or three other lads already in the shop, so I sat down to wait my turn. I had rather a good game that I had been perfecting at home, and to while away the time I thought I would play it. It went like this: I would pretend to be a singer on the radio, and while I was singing I would switch the radio, or rather me, off. I, or rather the singer on the radio, would carry on with the tune silently in my head till such time as I elected to switch the radio on again. Then I would resume the tune out loud. I kept switching on and off, while keeping the tune going:

> Beautiful dreamer . . . . me
> Starlight and dewdrops . . . . thee
> Sounds of the rude . . . . day
> Lulled . . . . have all . . . .
> Beautiful . . . . queen . . . .
> List while I woo—

I concede that to anyone not *au fait* with my game my rendition might sound confusing, not to say irritating. I was completely un-mindful of my surroundings, however, and it gave me quite a jolt when the barber swooped down on me, got me by my jacket collar and led me firmly out of the shop, saying as he did so, 'That's enough of that bloody row.' I reflected on the way home that he would probably have preferred it if I had done the whole song out loud.

When I finally got home there had been plenty of time to have my hair cut. I had stopped outside a house where an ambulance was parked and waited expectantly for the hospitalee to be carried out and put into the ambulance's great maw. It was very impressive. An ambulanceman at either end of a stretcher bearing an elderly man who looked pale and ghastly – very ill indeed. I reflected bitterly on how I had been denied a stretcher when I got scarlet fever, and that my being carried to the ambulance in a blanket must have made no impact whatsoever.

Back at number 29, I returned Mother's threepenny bit. 'Why haven't you had your hair cut?' she asked me.

'The barber threw me out.'

'He threw you out?'

'Yeh.'

'What for.'

'Singin'.'

'Singin'?'

'I kept stoppin' and then startin' again. Like I was on wireless an' bein' switched on and off. "Beautiful dreamer . . ."' but Mother had heard enough. She grabbed her coat and me, and off we marched back to the barber's.

'What do you mean by throwing him out?' she demanded.

The barber, standing over his chair with scissors and comb, looked aghast and found no words.

'You miserable sod. He was having a bit of fun. He's only little. You must think very well of yourself when you can decide whose hair you'll cut and whose you won't.'

The poor barber still couldn't answer. At the door Mother had another shot: 'His hair'll be down his back before he comes in here again.' Nor did I. From then on I went to a barber's much further along

Hessle Road even though a haircut there cost fourpence. The following day Grandad Quest, having heard the story of my expulsion, called on the barber and told him, more in sorrow than in anger, that his nerves must be bad.

Mother once sent a young policeman packing. He had brought me to our front door for playing in West Dock Avenue schoolyard during the school holidays – something we weren't supposed to do. 'Where the hell's the harm in it? Where else can they play? They're not supposed to play in Langham car park. The streets are covered in dog muck. [I think she said 'muck' instead of 'shit' out of deference to the policeman's youth.] There's nobody works harder than our Tommy. He's doing homework every bloody night of the week. He goes in schoolyard for half an hour for a game of football and he's stopped by bloody police.'

Dad, embarrassed, was shushing her in the background. The young policeman looked abashed but tried his best. 'I won't say anything about it this time, but will you please make sure that he doesn't do it again?'

'Will I hell.'

'It's all right, constable, I'll see to that,' said Dad, enabling the young policeman to beat his retreat without losing face.

'What's wrong with 'em playing in schoolyard?' she asked.

'Nothing,' said Dad, 'but you can't go on at that policeman. He's only a kid himself. He's just doing what he's been told.'

But it was the meanness Mother didn't like. Stopping kids from playing in a playground.

'She was the most honest person in the world.' That was quite something from Uncle Pat because she was so scornful of his beloved religion.

Once when I was little I saw a pile of change on the kitchen table. There was a sixpenny piece on the top of it winking brightly at me. Mother was in the scullery. I put the sixpence in my pocket and looked nonchalant. Minutes later, she picked up the change to put in her purse.

'There's sixpence missing.'

She didn't accuse me. But all of a sudden I knew I had done wrong. Far too wrong to want to own up to her.

'Is there? I'll look for it.'

I got on my hands and knees and pretended to search for it. Checking I wasn't being observed (Mother was sitting patiently with an ever-so-slightly long-suffering expression), I got the sixpence out of my pocket and put it on the floor.

'Oh, here it is!'

She didn't say anything. But I knew she knew what I'd done. And she knew I knew.

Dad once said to me, 'Your mother was always very modest.' She once told me that on their wedding night Dad had passed out dead drunk. But I was too young to appreciate the significance of the story. I was still firmly of the opinion I had given to my friend Arthur, namely that grown-ups did it only to make a baby. I don't know why she told me. Maybe she was ruminating more to herself that life is never quite what you expect it to be. The Quests and the Courtenays were bound to have had a good celebration that night, and I bet Dad had started in the morning with Uncle Pat and his mates.

I always thought she was very innocent, maybe because I was. When I inadvertently mucked up her dark blue coat she seemed to have no idea what I'd been doing. I must have been about ten when I borrowed it to put on my bed for the winter. It saved her buying a blanket. One night when I did what Arthur told me gave me the white spots under my dick, to my great consternation stuff started to come out on my hand. First spots, now stuff! This had to stop. I vowed that it would and unthinkingly wiped my hand. On her coat.

Winter gave way to spring. I have to confess that though I had reined in I hadn't altogether managed to stop, and I arrived home from school one afternoon to find Mother looking extremely annoyed and mystified and holding her dark blue coat.

'What's this mess on my coat?'

The coat looked as though a hundred snails had used it for their Christmas outing. The dark blue background showed up the glistening residue of their merrymaking. I, like the barber before me, was at a loss for words. 'What the hell is it? How will I get it off?'

I had no explanation I cared to offer, but my luck was in. Dad, off work after his first accident, came out of the back-yard lavatory, weighed up the situation and started to shush her. She would not be placated, however, and it wasn't until he managed to get her into the scullery, presumably to explain to her what little boys sometimes do, that she let the matter drop.

She was very quiet that evening, however. Not only was I a dirty little devil, I had ruined her coat. She never wore it again, making two blue coats in her lifetime that, for different reasons, she didn't get much wear out of.

KINGY 'IGH

The Kingston High School colours were maroon and white. Mr and
Mrs Courtenay were sent a list of requirements. Minimum requirements were of special interest to Mr Courtenay, and he spelt them out
carefully: 'A cap and a tie.'

'That's all I'll get an' all,' I grumbled. 'Billy Spencer's getting a blazer.
And Norman got a proper satchel.' My cousin Norman had passed for
Kingston the year before. He was Dad's sister Ivy's son. His father,
Uncle Arthur, made better money than Dad as a cook on the trawlers.

I resented not getting the lot – blazer, satchel, football kit, gym kit –
everything. I did get an almost maroon and white scarf from Grandma
and Grandad, though it wasn't the official one. Official school things
came from a special shop in town. 'School Outfitters'. Apart from when
we bought my cap and tie, we never went near it. 'Too bloody dear
there,' said Dad. The official school scarf was maroon with elegant
lengthwise white stripes. Mine had crosswise stripes. Wearing it, it
seemed to me, I could easily be mistaken for a Hull Kingston Rovers
supporter.

Uncle Bernard bought me the official maroon football shirt, with
plenty of room for me to grow into it, and I was expected to feel very
grateful and indebted. It seemed to me then that a football shirt was an

essential, and that Uncle Bernard, a chief engineer, can't surely have missed the thirty shillings it cost. But now I think it was very generous of him. It lasted me for years. Mother didn't want me to be stunted, but, being so conscientious with the family purse strings, she would often express pleasure that I wasn't growing out of things.

Dad didn't like my ungrateful attitude, but since I knew how much it meant to them, as well as to me, that I had taken the great leap forward, I couldn't understand why they didn't celebrate by kitting me out with more style. I knew Dad had recently got his compensation money. But he had no intention of blowing it to dress me up. Mother thought the Kingston blazers didn't have much wear in them and when I got one some years later she was proved right. The beautiful white piping round its edges came loose and it didn't last long. They had too much sense to throw away what little they had got. They could remember the days before the war when there had been far less work on Fish Dock and money was hard to come by.

Life may not be perfect but it can still be beautiful. I loved my maroon cap. Nobody else in Harrow Street had one.

I got the bus at the end of West Dock Avenue. Along the Hessle Road towards Hessle. Off at Pickering Park. I walked through the park, and there it was, at the end of its L-shaped drive. The Kingston High School. A long, low, two-storeyed, pre-war structure standing in its own playing fields.

I had met some of the lads in Form One when playing soccer for West Dock Avenue. We had done quite well against the posher, non-Hessle Road schools. Arthur had scored the winning goal against Ainthorpe Grove. Jack Barnaby had played for Eastfield Road. He was a tremendous athlete. I certainly wasn't, but I talked a lot. Though I regretted my scruffy Fish Dock background, it helped make me a bit of a card. Billy, also from West Dock, didn't make as much noise as I did.

At the Kingston High School I was very conscious of coming from a family that was less well off than the majority. I suppose they would only have been lower-middle class, but the difference between them and me from Harrow Street felt very significant. Our intake sported heaps of blazers and shiny new satchels. Jacketed in homely tweed, I made do with a not even nearly new imitation leather attaché case in which to carry my homework. I thought it was a contemptible object with which to launch my grammar-school career, and it was a difficult thing to hide.

My secret weapon was our recent holiday. 'We went to Portchester on the south coast, near the South Downs. My uncle has a car, so we went to Brighton and Bognor Regis, Lee-on-Solent and Arundel.' Every bit as telling as having a dressing-gown. They might even have thought I was kidding when I said I lived in Harrow Street.

There was so much to report to Mother. So many classes – physics, biology, woodwork. Masters wearing gowns. (Though not, sadly, mortarboards, as they did in 'Smith of the Lower Fourth' in *Wizard*.) She loved to hear of any small triumphs. So did Dad, though he'd usually say, 'Don't be so big-headed.'

That summer my interest in classical music had started to grow, and I listened to it on the wireless whenever I could. The BBC used to broadcast lunchtime symphony concerts, which often included those innumerable Haydn symphonies. Mother and I would listen together, though musical as she was, she didn't always care for what was on offer – and with some justification. I was keen to become as knowledgeable as possible, believing that it would help my standing at the grammar school.

'Do we have to have that bloody row?' she would sometimes ask.

'But, Ma, it's 'aydn!'

My policy of self-improvement paid off. The music teacher played a record. 'Who wrote this music?' he asked. Silence throughout the classroom. I raised my hand.

'Yes?'

'Mozart, sir.'

'I was the only one who knew it was Mozart, Ma,' I announced later. She smiled happily. One up to Hessle Road. Dad just looked at me over the top of his *Hull Daily Mail*.

There was plenty to tell Arthur. 'In chemistry, Arthur, we've got these scales – they're so sensitive they can weigh things you can't even see.'

'Oh, we've got scales like that at West Dock Seniors. We throw them around.' And for a second or two I believed him.

I felt sorry for Arthur. West Dock Seniors seemed to me to be a living hell. Somewhere you waited without interest till you were fifteen and could become a barrow lad on Fish Dock. I don't think Arthur was as bothered about it as I was.

The major disappointment of my first year at Kingston, mortarboards apart, was the English teacher, Mr W. He was reputed to be a keen trainspotter, and his chief preoccupations in the study of English were spelling and grammar. He used to get very excited about whether you wrote 'alright' or 'all right'. What had been known at West Dock as compositions were now called essays. I think the former title suited Mother and me better. Mr W. set an essay entitled 'King for a Day' for homework, a subject surely giving us plenty of scope. Mr W. was very particular that we were to write no more than a page and a half of exercise book – perhaps he had a lot of trainspotting that week. That evening at home I was happily engrossed as a king from a bygone age when I suddenly realized that, with a page and a half of exercise book already written, I had yet to rise from my royal bed. My servants were still putting out my silken robes. Even if I got only as far as my royal elevenses, much more writing would be needed. I had yet to check through my illuminated vellum engagement book, and toy with my larks' tongues on toast. I knew, however, that when Mr W. said a page and a half he meant a page and a half. His trains would not wait. What was I to do?

'*Tommy, it's time to get up,*' I wrote. It was Mother's voice. I had been dreaming! It was dramatic and made perfect sense of my still being in my royal bed. Brilliant. Or so I thought.

Mother and I waited eagerly for the essay to be marked. What did I get? A measly six out of ten. 'King for a DAY,' wrote the literal-minded Mr W. The capitals are his. The two lads who had written the pieces considered by Mr W. to have cut the mustard were asked to read them out. This added salt to my wound. Reading aloud in class was something I loved to do.

SINGIN'

Look out, look out, Jack Frost is about.
He's after your fingers and toes.

That's what I sang in West Dock Avenue Mixed Infants' Christmas concert, aged five. I had on a paper hat and a white sheet round my shoulders – fair enough for Jack Frost. But the wardrobe department didn't run to footwear, so I had to wear my own boots. I clearly remember looking down as I leapt about, thinking they weren't sharp enough for Jack Frost. Far too galumphing. That's the first performing I remember doing at school. But I had already started at home.

Mother's piano, in our front room, was the backbone of the parties that were held at our house. 'Dos', as they were known. Christmas Eve was the big night of the year. Quests, Courtenays and friends used to come back to our house after Subway Street Club had emptied out, with a crate or two of Hull Brewery. Ann and I were put to bed while they went in Club and promised we'd be woken when they got back. This I loved, and a lifetime passed as I tossed and turned waiting for their return. Back they would come at long last in high spirits, and I was soon giving them a song. What with the Hull Brewery and maybe the odd drop of short stuff, not forgetting the appeal of my lack of years, they were a very good audience. The first song I can remember singing was 'Coming Home On A Wing And A Prayer'. Not my favourite but apposite, there being a war on. I much preferred 'I Don't Want To Set The World On Fire, I Just Want To Start A Flame In Your Heart'. More tuneful and romantic. My greatest wartime success went:

> In an old Australian homestead with the roses round the door
> A girl received a letter it was newly from the war.
> With her mother's arms around her . . .

And the chorus:

> Why should I weep, why should I cry,
> My love's asleep, so far away . . .

I sang it on the eve of Uncle Jack Stathers' return to duty. His status as a Desert Rat was, to me, extraordinarily impressive and moving. Such a long way from Harrow Street to the desert. He was full of beer, and I don't know which of us cried the most. It must have been very irksome to Dad, a mere Home Guard, for Jack Stathers wasn't the man that he was. But he didn't complain.

The 'dos' continued well after the war. I wasn't the only one who sang. Grandma and Grandad Quest often used to give us a duet, their favourite being 'The Old Rustic Bridge By The Mill'. Our proximity to the Fish Dock made its pastoral quality especially appealing. I loved it when they sang 'around us the stream gently rippled'. It went on, 'It was there, Maggie dear, with our hearts full of cheer' and everybody would shout out, 'Beer, more like!'

Grandad taught me his favourite song:

> 'Twas the ring your mother wore
> On the day she took my name
> 'Twas a plain gold band
> That I placed on her hand
> As partners in life we became.
> 'Twas a simple gift I know

> And a simple gift to show
> May it bring the joy
> To you and your boy
> That it brought to your mother and me.

When I sang it my audience didn't seem to care that, being forty or fifty years too young, I wasn't well cast.

The songs weren't always sentimental:

> Oh, this is number one and the fun has just begun.
> Roll me over, lay me down and do it again.

This was sung communally with much laughter. Ann and I joined in, though we didn't know why they were laughing.

> I'll take you home again, Kathleen,
> Across the ocean wild and wide
> To where your heart has ever been
> Since first you were my blushing bride.
> The roses all have left your cheeks
> I've watched them fade away and die
> Your voice is sad whene'er you speak
> And tears form in your loving eye . . .

I used to make mincemeat out of Uncle Pat with that one. 'He likes to think he's Irish,' explained Mother. Dad would occasionally give us a song, when he'd had enough to drink. His favourite was called 'Sad Or Glad', because he used to get the sads and the glads mixed up, to everybody's delight.

While I was still at West Dock Avenue School the Latin version of 'O Come All Ye Faithful' was written out on the blackboard by Mr Brabbs, even though we didn't learn Latin. With Christmas approaching I thought this might be a useful and impressive addition to my repertoire, so I took the trouble to learn it. Sure enough, come Christmas Eve, 'Adeste Fideles', not to mention the Hull Brewery and the short stuff, worked its spell on my audience and they responded with a whipround. Grandad's friend

Mr Boynton went so far as to give me a threepenny bit on the sly – 'Don't tell your father, Tommy.' I was expected to share my takings with Ann, which I usually did, albeit reluctantly. On this occasion I managed to keep the threepenny bit to myself. I had sung in Latin, after all.

At West Dock Avenue School performing opportunities had been limited. I think Jack Frost was a one-off. My chief outlet was the odd bit of reading I could do in class. But Kingston High School was a different matter. The school hall where we assembled for prayers every morning was really a theatre, complete with stage and balcony. Dr W. Cameron Walker, our headmaster, used to take prayers from the stage, and during my first term, on the side stairs leading up to the stage, the then Head Boy, Goodwin, made a little speech. I really fancied the thought of making a speech from up there, and I was silently critical of his delivery.

The most fascinating teacher was Mr Large, the senior English master. He was slim and dark, with piercing brown eyes and a far more histrionic manner than any of the others. He produced the school play every year before Christmas. It was cast from the sixth form only, but I was determined to let Mr Large know of my existence as soon as I possibly could.

To my great delight, in our second-year English classes, the prosaic Mr W. was replaced by Mr Large's partner in life, Mrs Large. She was much more sensitive to artistic pretensions, literary or histrionic. She told us that their name meant generous as in 'largesse'. She could be strict but she could also be charmed. And she could, I imagined, pass on to Mr Large reports of any good bit of reading done by her charges in 2S. 'Oh, John, Courtenay did a very good reading from "Sohrab and Rustum" today. I was moved to tears. Are you sure he's too young to be in the school play?' Or something like that.

In the fourth form, aged fourteen, when we were streamed into A and B forms, to my great joy Mr Large became our English master. No other master had his way with a gown. He would meticulously draw it round his sleeves as though protecting his suit, or round his body as though protecting his whole being. Sometimes he would hold it open like a pair of wings as his thoughts took flight. He loved the theatre. He went every week to the New Theatre in Hull, and he had seen plays in London and Stratford. He had sat next to Paul Scofield in a teashop in Stratford, and he told us how marvellous Scofield was.

I always think of Mr Large when they talk on the news about a 'tragic accident'. Tragedies can't be accidental because they are inbuilt, he told us. The great tragic dramatic heroes have some flaw that leads to their downfall. There's nothing accidental about it. It's inevitable. Accidents are just accidental. They don't lie in wait, they hit you out of the blue. They can't be tragic even if people on the news say they are. 'Aggravation' was one of his hobbyhorses, too. From the Latin, it means 'making worse' not 'annoyance'. I have always remembered that.

I got my first chance to speak from the stage in the fourth form, delivering a vote of thanks to Alderman Science, a school governor, on Junior Speech Day. Mr Large helped me to compose it. As there were local elections that day he suggested I imply that the good Alderman might prefer to be elsewhere. As I did this, I leant forward to look quizzically at the Alderman round a floral display placed on the stage specially for the occasion, and got quite a big laugh. I thought I had done well, but Bernard Mudd told me I was too cheeky by half, so I wasn't sure whether I had been a success or not, and didn't like to ask anyone else. Bernard was my pal. He was serious minded and a very good distance runner, and small like me.

I didn't appear in the school play till my penultimate year at KHS. It was *The Stars Bow Down* by Gordon Daviot, and I played an Arab named Ishmael. I can still remember my first line: 'All the wonders of the east, lord.' The leading part was played by Ian Hamilton. He was very handsome with blue eyes and black hair, which gave him a distinctive air. As Head Boy he often read the lesson in assembly. He had played the leading part the year before in *The Admirable Crichton*. The leading part two years in a row! I thought that was really something. I think he was much more Mr Large's idea of an actor than I was.

In the first-year sixth form I had done well in the debating society, and in spoken English, so it was no great surprise when I was made a prefect at the beginning of the second-year sixth – our last year. Nevertheless, Mam and Dad gave me the money to go to the New Theatre in recognition of my achievement. Dad was pleased enough. 'Jack Barnaby will be Head Boy,' he said. The Head Boy was to be announced the following day and who could doubt the accuracy of

Dad's prediction? Jack was school captain at cricket and football, as well as being outstanding in science.

When I got back from the theatre I had quite a bit to say about the play I had just seen. I can't remember the name of it or indeed anything about it, except for the performance of the youngest member of the company who, poor lad, had been burdened with the part of an old man. I hadn't much sympathy. 'He was terrible. I could do better than that and I'm a lot younger than he is.'

'All we hear about is how good you are,' said Dad. 'You haven't done anything yet. That actor lad has got a job, which is more than can be said for you.'

The next morning in assembly we newly appointed prefects sat in our positions in a row at the side of the hall, next to the masters. Jack Barnaby had been summoned to see Dr Walker, the headmaster. It was assumed he was being told of his elevation. Then Jack appeared, walking thoughtfully towards his seat. As he passed me he swung his arm vaguely in my direction but didn't look at me. Moments later Dr Walker announced that I was Head Boy. Jack had been told first as beaten favourite and out of deference to his outstanding qualifications.

On the way home after being made Head Boy I decided that after the previous evening's rebuke I would be as cool as possible when announcing my triumph. I thought a throwaway technique would work best. I pretended to be occupied with a book.

'Oh, I forgot to tell you. I'm Head Boy.'

Dad looked up sharply from his *Hull Daily Mail*. 'You.'

'Yeh.'

'Why you?'

'I dunno.'

'What about Jack Barnaby?'

'I thought it would be him. Everybody did. He's the best in the school at football and cricket. And he's very clever.' Dad, after our recent difference, could hardly punch the air in triumph, though a huge blow had undoubtedly been struck for Hessle Road. It was left to Mother, glowing with quiet pride, to fill the silence and get things in perspective. 'You're clever as well, Tommy. And you're the best at reading the lesson. If they want any speeches made, you're the one who can do it.'

I don't remember Dad saying anything very much, but I'm sure he would have told Uncle Pat at the first opportunity, 'Our Tom's Head Boy at Kingston.'

Dad had been off work for months with his broken leg. He had been knocked flying by a car when leaving a club with Mam and Uncle Bernard. They had been on a special outing. Uncle Bernard was as white as a sheet when he came to tell Ann and me that Dad had been taken to hospital. He thought Dad had been killed. His leg took ages to mend. I can remember walking home along Harrow Street just as he was getting out of an ambulance on the day he'd hoped to have his plaster removed. His leg was still encased and he shook his head sadly at me as he swung on his crutches to our front door. Eventually they decided to put silver pins in it. 'I'm worth something at last,' he said.

All the time I was Head Boy, because Dad was off work, we were on National Assistance. Dr Walker showed great sympathy and kindness. He often asked after Dad when I went to get the lesson to be read in School Prayers, and when I eventually had to go to London for an interview with University College English Department he arranged for me to stay with a former Kingston High School teacher. He told me what bus I needed to get from King's Cross and gave me a ten-shilling note to take with me in case I got short. Dad thought it was very good of him and urged me not to spend it if I didn't have to, so I gave it back on my return. 'I didn't need it, thank you, sir.'

The teacher I stayed with in London was very genial, though having been asked by Dr Walker to put up Kingston High School's Head Boy for a night he was possibly expecting someone more imposing than me. He asked me what I wanted to be.

'Well, I'm quite interested in acting,' I said modestly.

'A shrimp like you!' In the sixth form I was small for my age. 'I don't think so. We've just done *Henry IV, Part 1*. You should see the lad who played Falstaff. What a character! Brilliant! He's not even interested in the stage. And the Prince Hal. Superb! He's not interested either. Great strapping lads, both of them. No, you don't want to think of being an actor. A shrimp like you!'

I didn't say anything.

I scored some points, however. I told him I was from the Fish Dock area of Hull.

'A friend of ours used to teach there,' he said. 'West Dock Avenue. What a rough place that was.'

'That's where I went before Kingston.'

'Did you really?' He seemed impressed that a shrimp could have survived such a hell hole.

'Mr Beeken was our headmaster.'

'That's him. Dear old John Beeken. West Dock Avenue! Dear oh dear. He had his hands full there.'

Mam and Dad must have been both puzzled and worried by my wanting to go on the stage. Where had such an absurd notion come from? (Where indeed?) They had always been aware of their own lack of education, and therefore of opportunity, and they believed that I would be better equipped to make my way in the world if I went to a university. My getting a good education was very important to them. Nobody from West Dock Avenue School had ever been to a university. I was the first, and I think the last. All I knew was that I wanted to be an actor. But I had no way of knowing whether it was a good idea, or whether I had any hope of success. And no one who knew me and felt any degree of responsibility towards me would have recommended a career on the stage. It was the most precarious living imaginable. And for a shrimp like me whose father worked on Fish Dock it was unthinkable. It wasn't as if I could ask anyone. 'Would I be able to become an actor?' I wouldn't have dared to ask Mr Large. I was certain he wouldn't have encouraged me. And who else would know anything about it? I once asked him if he thought I could become a journalist. Mother always hoped I'd be a writer. You could start writing while you had another job, while you were a schoolteacher, say. (I had been quite keen on the idea until my best efforts were given 6 out of 10 by Mr W.) I used to like asking Mr Large things, and it was easier to talk about something that didn't concern me so much. 'I can't see why you couldn't become a journalist,' he said. 'But don't they have to be very good at writing, sir?' 'No gooder than you,' he answered quaintly.

It was Alan Plater, my best friend from Kingston and my dear friend to this day, who was the writer among us. Although he was two years ahead of me at Kingston we had become friends, and when he founded an eccentric society, the Old Kingstonian Society of Genii, or OKSOG, junior though I was, I was invited to join – much to the annoyance of my classmates in Lower Sixth Arts. The main thing in OKSOG was to be humorous and laid back. So laid back was Alan that although he was the youngest boy in the school ever to play for the second eleven at soccer, he never made it to the first eleven. OKSOG members had a special greeting for one another: 'How nice to see your bright and shining face bringing a touch of gladness into my humdrum, everyday life,' which must have been quite irritating to the uninitiated. And they were very partial to catchphrases. Such as 'It's a green 'un,' which had to be delivered in impersonation of Mr Hicks, who was in charge of cricket. They invented a character called Wulfric Hatrack and entered him in competitions in newspapers. And the unhumorous among their contemporaries were known as 'nignogs'. I ordered *Punch*, which was required reading, from Brooks' shop next door, and tried my best. I couldn't abide being thought of as even remotely nignoggish. Two years is a lot to make up and I had to be cunning. I discovered, by trial and error, that the best way to get laughs was not to try. Or indeed to reason why. If they thought I was funny, even though I didn't know why, then that was good enough. Just be thankful. (A bit like being in plays.) I can remember determinedly ploughing my way through *Punch*. I got some of it, but by no means all. Alan had assured me, however, that the magazine was the bees' knees, so I wasn't going to admit, even to myself, that I didn't get half the jokes.

He really had me baffled about the advertisements on the London Underground. Just before I left for London, Alan, who was by then two years into an architectural course at Durham University, observed, during one of our many aesthetic discussions, that some of the advertisements on the Tube were works of art. I looked forward to seeing them, confident I would be able to pick out the humdingers, but I never did. No matter how hard I tried, up and down the escalators, I never found out which were the good ones. They all looked much of a muchness to me. Posters. Of course I didn't say anything. Only in recent years have I got to the bottom of this mystery. Men who in later life are clever and wise talk tripe when they are twenty, especially to their younger friends who they know are inclined to believe anything they say.

Alan lived near Pickering Park, not Fish Dock. His father was a chain inspector on Hull's commercial docks. I can remember thinking how canny Mr Plater was. I always felt he had got me weighed up, and knew my weakest link. They were, I suppose, lower-middle class, though to me they seemed posh. (Just about everybody at Kingston did.) Their cups and saucers were very much nicer and more plentiful than ours, and they had a little linen cover, edged with beads, that went over their sugar bowl. It never failed to impress me.

I wouldn't have dreamt of admitting to Alan that I wanted to become an actor. The one bit of encouragement I got concerning my longed-for career came from a comparative outsider. Mr Stannard, the art master, was away ill, and the teacher who took his place for a few weeks saw me reading the lesson in prayers one morning. I had to call in the art room and he was sitting at his desk surrounded by several sixth-form girls. 'You were terrific in assembly this morning. I've never seen such a young lad so at home on a stage. You should become an actor.' The girls' proximity made his remarks all the more magical. 'Thank you, sir, but everybody says you can't make a living as an actor.' 'I have a friend at Liverpool Rep who earns twenty pounds a week. If that's what you want to do, don't let anybody put you off.' His words were so un-expected and so much what I wanted to hear that they took my breath away. I used to love reading the lesson in assembly when I was Head Boy. They would all listen so quietly, and the lectern was on the girls' side of the hall, which made it even nicer. And of course we had the Authorised Version then. 'Faith, Hope and Charity' from Corinthians was my favourite passage. The three syllables of 'Charity' are much more expressive than the single syllable of 'Love', which is in use today.

My second appearance in the school play, in my final year at Kingston, was in an adaptation of Jane Austen's *Emma*. I had graduated to Mr Knightley, and greatly preferred being the leading man to being an Arab. I loved my costume, especially the hat. I didn't have a nerve in my body when I acted at school. That temporary art teacher was right to say I looked at home on the stage. It was just something I loved doing. The photo of Mr Knightley bears him out. I look very serene.

I can remember both costumes, Arab and Mr K., being got out of the huge wicker basket that came from London, Mrs Large helping and smiling at my excitement. Can a basket be an Aladdin's cave? It was full of magic, that's for sure. And when the costumes were put back in the basket after only two performances, the most beautiful and exciting part of the whole school year was over. With two terms to go.

I was in no position to do anything directly about going on the stage. It was unthinkable for me to do anything other than what Mam and Dad wanted me to do. I nevertheless had a scheme I thought might satisfy my parents' hopes for me and at the same time help me towards my goal.

Madeline Blakeney, opposite whose Emma I had given my Mr Knightley, had told me that University College London was in the same street, Gower Street, as the Royal Academy of Dramatic Art, the most celebrated drama school in London. Her father was a passionate amateur actor in Hull, and they didn't come from Hessle Road. This information made UCL my preferred seat of learning. A step nearer Mecca – though I didn't tell Professor Sutherland that when I went for my interview with the English Department. I can't remember what I said when he asked me why I wanted to go to UCL, but it must have been politic because he said, for some reason memorably, 'We'll just purr round that if you don't mind.'

My interview 'having been', as I used to write in Latin translations, completed, I strolled along Gower Street to make sure Madeline hadn't been kidding me about RADA. Its frontage took up a fraction of the space that UCL did, but there it was. In my childish way I imagined that while working to get a degree I would be able to weigh up the students coming in and out of RADA. Who knows, I might even meet some of them and get an idea of how I measured up.

The English Department at UCL, innocent of my cunning scheme, offered me a place – on condition I got three A levels including Latin. I worked very hard – I had to, I wasn't a natural scholar. Especially at the Latin, for which I had no flair whatsoever. I did four A levels at Kingston, namely English, History, Latin and French. Some universities required only two A levels and no Latin, but they weren't next door to RADA in a city full of theatres, so there was considerable point to my exertions. When the exams were over and I said a sad goodbye to the Kingston High School, Hull, I went off with a bunch of sixth-formers to work in school governor Alderman Science's café in Bridlington, one of the many vacation jobs I had when I was young. Our exam results were duly posted to us, and I was able to send Mam and Dad a telegram from Bridlington to Portchester where they were on holiday, saying simply: 'Passed in everything.' So I would soon be on my way to London.

Amy Johnson, the Hull-born flying ace, had been a pupil at Kingston in its previous existence as the Boulevard School. In her memory a prize was awarded each year. It was called the Amy Johnson Memorial Prize for Grit. In my last year at Kingston I won that prize. What particularly gritty thing I did to deserve such an honour I can't say for sure. I have always fancied that the prize was something to do with my father's broken leg – because I had been Head Boy while we were on National Assistance.

At the beginning of October 1955 I set off for University College London. I gave Mother a hug and a kiss and began lugging my case along Harrow Street. I glanced back before turning into Hessle Road. She was standing 'again door', as she used to say in her letters, looking as forlorn as I felt. I waved one last time before I rounded the corner and I thought my heart would break. I didn't want to go to University College London, and I didn't want to leave her. I was astonished by the intensity of my feelings. It was as though the cord that once joined us was being cut yet again.

Our parting must have been ten times worse for her. Earlier that year, when she thought she discovered I had a girlfriend, she was terribly upset. And it was a false alarm anyway.

In the sixth form we used to have occasional parties at people's houses when, at a certain stage, the lights were turned off and kissing and cuddling took place. There had been one party when I had thought I was being allowed to put hand directly to breast, only to discover a further layer of clothing I hadn't expected. I couldn't feel too disappointed because it would have been really quite something to have reached the breast itself. At one particular evening, however, Hetty, let's call her, with whom I had flirted in the sixth-form library, told me that such was her depth of feeling I could feel her breasts, but not here. Where, then? There was no place but her front porch.

It was winter and the night was dark and cold. Nevertheless, I couldn't wait till the party was over and I walked her expectantly home, thinking that life was going somehow to open up for me. It must have been about two in the morning. My hands were very cold and Hetty was very cold. But she patiently let me do what she'd promised. I had great difficulty reaching the objects of my desire because I wasn't used to dealing with bras, and when I reached my goal, or rather goals, they were covered in goosepimples. Hetty said she would always love me, and I walked the two or so miles back to Harrow Street, thinking that it was very late and that the new term would soon be starting with four A levels including Latin.

A few days after the latest night I had ever stayed out, I got back from school to find Mother very dejected. She could hardly speak. She indicated a letter on the mantelpiece. She had opened it by mistake thinking that because it was addressed to Tom Courtenay it was for Dad. It was, in fact, for me, from Alan Plater, whom I have since forgiven, and it began, 'Dear Tom, I'm so glad to hear you're going out with Hetty B . . .'

God knows what she thought I'd been up to. I couldn't explain that there was hardly anything between Hetty and me, and that what little there was I had already called to a halt on account of my A levels. I couldn't explain that I loved Mother most in the whole world and would for ever.

LONDON

Arriving in London for my first term I wasn't alone. Geoff Tindle, from Kingston High, had won a place in the Physics Department at UCL, and we shared the same digs in Muswell Hill for our first year. Mrs Anderson, our landlady, was solicitous, going so far as to watch us eat our breakfast. We were expected to chomp through every bit of toast. I found it a struggle so early in the day. The evening meals she did for us on Saturday and Sunday at 6 o'clock were, by contrast, salady and not very filling. I could have done with the morning toast then. We got our accommodation at a reasonable rate, however, because the bath was in the kitchen – a fact of life to which I was perfectly adapted.

The first thing I did on passing through UCL's huge forecourt on Gower Street was buy a College scarf from the College shop. I thought I might as well look the part even though I felt miscast from the start. I didn't want to learn how to analyse English literature. At school I loved it, but as something I understood through my feelings. My favourite way of showing how I felt and understood it was to read it aloud. Chiefly Dickens and Shakespeare. Suddenly I was surrounded by brainy young men and women who were longing to hurl themselves at Eng. lit. and analyse the hell out of it. All of it, from early, horribly early, to modern. Nothing wrong with that, of course, but it wasn't what

I wanted to do, and I felt I was the worst equipped student intellectu-
ally in the whole of the English Department. I had been posted to the
right street in London, but to the wrong educational establishment.

And did I feel homesick! I had left two homes: 29 Harrow Street and
the Kingston High School, Hull, which during the previous few years I
had made my second home. The school had been so good to me. I wept
when I said goodbye to Mr Large. My childhood in Hull was made of
hopefulness and promise. Of unwavering progress built on encouragement and support. And then I left Hull for London, to study something
I didn't want to study, at the biggest university in the world, and
progress stopped.

What was I doing there? Well, didn't anyone who was anyone know
that university was the place to get a proper education, and wasn't a
proper education the best way to get started in life? It wasn't only Mam
and Dad who thought that. All our teachers at Kingston thought it.
And all our teachers, with one temporary exception, thought that the
one place not to study in order to make one's way in life was the Royal
Academy of Dramatic Art. It now seems to me extraordinary but true
that at school I knew better than anyone else what I should do with my
life. Before being free to do it, however, I had to serve my time doing
what others thought I should do. I had three years of trying to become
a Bachelor of Arts.

One of the oddest things at UCL was being addressed by the lecturers
as 'Mr Courtenay' instead of 'Courtenay'. It suggested an authority, a
gravitas, I didn't feel I had. And the comparative freedom. Nobody
bothered to check whether we went to lectures or not. Not that I would
have dared to miss the ones we were advised to attend. The lectures
lasted about fifty-five minutes. Some lecturers were a bit dry in their
delivery. I often thought it would have been much easier if, say, 'The
Metaphysical Poets' or 'The Nineteenth-Century Novel' had been
printed out and handed round to us rather than read out. We could have
studied them at leisure instead of having to scribble so furiously. But
then what would we have done all day? There were classes as well as
lectures, when we had to take part. I'm shuddering at the thought. We
had to study Anglo-Saxon, or, as they preferred to call it at UCL, Old
English. Middle English came after Old, with Chaucer and the

anonymous (certainly to me) *Sir Gawayne and the Green Knight*. Mother had already been introduced to Old English. We were advised in advance of my first term to purchase a copy of King Alfred's *Anglo Saxon Chronicles* which I ordered from Brown's bookshop in Hull. Mother and I peered at its funny writing together, equally bemused. 'Well, Tommy,' she said, 'if you're going to study English you've got to know it from when it started.' I think she still hadn't given up hope that I might one day become a writer. During Old and Middle English classes we were subjected to having to translate out loud when picked on, which I dreaded, so convinced was I that I was the stupidest in the class. I didn't have to do it many times, thankfully, and just about passed muster when I did. The *Anglo Saxon Chronicles* had no literary value whatever. I remember that King Alfred was worried about the Danish fleet in the Thames. Or was it the Wash? I'm not going to look it up. The early manifestations of our wonderful language threw up some real purlers. The 'Ancren Riwle' or Rules of the Nuns for one. I don't remember the nuns' doings in any detail, only that their rules were very strict. The most horrible thing of all, though, in the study of the birth pangs of our literature, was *Beowulf*. That took up an awful lot of space in the degree curriculum – far more than it deserved. We were expected to study the beast with great care and attention. Why? Why?

Usually when I studied a poem I liked I would automatically learn chunks of it. I remember half a line of *Beowulf*: 'Ne was him Fitela mid' (Fitela was not with him), the first two words pronounced 'nay wass', and there were thousands of them, a great many of which stayed unperused by me. The longer I studied at UCL, the more threatening the huge black rock of *Beowulf* became to the fragile barque that was my BA.

Professor Smith was the head of the language, as opposed to the literature, side of the course. Tall, thin, balding and bespectacled, he was perfect casting for the part of absentminded professor. He had a great fondness for a book called *The History of the English Language*, by Wren, which he constantly referred to as 'Wren's little book'. Little as it was, I never did finish it. Its high point concerned something called 'the great consonant shift'. I liked the idea of consonants rather than continents shifting, even though I wasn't sure why they did, but after that bit the book soon relinquished its hold on me.

One class, called simply 'English', taken by Miss Jones, who was frighteningly clever and sharp, made me feel the most stupid of all. 'Write a description of a telephone (a 1950s one) for the benefit of someone from another planet,' she demanded. 'I can't,' I soon thought, or 'I don't want to,' or both. 'It's made of bakelite, it's got a dial on it with numbers that you . . . no, you put your finger in one of several holes in a circular disc and turn it clockwise till it stops. They've got numbers under them, the holes, that is . . . the numbers are on a fixed disc below the other disc . . . Oh, Christ, save me from this punishment.' I met her some years later when I was first successful as an actor, and I can still feel the relief that I was by then being tested not in her field but in my own. A very demanding and treacherous field, but one that I had chosen myself.

When Don Revie was manager of Leeds United he told me that he had players at the club who had got their A levels but seemed slow-witted on the pitch alongside uneducated Billy Bremner from the back streets of Glasgow, because Billy was in his element more than they were. We all need our element. His brains were in his feet. My brains weren't in my feet, but neither were they entirely in my head. They had slipped down a bit towards my heart and my stomach and had spread close to my skin, greatly dissipating the power required for describing telephones, ploughing through *Beowulf*, and analysing literature.

At the end of the first term we had to write some sort of essay as a test of our progress. I don't remember the subject, just the feeling of being in the dark, of writing about something on which I had no opinion but had to appear to have one. I can remember the relief of being given a B and being allowed to go back home to Mother. That was one of the two best things about my first term at university – going home to Mother. Once there I showed her some photographs from a play I'd been in. That was the other best thing.

After buying my College scarf at the beginning of my first term I set about unearthing the College Dramatic Society. Dramsoc, as it was known. I found its noticeboard behind a large sofa in the Students' Union. A noticeboard among many. The Catholic Society (Cathsoc), the Music Society (Musoc), the Classical Society (Classoc), the Jazz Society (Jazzsoc). In subsequent terms, as Dramsoc took over my college life, I used to like to see from the other noticeboards that I wasn't the only student bound up in extra-curricular activities. The Dramsoc board announced that auditions would be held for *Dark of the Moon* in the gymnasium coffee bar at 5.30 later that week. Roy Battersby, a tall and impressive second-year economics student, heard me do a piece of something or other and duly offered me a part. I don't think the competition was fierce. *Dark of the Moon* was the story of Barbara Allen, who marries a witch boy. My 'finding out about RADA' policy was quickly underway because Barbara was played by a student from RADA, Joanna Dunham. Not that she took much notice of me. I played Barbara's brother – the family were hillbillies – with a southern American drawl which I loved doing. He was a bit of a layabout, as I recall, and quite funny. I had a good time in *Dark of the Moon*. The part wasn't demanding but was long enough to make its mark, and I felt like something of a bright spark in the Dramsoc fraternity, if a dull one in the English Department. I made two friends in the show: Corinne Lambert, like me reading English, a very bright girl from north London who became my pal and confidante, and Roy Battersby, who became like my older brother. He was working-class, from Willesden. He hadn't known his father. When, later on, I went to visit his mother's house I was delighted to find that, though tidier, it was as homely as ours in Hull. She lived with her sister Flo and Flo's husband, known as Ebb. I remember telling that to Dad. He had a liking for what he thought of as cockney humour. (Once, years later, on a London bus, he was delighted when, as the bus approached its terminus, a lady asked the conductor what was the next stop but one. Dad loved the conductor's response: 'Bladdy Jerichow, missiz.' He did the accent, too.)

When thankfully I got back home to Hull, Mother was in the middle of a losing battle with housework, intensified by the onset of Christmas and my imminent arrival. 'In between Christmas' she once described the chaos that the extra cleaning brought about. Our front door wasn't locked and I lugged my case along our dark passage calling out, 'I'm back, Ma.' We were both taken by surprise for a moment, so suddenly was I there. The rag rug was folded up against the sideboard, the hoover alongside it. And it was washday as well. Wet things on the clotheshorse. Mother had over-reached herself on account of my returning home. She must have been thinking of it for days, so had mucked up her preparations. Just for a second I thought, 'Is this what I've been longing to come back to?' But there was that slim little figure and those beautiful eyes that affected me like no others and I knew I was home. We hugged, housework stopped, we had a cup of tea and I showed her my photos of *Dark of the Moon*. She drank me in as I paced excitedly around, so happy that I, too, was happy to be back. And then Dad and Ann came home from work and we were all smiles and had our tea, the four of us. I remember pointing out that the long summer vacation was longer than any term, that I could get work on Paragon Station then, in addition to my Post Office Christmas work due to start in a couple of days, and that Hull was where my heart was. I did my hillbilly accent, which made them all laugh. Whether Mam and Dad read anything into my talking mostly about Dramsoc at that time, I can't say.

More than any other city in the world, London was the home of theatre. That was another reason for my being drawn towards UCL. One of the first things I had done on arrival was to go to the Old Vic. 1/6d in the gallery. *The Merry Wives of Windsor* with Paul Rogers as Falstaff on my first Saturday night, *Julius Caesar* with John Neville as Mark Antony the following Saturday night. He wore a huge red cloak I wrote to Mr Large about, and in the programme his photo sported a crewneck pullover, his shirt collar turned over it – a style I was to make my own. Some West End theatres had small portable seats outside the gallery entrance that you could book on the day of the performance and so be first in the race for the unreserved gallery seats. That way I got to see Edith Evans, John Gielgud, Peggy Ashcroft and Sybil Thorndike. From afar, but magical enough. One of my great thrills was seeing Paul Scofield at the Phoenix Theatre, not once but three times: *Hamlet*, *The Family Reunion* and, my favourite, *The Power and the Glory*, in which he played the whisky priest. For days afterwards I went around chanting, 'We must have a mass, Maria.'

In my second term at UCL I got the part of Ferdinand in *The Duchess of Malfi*. A step up, but not nearly so much fun as being a hillbilly. Ferdinand, as I recall, was an unreasonable duke. 'Rhubarb, oh for rhubarb to purge this choler.' He was also said to have the most beautiful line in Jacobean drama outside Shakespeare. Remorseful over the body of his sister whose death he has engineered, he says: 'Cover her face; mine eyes dazzle; she died young.' Anita, our director, couldn't get me to do this line to her satisfaction. I found the line's fame something of a burden and never did get it licked. I am happy to say that now it would give me no difficulty whatsoever – as long as I didn't have to do the rest of the part. My reading in 1956 was too deliberate, because I was thinking, 'Here comes the beautiful line.' What's needed is a beat after the second phrase. Then the remorseful, personal bit: 'she died young.' If I had only known . . .

With *The Duchess of Malfi* my 'finding out about RADA' policy took a prophetic leap forward. Our director, Anita, had a friend who was a RADA student, name of Bill, who came to see her production. He was tall, handsome and laid back, with a soft Scottish accent, and he had a lot of authority because he didn't gush. I was very pleased when he told me I would have no difficulty getting into RADA, even though he thought there would be plenty for the teachers to work on. I didn't in the least mind being raw material. No point in going there otherwise. He went on: 'There's a wonderful boy at RADA at the moment. He's very charismatic. Strangely enough, you have something in common with him. You're not at all like him temperamentally and I can't really say why you remind me of him. But you do. I suppose you could be his younger brother.'

Intrigued, I asked his name.

'Finney. Albert Finney.'

Bill cannot have known that the New Wave was just around the corner. But maybe he sniffed it on the wind.

Dramsoc became the centre of my undergraduate world. I was in a play every term, which didn't help my admittedly slack grip on what I was supposed to be doing. At home in Hull, where I felt secure and happy, I had been able to grind away at my four A levels. Sitting in our front room in Harrow Street, I learnt our Latin master's translation of the Virgil set book by heart, so that no matter which piece of it the examiners selected to catch us out I would be ready. Not much flair but plenty of application, not to say grit. But at UCL my grit gradually dribbled away, and with it application. I can remember in my second year putting off essays I was supposed to be writing till the very last moment – having to wake up at five in the morning to finish my piece due to be presented to Mr Warburg at eleven. Or asking for a week's grace till the production of *Nightmare Abbey* had completed its short run. And I can remember the puzzled expression on the faces of the middle-aged couple I then roomed with in north London. There were two other students boarding there, each with his own room, and we were invited to sit with them in the evening for cocoa to help us relax after our hours of study. Involved with Dramsoc every evening, I would put my head round their living-room door to say goodnight. The couple and the two studious lads having finished their cocoa long since, they would gaze in wonderment at the one who never came among them till it was time for bed. When did he do his studying?

For two years I got away with it, managing to wing my way through my college work on a steadily decreasing supply of grit, and I did get better at giving my opinions on drama and literature even though they weren't heartfelt. In fact my literary critical career reached its high point in the long vacation between my second and third years. Having completed a stint of portering on Paragon Station I settled down to four weeks of Henry Fielding for an essay for Professor Sutherland. I decided I would say why I thought *Tom Jones* was a better novel than *Amelia*. I thought it was, by a long chalk. *Amelia* was sentimental and not so life-like. The fruit of my endeavours, while secure at home in Hull, with no Dramsoc to distract me, was 'A– –' Minus, minus. Was that better than B++? I wondered. And lest I give the wrong impression, I have to admit that Professor Sutherland was known to be a generous marker, and I had only to read two books, albeit long ones, one of which I liked. I hadn't been sharpening up on my *Beowulf* and *Sir Gawayne*. Mother, seeing me reasonably contented that summer, must have been quite unprepared for the year that was to follow.

By the third year I had had enough of both Anglo-Saxon and Eng. lit., and Nemesis, in the form of Finals, was approaching without pity. More than winging was going to be required. The Shakespeare Paper, for example. There were four or five plays set each year. There are many bits of Shakespeare where there is no certainty about what he

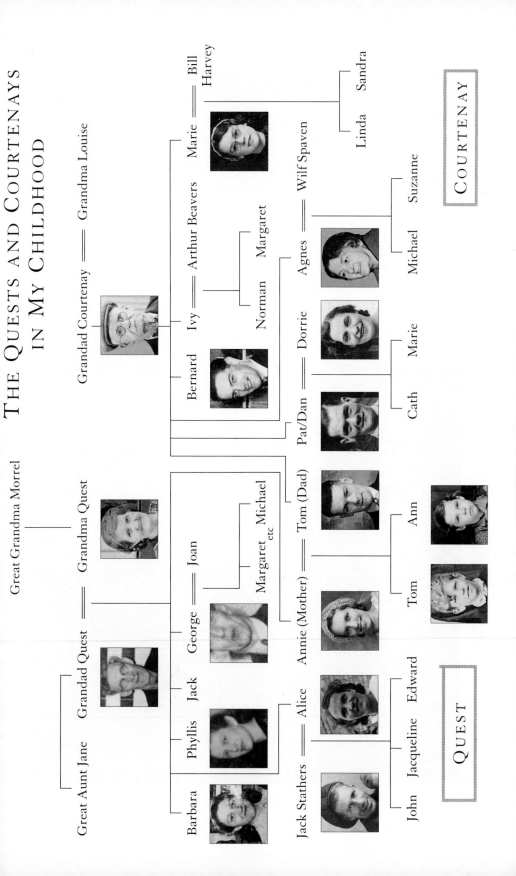

The Quests and Courtenays in My Childhood

Quest

Courtenay

Great Grandma Morrel

Great Aunt Jane — Grandad Quest ══ Grandma Quest

Barbara   Phyllis   Jack   George ══ Joan

Jack Stathers ══ Alice   Margaret Michael
                                    etc

John Jacqueline Edward

Grandad Courtenay ══ Grandma Louise

Bernard   Ivy ══ Arthur Beavers   Marie ══ Bill Harvey

Norman   Margaret   Linda   Sandra

Agnes ══ Wilf Spaven

Michael   Suzanne

Annie (Mother) ══ Tom (Dad)

Pat/Dan ══ Dorrie

Tom   Ann

Cath   Marie

Annie Eliza before I knew her.

December 1935. Left to right: Aunt Marie; Uncle Pat; Aunt Phyllis; Dad;
Mam; Aunt Barbara; Grandad Quest; Aunt Alice.

Tom the Tiger and
Bernard the Bull.

Grandad Courtenay.

Uncle Pat and Aunt
Dorrie, newly wed.

On holiday in Portchester with
Uncle Bill and Aunt Hilda.

Ma and Aunt Alice. Ma had just
learned that I was on the way.

On the Downs: Mother, Aunt
Barbara, Mary-next-door, Ann, me.

Tommy and Ann.

Home from the desert?
Uncle Jack Stathers, Aunt Alice,
cousin John.

ABOVE: In front of the defunct Quest shop: cousin John, Grandma Quest holding cousin Jacqueline, me.

Net braiding, *c.* 1941. Mother's work between school and marriage.

Courtesy Lily Rylett/Alec Gill

The only bit of our back yard that (sometimes) caught the sun.

West Dock Avenue Junior Rugby League team. Captain for the day.

Grandad and Grandma Quest
with Aunt Barbara.

Ann, maroon cap, Dad and little lad
in Portsmouth, *c.* 1948.

LEFT: Dennis, Dad, me (in dressing-
gown), Ma, Uncle George, Grandad
and Grandma Quest. Dad looks as
though he's had a few. And
Grandma too.

Hessle Road, 1960s. *Courtesy Hull Daily Mail*

The most soulful eyes I ever saw.
Mother with Uncle Bernard, Grandma
Quest and Uncle George.

The Star & Garter pub – Rayner's to
all who knew it. *Alec Gill*

Pre-match, Wembley 1959: Wigan 30, Hull 13.

actually wrote, which gives scholars endless opportunities for study, surmise and debate; reams of scholarship about whether he wrote 'solid flesh' or 'sullied flesh', to name but one of thousands of textual cruxes, not to say cruces, as they were known. We were supposed to know the history of the scholarly debate that had piled up around these said cruces since the plays were first published. Such knowledge required a lot of studying, of really getting down to it. In my final year at UCL I was even less up to it than during the previous two.

Had I been a prince with my own private tutors, I would have coped much better. I could have sent the Anglo-Saxon and Middle English tutors packing. 'Sorry, chaps, that's not for me!' And I could have taken just what I wanted from the Shakespeare scholars. I would have recorded Mrs Nowottny taking us unforgettably through Shakespeare's Sonnet 56: 'Sweet love, renew thy force.' The argument is that love is superior to appetite ('do not kill/The spirit of love with a perpetual dullness'), and it is carried triumphantly through to the last two words, 'more rare.' She talked quietly and with hypnotic intensity. She said something about *King Lear* that I never forgot. 'Our parents become our children.' And about Dogberry in *Much Ado* and the nature of language: not once is he able to say what he means, but we always know what he means. Paul Turner, my kindly tutor in my final year, was actually funny when he lectured, and helped me to see that literature was to do with life, not school. I can remember when the penny dropped. He was gleefully describing the old couple in *Bleak House* who sit feebly facing each other. When strength allows, they vent their feelings by hurling cushions at one another. That was what marriage was like, he pointed out, and we all laughed.

I know I learnt about one book at UCL. In my first year I went to a lecture on *The Catcher in the Rye*, and understood not a word. In my third year the book became my Bible. Holden Caulfield, plus James Dean in *East of Eden*, were by that time my soulmates in youthful anxiety. I was playfully warned against going to see *East of Eden*. My friends in Dramsoc knew how it would affect me. I took to running up and down between imaginary rows of plants, imploring them to grow, as James Dean had done. And in the UCL coffee bar I did Dean for whatever comely art student might be paying attention, moaning and rolling a milk bottle against my face.

I felt terribly guilty at no longer being able to apply myself. Mam and Dad so wanted me to get a degree. They knew by then that I was set on going to RADA if I could get in, but that ambition of mine worried them greatly, and understandably so. 'Don't put your daughter on the stage, Mrs Worthington' – or your son, come to that. Especially if his father is a chipper and painter on St Andrew's Fish Dock, Hull. They wanted me to have that degree to fall back on. 'To fall back on.' Deary me. The Dramsoc fraternity was crawling with people who had got their degrees (usually in arts subjects) and were finding them no use at all. They didn't know what to do. I was one of the few who did know what he wanted to do, though encouragement was not easy to find. The overriding feeling was still that the theatre was an impossible career. I was always hearing of past Dramsoc stars who had been brilliant and had got nowhere. It didn't stop me from applying for, and getting, an audition at RADA. It was to take place on a Saturday morning in July, one week after the ominously named Finals.

In the first term of my final year at UCL (1957–8) I was invited to share a basement flat at 408 Camden Road with three graduates, one of whom, Mike Lee, I had got to know through Dramsoc. We had appeared together in an adaptation of Thomas Love Peacock's *Nightmare Abbey*. Having completed the much-derided teacher's training course – thought of by all and sundry as a way of having a year's grace before facing the outside world – Mike had got a job as a French teacher, as had his flatmate, Mike Lunnon. His other graduate friend, Arthur Brooks, worked in a public library. My sharing a flat meant that I now had access to a kitchen – though maybe that is putting it too high. In the hallway leading to the tradesmen's entrance of the house, our front door, was a gas cooker and a narrow table. Though I ate mostly in the refectories at UCL or the neighbouring Birkbeck College, I learned at Camden Road how to make a fried egg sandwich. The first (and near enough the last) cooking I ever did. And I was introduced to Schubert songs. A ten-inch LP featuring the French baritone Gérard Souzay. I already knew and loved Schubert's String Quintet, but at first I couldn't understand why my flatmates were so enraptured by his songs. Then suddenly a curtain lifted and I was as taken as they were. There was a lot of music played on Mike Lee's record player. New to me, and greatly loved, were Beethoven's Violin Concerto, Brahms' First Symphony, and Shostakovich's Fifth. Mike Lunnon could play the piano after a fashion and we would occasionally try to sing a bit. Schumann's 'Du bist wie eine Blume' comes into my head. (Sounds better than 'You are like a flower'.) It's very pretty. Mother smiled when I sang the beginning of it to her, and told her what it meant.

The bedroom I shared with Arthur was very large, so there was plenty of room for the three beds it contained, though its size and position at the bottom of the house made it cold and dank. There was a gas fire in the sitting room, but we were chary of over-using it. I didn't like to put it on when I was on my own – I felt a quorum was required to justify the expense. A bit of Mother there. As a student, for much of the time I was either too cold or too hot. Roy Battersby had observed me from the top of a bus in my first year, walking along the Tottenham Court Road and looking, he said, like a bank clerk. I was wearing a very square-shouldered mac I had bought in Hull. Clearly my wardrobe had had to be rethought. In my second year, duffel coat and narrow dark grey trousers à la Roy, with shirt collar turned over my crewneck jumper. In my third year a College scarf was considered a very uncool thing to wear. So I had my look by now. Having one attire for all seasons, however, for only some of the time did I suit the prevailing temperature.

So there I was living in Camden Road opposite Holloway Prison with three who had their degrees to fall back on. Arthur, in a public library, wasn't using any of his degree; and the other two were teachers. And here is where I felt my world had turned on its head. These two teachers hated marking. They found it a strain to be punctual. Mike Lunnon especially found the going very tough. He had rather an odd mannerism: he would stick his chin out and up, lift his shoulders and stick his arms out sideways – like a grounded bird giving its wings a stretch. He did this quite frequently, and one day he caught the lads at his school mimicking him doing it. He laughed in rather a pained way as he told me. He saw the joke, but I think it hurt him. He had great difficulty keeping order in class. 'The lads think I'm a bit of a cunt. They may be right.' And he laughed again.

But at school, teachers had been the pillars of my world order. I never thought of them as people – except perhaps a couple of the older spinsters who were said to have lost their young men in the Great War, and that seemed romantic. I had imagined they were all so happy marking our homework during term time, and aimless during school holidays – counting the hours till they could face us with yet stiffer tests. They were superior beings, not normal flesh and blood. But here was my teacher friend and flatmate Mike Lunnon, who I liked a lot, with his vulnerability, his odd mannerisms and his derisive pupils.

At school I had had the magic of Mr Large, who I thought knew everything. Even the prosaic Mr W. had seemed so sure of himself: 'Six out of ten. King for a DAY.' But now it was 'The lads think I'm a bit of a cunt.' The world had become a very different place.

When I think back to my last, unhappy year at UCL I can't help thinking also of the Slade girls. They were the salt in my wound. Adjoining UCL is the Slade School of Art, and the art students used to frequent the College coffee bars. The female art students I found very disturbing. At school the girls had just been a delightful presence. One was happy to love them from afar. We were all getting on with our A levels and saving ourselves for the future. The girls of the English Department were wrapped up in *Beowulf* and literary criticism. But the girls from the Slade! So bohemian. And no *Beowulf* to worry about, just art. Plenty of time on their hands, in wicked London. They made me feel very Hull-born and awkward. Oppressed by the awful weight of Finals, of Mam's and Dad's expectations, by the guilt and misery of striving to do work for which I had no stomach, and for which I was getting a generous grant, I had no choice but to love them, too, from afar. But they were very alluring, and I wasn't at all happy about it.

Mother wrote to me every week when I was in London. It was during my last year at UCL, when the hope and joy of my childhood seemed to have evaporated, that I started consciously to save her letters. My unhappiness worried her deeply and affected the way she wrote. 'I wanted to know where I'd gone wrong, hence the change,' as she put it. All I knew was that the letters became very precious to me because there seemed to be so much more of her in them.

19th February 1958

Dear Tom

A week today is your birthday. The weather here is very cold after some spring like weather.

Your father didn't send the Sports Mail as no Hull teams were playing.

Alice called last Saturday to tell us how much she likes her new house at Longhill Estate. It's two bus rides East Hull way. Also Granny wanted a sub. I was very angry. She'll never learn.

I shall be glad when you have got your exams over, also your July test at RADA. Everything seems unsettled lately. Ann moons about. You seem to be concerned about who you are working to please. Whatever you have wanted to do never have we objected. As long as you can be happy also Ann, that's enough for us. But when you are unsettled we are bound to wonder.

I am pleased you think of us. I think of you when we have dinner to spare. Tonight we had baked haddock with sage and onions, mashed potatoes and sultana scones. You would have liked it. Your father is busy mending Ann's sewing machine, something wants straightening so he is filing it. I daren't say anything.

One thing has stuck in my mind and that is Jack Stathers. I am not standing for him coming to our house and insulting people. I shall let our Alice know. I think it is about time he grew up.

I hope you are keeping well and happy and having plenty of friends to see you. Too much of one's own company is not good.

We shall send your gifts on Monday so you can get them on Tuesday and the best of luck.

Love Mam Dad and Ann

In the first term of my final year I had gone, with a cold and feeling low, to see one of the College doctors, Dr Linken. He thought I was in need of some psychological help. I was allowed, indeed encouraged, to tell him my troubles. He was very kind and patient with me and only got annoyed when I forgot one of our appointments because I was mooning about dreaming of one of the Slade girls, Susan. I had had a bit of success with Susan. When I told Roy this he confidently assured me I would be able to have all the success I wanted. Roy had a steady girlfriend, Audrey, and was my adviser on many matters, not only those sartorial. I had placed Susan on hold while appearing as Orestes in Jean-Paul Sartre's *The Flies*, my last big part before I intended to concentrate on Finals. Roy played Orestes' tutor, wearing an over-large, solidly made bald wig. When he swatted an imaginary fly on it, the hollow thwack he made echoed all the way round the gymnasium that served as our theatre. Once our final performance was over I resolved to put Roy's assurance to the test. Susan didn't look like a typical Slade girl. She was pretty but not bohemian and intimidating. While I was taken up with *The Flies*, however, she had not marked time and on presenting myself hopefully before her I was told she couldn't see me because there was another, and though I hadn't given her a second's thought while I was working on *The Flies* I suddenly found myself love-lorn. My already slack grasp on *Beowulf* loosened completely. When Dr Linken got over his annoyance that I had forgotten one of our appointments, he hit on the idea of trying some group therapy on me. I didn't care for it. I didn't find the other group members nearly so interesting as I found myself.

[27th February 1958]

Dear Tom

I'm pleased your greetings arrived safe in spite of the weather. I bet you had a whale of a time opening the cards. Don't worry about the pen we bought you, it isn't often one's son is 21. We thought it looked nice with your name inscribed on it.

I had Aunt Alice in on Friday. I felt a coward about telling her about Uncle Jack, but I quietly plucked up courage. I said what a nuisance he is coming in drunk. She said I should tell him. 'How can I when he's like that,' I said. I told her he mocked you and said something awful to Ann and that he used bad language. But she didn't want to know. I said 'It's time he grew up.' I said I thought she had a shocking life with him and I really meant it. She left in a huff, but I'm glad. If he comes anymore I shall tell him he's 'ugly vulgar and insulting'. I said if he spoke to you while he was sober he might learn something.

I suppose you have got settled down to work. By now you will know if you have passed your medical. I am pleased your Beowulf classes are finished.

I told Grannie how the stockings she bought Ann were 4 times too big for her and a waste of money. Ann told me it was none of my business. Your father's leg was playing him up. I suppose he has tired himself and is now feeling the effects. But he wont have it and still thinks he's 21.

I was thinking this morning does Tom want to come home to see his mother and father? The funny part is I don't really feel like anybody's mother. Sometimes I do. Sometimes I don't. I suppose one feels more like a mother when one's children are young. Sometimes I'm frightened at the outcome of all your struggling and striving. All for now.

Love Mam, Dad and Ann

The pen was a Parker 51, an expensive thing for them to buy me. I still have it. The barrel, with my name on, had to be replaced in the late Sixties, when my Dalmatian, Wagstaff, tried to eat it. (He was named after the left side of Hull City's legendary strike force Ken Wagstaff and Chris Chilton, a.k.a. Waggy and Chillo.)

Did I still want to go home and see them? Of course I did, though as I got more unhappy I sometimes wanted to shout, 'Please stop being so interested in me.' Or, 'It's your fault that I'm at UCL.' Leaving Hull for a new term was always painful. It was the feeling of desolation that came from Mother for all she tried to hide it. We would pretend to be interested in something on the radio till, thankfully, it was time at last for me to get the bus to Paragon Station.

The 'medical' was for the army. Should my RADA audition be successful, there remained another obstacle between me and the start of a career on the boards: National Service. It was about to be abolished. Lads of my age were the last who were due for call-up. Had I been a year younger I wouldn't have been eligible. This made National Service seem even more of a waste of time. Even the government had realized it. I had been treading water for three years already, and a further two trying to be a soldier would have been more than frustrating. How to get out of it? There was a great deal of talk at College about how it had been or could be done. It was said that Marcus Toulmin-Rothe of the French Department – a sweet member of the Dramsoc fraternity and quite supportive of my theatrical ambitions – got out after only two weeks because the uniform gave him a rash. I can well believe it. Rumour had it that the aforementioned A. Finney, who was by this time making a name for himself, had got out by pretending to be crazy. In 1998 I asked him if this was so.

T: 'Albert, I'm working on a book about the Sixties and would like to ask you a few questions.'

A: 'I don't give interviews.'

T: 'I'm going to take the lid off what was one of the most influential decades of the century. You would hate not to be included.'

A: 'Mmm.'

T: 'Is it true that you got out of the army by sitting on top of your locker? That's how rumour had it.'

A: 'I sat on one of the rafters in our Nissen hut. I didn't eat anything and from time to time I fainted.'

T: 'You fell off the rafter?'

A: 'I didn't faint while I was on the rafter, silly bugger. I waited till I was on the ground.'

T: 'How soon before they let you out?'

A: 'Eight weeks. They would have let me out sooner, but they knew I was a drama student and the officers wanted me to direct their Christmas play.'

It seemed to me that my best way out of the army would be via Dr Linken, so on being summoned to a medical by the army authorities I went to see him to find out whether I had any natural impediment to my being called up. Fallen arches or some such. My arches were fine – in fact he couldn't find anything physically amiss. 'The only way you will avoid being called up is if I write to them saying you are emotionally unstable.' Without hesitating I saw this was the answer. 'But it's not a good thing to have on your record. If ever you went into industry they would want to know why you hadn't done National Service. Any company would be reluctant to employ someone who had been thought temperamentally unsuitable for conscription. I think I could get you out of it but you must think very carefully of the consequences of my writing such a letter.'

I discussed the matter with my tutor, Paul Turner. He didn't think the letter was a good idea. And I wrote to Mam and Dad about it, eliciting the following reply.

9th May 58

Dear Tom

I really do hope you haven't to go in the army. So let us know as soon as you can. I hope you got the RADA card alright. If you haven't to go in the army shall you still go to RADA? I don't like the idea of your being labelled 'emotionally unstable'. If you don't act or write there are lots of jobs including teaching that wouldn't have you with that label so think seriously about this. I read in the paper where students with degrees will be accepted in the army as officers straight away. I don't want you in the army but think very carefully about it.

Love Mam Dad and Ann

It seemed to me, however, that I had no choice in the matter. I couldn't abide the thought of two more wasted years. I asked Dr Linken to write the letter.

The day of the army medical arrived. I got through it satisfactorily enough, including the infamous 'Now cough' sequence. This had been made memorable for me by a student at Alderman Science's café in Bridlington. The medical orderly, placing a finger under the pertinent spot, had said to him: 'Now cough,' then added, 'I bet this bird's been in a few cages.' To which the student replied (he said), 'Yes, but it's the first time it's been on a perch before.' In my case, the orderly made no comment on any part of me, but picked up Dr Linken's letter from a desk and read it carefully. 'Don't you want to go in the army, lad?' 'No,'

I replied, with some feeling. He studied the letter a second time, then looked me in the eye. 'You know you'll have to see a psychiatrist,' he said as ominously as he could manage. 'I know,' I said. Dr Linken had told me as much, and I couldn't wait.

When I saw the psychiatrist, in a room in a vast government building somewhere in Ealing, I didn't have to put on an act.

'I don't want to go in the army. It's such a waste of time. I want to go to drama school. I've already wasted three years at university. I don't want to waste two more. In the army I wouldn't be able to react as I would want to. If a sergeant shouted at me I wouldn't be allowed to shout back and I wouldn't be allowed to run away. I don't know what I would do.'

I was speaking from the heart, and the psychiatrist believed me. No fainting necessary and no National Service. I got a card from the army authorities. I was marked either C3 or D4, I don't remember which. Temperamentally unsuitable. A blot on my escutcheon, I dare say. But no employer of mine has ever wanted to know why I didn't do my National Service. And having wriggled out of the army, the prospect of finally getting to RADA was clouded only by the dreaded Finals. I wasn't yet free from care, and I could never hide that from Mother.

[5th June 1958]

Dear Tom

Ive been thinking a lot about Saturdays letter and I think its quite understandable to feel like you did. Isnt it true when one has some hard task to do and it makes one angry and miserable one wants others to have a large lump of the misery. I think I know all about that. Your father isnt nearly so anxious for others to suffer with him.

Your father and me were talking about TV Friday night. He seems to think he can get one that gradually reduces to 1/- a week. So we nearly ended up arguing. I thought I would go to bed. I was just getting undressed when our Phyllis trips upstairs to say she'd left home. I wished her in hell. I offered her a bed but she prefered to take a taxi to our Alice's. She thought Mother Joe and Jack would be looking for her. Did they hell, they had all been rowing. I was glad she went. Poor Phyl. They are all friends again now. Joe is drinking mild instead of bitter.

Sunday morning the Salvation Army got going so I got up just in time to hear Mrs Middleton read the lesson. She said people think they can find their happiness drinking beer and she found her happiness when she was saved 6 year ago. I shall quietly find something to say to Mrs M. I also think Salvation Army uniforms are comic and I think a lot of people they help shouldn't be in that state. What qualification has Mrs M. got to tell me where to find happiness? Ive heard she has a vile tongue.

Your father backed the Derby winner and won £1 15. I reminded him when I got 4/- rebate out of the gas I gave him half, 2/-. So he said all right I'll give you 2/- back.

Love Mam Dad and Ann

I last saw Aunt Phyllis at my nephew John's wedding, in the early Nineties. She liked a good do and was in excellent spirits. She had always been some sort of skivvy, and was working in a menial capacity in the canteen of some firm or other. She was very pleased to be on the darts team. She had been a victim of diphtheria when she was seven. This had rendered her right hand fairly useless, though she was very adroit with her left hand. When I was little I used to be fascinated by the way she wiped the crumbs off Grandma's oilcloth table covering. I just knew she did it differently. Her right leg had been affected too, but she could hobble about at quite a lick. 'Our Phyllis trips upstairs' is perfect. Her hair, which Mother always said was so beautiful before diphtheria struck her, was represented at John's wedding by a National Health wig. She was keen to point it out to me and thought it a bit of a hoot.

She was regretful only about the fate of Joe, her beau. He had lost both legs. First one, then the other. After a life of drinking and smoking, his heart couldn't manage to pump all the way to his toes and back. 'It's pitiful to see him, Tommy.' For her sake, I gritted my teeth and went round with her to see him, but he had gone out for a drink. She was disappointed that he had missed me, but proud that he hadn't given up trying. 'Nothing'll stop him. He's mustard in his wheelchair.' Ann thought he led her a hell of a dance, especially since losing his legs. She was selflessly devoted to him, but he'd never married her. 'I'm the black sheep of the family,' she confided, though it made her laugh not cry. I thought my little Aunt Phyllis had a big heart, and I wished I had seen more of her. She had a hard life. She died in 1996. When Ann went to see her in hospital, she finally seemed to have given up. 'I'm no good, I'm no good,' she muttered. But it wasn't true.

Thursday, 14th July 1958

Dear Tom

The weather is awful today rain and dullness again.

Did I tell you about my cousin Rosie and family who are emigrating? Well they all came to see me today just as I was resting with feet on chair after dinner. They are a very nice family and their daughter Ann is very much like you. Their other daughter Margaret is married. She admired my Renoir and said she had seen a Van Gogh exhibition in Shields. She's fond of art and good music. Van Gogh used to get very depressed and tear his hair out. This shows in some of his works I understand. I felt a little sad when they went, to think I have some cousins on the art side and when I find out they have to emigrate to bloody Australia.

Thursday is scrubbing scullery day. How can one feel like such a job when one's relatives are en route abroad to a land of sunshine. (Still raining.)

It's funny to me, Rosie has had a big operation, her daughter a bigger one, Rosie's husband has also had a big operation. I just don't know where they get their enthusiasm for all this change. What's the matter with me? I think I'll emigrate. I'll tell your father.

I don't think your father is talking to me and rightly so. Last night he suddenly got angry with me because I hadnt repaired the chair cushions (how I hate sewing). I wanted to run away always do at the thought of a sewing job. He said do I think he's an idiot and I said Yes! And I told him not to speak to me. Arent I an awful person. (Still raining.) Your father has taken me at my word and is not talking. I should not have got married one should not marry if one can't sew. What looks nicer than a neat patch or mending job well done. Well Tom enough of that.

Love Mam Dad and Ann

I never met Rosie, nor can I recall her ever being mentioned. She must have been very thorough in saying farewell to her relations.

I would sometimes prevail upon Mother to darn my socks. I used to like watching her do it. Very neatly. I had no idea she was so averse to the task. I would sometimes try to do it myself, but I couldn't get the strands of wool close enough together.

[21st July 1958]

Dear Tom

Thanks for your letter. I am writing early so as to send you £2.

Your father came home yesterday and said Uncle Dan [Pat] was in an awkward situation. It appears Yvonne his sister-in-law asked him to get her some paint, she doesn't want him to pinch it. She was willing to pay. The paint cost £1 14 10d, so he charged her 30/- as a kindness. He went home on bus and took the paint with him upstairs and placed it on a shelf. Unluckily one tin fell off and emptied itself all over the place including a young ladies coat. Your father understands the bus was in such a mess it was in garage for a whole day men had to clean it and it lost money being laid off the road. Of course several people wanted your Uncle Dan's name and address and for some unknown reason instead of saying 1 Springville Ave. he said 1 Preston Rd. which later on no one could find. Eventually two policemen found his house and accused him of giving a false address and also wanted to know what he was doing with the paint and if it was stolen.

Poor Uncle Dan. He will have to buy the young woman a new coat at least without the bus company suing him. Aunt Dorrie will have a frown on her face for six months. When your father told me I thought I'd have died laughing. The other week Uncle Dan knocked over some kid's bike and the damage cost him 13/6. Soon he won't be able to take any more punishment.

Well Tom write and let us know if you will be coming home and when. When will you know your exam results.

I am a bit mad at your father tonight, because I was saying something about you, like how clever you are. He said 'Anybody would think there was only our Tom in the world.' So I said I wasn't speaking to him. Anyhow I told him I would tell you. (I think he was a bit frightened.)

Love Mam Dad and Ann xxx

Good luck next week.
PS. I wouldn't mind seeing the Queen Mother hand you your B.A. paper. I should cry I think.
PPS. Why can't I get it for you.

Even though Dad was by this time working in Webster's paint store, on Dock, it wasn't often that free paint was come by. The policeman at the end of the Fish Dock tunnel kept a watchful eye on what the workers brought off the dock, though they could be fairly easygoing when it was fish. Grandad Courtenay had once got to the end of the tunnel with the tail of a haddock sticking up at the back of his neck. A policeman told him to make a better job of hiding it. He loved that story. It was thoughtful of Uncle Pat/Dan's sister-in-law to say she would pay for the paint, otherwise he might have been tempted to risk getting some off the dock without buying it. It would have appealed both to the daredevil and to the socialist in him – putting one over the bosses. Unlike Dad, who walked from work, Uncle Pat/Dan lived in Hessle and had to get a bus home. It took all his powers of concentration on some Saturday afternoons if he and Dad had gone straight from work to Subway Street Club.

In July 1958, having completed my Final examinations the previous week, I returned to Gower Street for my RADA audition. It took place in a small theatre in the bowels of the main building. I was ushered in by 'Sergeant', a thin man with a grey moustache and a green uniform with a stand-up collar, and told to wait my turn in a basement corridor outside the stage area. There was a tall young man also waiting. He would be tall, I thought (even though I had shot up while at UCL to medium height). He told me he was from New Zealand. He was summoned onto the stage. Very loud, I thought he sounded, and not very believable. He reappeared looking hot, and then it was my turn.

Auditionees were sent a selection of pieces. You had to perform one of them and one of your own choosing. I had chosen Trinculo's speech from *The Tempest*. There were six or seven people listening, about ten rows back. I was nervous. Later on, in the profession, auditions never scared me. I always thought they were looking for what I had, not for what I didn't have, unlike critics. But this audition was for a lifetime, and it had been a long time coming. Had I auditioned straight from school I would have been in better shape. More confident. My three years in London had unravelled me.

I told my audience who I was and what I was going to give them. As I started 'Here's neither bush nor shrub to bear off any weather at all, and another storm brewing,' the central of the figures sitting listening leant forward. My right arm was swinging about, but I knew it didn't matter. They didn't want the finished product, I told myself. And I felt instinctively that the figure leaning forward was John Fernald, the principal of RADA, and that he was on my side. I was right.

As I was about to leave, Sergeant, as he was always known (he never had a 'the'), asked me if I wanted to return the following Saturday to try for a RADA scholarship. 'Does that mean I've got in?' I asked him. 'I suppose it does,' he said. So I duly returned the following Saturday and with the aid of Hamlet's 'How all occasions do inform against me' won a scholarship. Things were looking up. I had got into RADA, and, provided I got a degree, the Hull Education Committee would continue to help me for two more years. The money from the RADA scholarship, though it would pay for my tuition fees, was considerably less than the grant I had been getting from Hull and would need to be supplemented.

The essays I wrote at College on literature or drama were usually well enough received, and once I knew I had evaded the military digression I had managed to settle down to some work for the weeks preceding Finals. It wasn't the time of my life, exactly, but I did think I had been not entirely unsuccessful. Not perhaps as successful as Mam and Dad might have wished, because I had always done so well in Hull, but I did think I had scraped by.

[29th July 1958]

Dear Tom

Received your letter this morning. I am not going to pretend it wasn't a shock, it was. Why didn't they sack you after the first or second year. But one thing I am pleased about I would sooner you got no degree than a low grade one. I think the examiners are a lot of Fuddyduddies and they are frightened you will be a radical or extremist. It seems very funny to me anyone passing a scholarship for RADA including Hamlet doesn't know what he is talking about. I think you have given them all a headache. We know you are clever.

I've read 'Catcher in the Rye'. Your father bought it. I enjoyed it. The young man seemed to have too much easy money and could have been in a run down condition but (nearly) all he said and thought was true. But how can one be right against so many?

Love Mam Dad and Ann.

And from Dad.

Dear Tom

I am sorry you failed your Finals, but I must try to be honest and say only perhaps for my *own personal pride*. I have got the impression that some of your essays could have been misleading and the examiners have not seen eye to eye with some of your views. I have got that impression from how you express yourself and after what they said was their 'thorough discussion' on the postcard they sent you.

Still I have known for a long time you didn't see eye to eye with a lot of things at College and have been bent on trying to get some-where in the Acting Profession. Well at least Tom you have made a good start. I have been told on good authority that only people with outstanding talents can hope to get a scholarship to RADA. But will the fact that you failed your Finals have any bearing on getting a grant from Hull?

Love Pop

Mam and Dad were terribly upset that I had failed. Their letters are very loving and generous. From Mother it was to be expected because her love had always been for whatever I was, not for something I might become. But Dad had always thought of me as the emblem of his family's worth. I represented the Courtenays in his eyes, so his generosity over my failure is huge. He would have hated telling Uncle Pat and Uncle Bernard about it. He had always longed for me to be successful. My school reports at Kingston were scrutinized with the utmost care and pride. I was not discouraged from showing my first term's report to the whole street, starting with Grandad Quest. I was even told to take it to the staff room at West Dock Avenue School to show Mr Beeken.

When in the fourth form at Kingston we were streamed into clever and not so clever, Dad couldn't wait for my end-of-term report, so keen was he to see how I got by against stiffer opposition. At the end of the first term in 4A, four of us were given an A. I took my report home as usual.

'How many As were there?' asked Dad.

'Four.'

'Who was top?'

'Atkinson.'

'Where did you come?'

'Fourth.'

Not a word from Father.

He may have been hard about my fourth place then, but now, when I really had failed, and was in need of his love, he could not have given it more generously.

I don't think, by the way, that Mother liked *Catcher in the Rye* as much as I did.

The first time I saw Mam and Dad after getting my exam results, they were sitting together in Rayner's. It was strange being a failure for the first time in my twenty-one and a half years as their pride and joy, and I felt sheepish and didn't know what to say. They were very sweet and welcoming in spite of their great disappointment, and I couldn't help feeling relieved that my university charade was over, however unsuccessfully. It was very hard for them. My having the chance to do something with my life meant so very much to them. After my years of study I had ended up with bugger all. Nothing whatsoever to fall back on. I might just as well have been a barrow lad on Fish Dock, bringing good money in. They couldn't resist trying to persuade me to go back to UCL for another year, to get my degree. But I would have none of it. They were very concerned that the Hull Education Committee might not be keen to help me through a second course of study, when I had failed the first one. And they were right.

I had found myself employment as a labourer in Finsbury Park, north London, for the weeks before the start of the October term at RADA. It was better paid than portering on Paragon Station, and the Camden Road flat was rented for the whole year, not just term time. That was the first long vacation I spent away from Hull. Very hard on Mother. And labouring in Finsbury Park can't have seemed to Mam and Dad to be much of an outcome for all that homework in our front room in Harrow Street, for all that 'struggling and striving'. The eternal student with yet another vacation job.

22nd August 1958

Dear Tom

Everything is rather quiet here, although I enjoyed the week-end and was sorry when you had to go back. I wish you had got things a bit more settled.

I hope you are enjoying working in the park. I didn't mean to be snobbish when I said you ought to be doing something different. People think that when young men and women go to university they are secure but by hell they are less secure than youngsters leaving school at 15 or so it seems.

Don't be angry if we seem to go on at you about taking your degree. I suppose we have to get it out of our system. Enough.

I feel sick as hell of Harrow Street today. I'm always seeing kids nearly getting run over.

Have you any more news from Hull Education. I wonder if they will help you and if they won't. What shall you do? If you go to RADA and have to work as well you won't be able to do your best at RADA. It's all a mix up and not the pattern you think it is. Never mind we'll have to wait and see.

All for now.

Love Mam Dad and Ann xxx

The man I saw at the Hull Education Committee's headquarters said they were prepared to give me a grant for another year at UCL, so that I could get a degree, and then to give me a grant to supplement my RADA scholarship. I had to explain to him, however, that I could in no way contemplate another year of academic work, and that I would go to RADA come what may. It was decided, therefore, to give me an Intermediate Grant, quite a bit less than the one I had been receiving at UCL. It was worth hardly more than the RADA scholarship, the value of which they deducted from what they granted me, so I was going to have to manage on a lot less than I had got used to at College – £150 a year instead of £250, making my vacation job even more essential.

I had had several vacation jobs, starting in my fifth year at Kingston when I helped deliver the Christmas mail. I prided myself on the accuracy of my work. My friend Alan Plater, a fellow postman and then in his last year at Kingston, was conscientious, too, but told me that, on reaching the end of the first street he delivered to, he glanced back and saw a long row of housewives exchanging their envelopes. He had got out of sync. So accomplished a postman did I become, however, that I was invited to help with the Christmas mail much later, when I had become a member of the Old Vic Company. I had to tell the Hull Post Office that there was nothing doing.

The following summer I managed to get a job for a few weeks as a clerk with the Eagle Star Insurance Company. The manager was extremely kind and let me have an hour after the lunch break for my studies. I read *The Uses of Literacy* by Richard Hoggart, who was a working-class hero of mine. My clerical duties had something to do with claim forms. Acting must have been very much on my mind because I can remember explaining to one of the office girls that it was perfectly possible to say 'We shall meet again at Philippi' without being too grandiloquent – as though you meant it, in fact. She wasn't in school uniform, which made her very attractive. It can't have been the usual topic of conversation at the Eagle Star and I think she thought I was funny but not quite right in the head.

The next summer, before my last year at Kingston, I worked for a few weeks with several other sixth formers at a harvest camp outside Driffield. We were doled out to farmers in the locality. The rates varied according to the farmer. I got one and six an hour, which was average, but some got one and ninepence. Jack Barnaby got one and ninepence. Christ. Best athlete in the school, sure to be made Head Boy the following term (oh really!) and getting threepence an hour more than me.

I have remembered the hourly rates of so long ago because Mam and Dad couldn't help occasionally reminding me that, unlike most of the lads of my age on Hessle Road, I wasn't bringing any money into the house. Of course, I knew how much they wanted me to stay at school, and I dare say they only did it when I was being full of myself, but it did affect me. I can remember working the vast length of a huge field, lifting the sheaves of wheat and propping them up against one another. Stooking, it was called. My arms scratched to buggery, covered in beetles, thirsty as hell, and fuelled by rage. Some lucky sods were getting threepence an hour more than me. But when I remembered that Bernard Mudd was only getting one and threepence an hour at his farm, my rage subsided. Come the evening, back at the camp, I told him we weren't really doing it for the money, were we? He may well not have believed me, but that was all I could think of by way of comfort.

(In 1999 I stood with David Hockney in front of a painting he'd done of the Yorkshire Wolds near Driffield. 'When I was at school I worked at a harvest camp near there,' I told him.

'So did I,' he said.

'I got one and six an hour.'

'So did I.')

*

The following year, while we awaited A level results, it was Bridlington's turn to offer employment, at Alderman Science's café. He was the school governor to whom I had once delivered a vote of thanks. Several sixth formers were enrolled to help with the summer rush. Some worked in the kitchen; I was in the front line as a waiter. Waiters wore a white jacket. The main lunch meal was always 'roast lamb', though backstage, before it was anointed with gravy, it looked like mutton and it didn't look roasted. 'That's been skipping around for a year or two,' observed one customer sagely, and I could not demur. The place came into its own with high tea. Fish and chips. The first sitting went well enough with the places all nicely laid, but thereafter chaos ensued. There wasn't the back-up in the kitchen. Never enough plates and cutlery, never enough washing-up. I felt unable to do myself justice. The menu also announced 'fruit salad', which was often requested. On a mantelpiece in the kitchen stood a sweet jar. Lying in a few inches of liquid at the bottom of it were some sad-looking segments of tinned fruit. Nobody seemed to know how this could be refilled.

I got enough out of it once for a single serving, but thereafter that jar bothered me greatly. 'Fruit salad,' I used to tell customers. 'You don't want to have that. It's awful.'

I did pretty well for tips. I think they felt sorry for me. None more so than the lady on whom I spilt soup. 'Please don't worry, love. It couldn't matter less.'

As I waited for a clean plate, so I could re-lay a table, the poor little old woman who did the washing-up used to engage me in conversation. Her wedding ring cut deeply into her finger – an effect of the washing-up water. She told me she had remarried not long since. 'He's eighty,' she said. 'I've had to get away from him. He won't leave me alone.'

The married waitresses used to like to tease me on account of my innocent air. A bit D.H. Lawrence. One of them was expecting her husband, a merchant navy man, back from sea. She was dark with a nice full bosom. I would have liked to rest my head on it. Her black and white outfit suited her. She used to flirt with me, I now see, and the other waitresses pulled her leg. 'She'll tell you all about what happens when he gets home, Tom,' one of them said. And I believed her and was looking forward to the account. Of course I never heard a word about it. People often confided in me during my vacation career, and usually on the same subject. I must have been a bit like Mother: 'They pick me out and I'm glued.'

In one summer vacation or other, I don't remember which, I served as a temporary porter on the Paragon Station, Hull. They gave you a porter's hat. I liked to keep a low profile on this job, though it wasn't always possible. I had sometimes to sweep the main concourse and I was mortified by the thought that I might be recognized. My fish merchant uncle, Wilf Spaven, saw me once as he waited to board a train. I longed to explain that my portering was only a temporary engagement, but I didn't really know where to start and Uncle Wilf had a train to catch.

My haven on Paragon Station was the place where the railwaymen had their tea and sandwiches. One of the ticket inspectors, the porters told me, had been a prisoner of the Japanese, though he himself never mentioned it. He was interested in the state of the railways and what the world was coming to: people trying to get away without paying – that sort of thing. He once told me he found a couple having sex in one of the compartments.

'What did you say to them?'

'Tickets, please.'

'What did they do?'

'The bloke reached in his back pocket and handed me their tickets.'

'Then what happened?'

'Well, they more or less carried on. I mean they stayed lying there. I thought about it for a minute, then I said, "Would you mind taking your feet off the seats, please?"'

I'm sure all the porters had heard this before, but it led the discussion in the direction of sexual mores. The most outgoing and energetic of the porters did not equivocate: 'It's a funny night I don't cock a leg over my old woman.' Nobody said anything for a moment. Could it have been that the energetic porter's lifestyle was the exception not the rule? The quietest of the porters, and my favourite, eventually spoke up. He had a slightly crooked back and his head was permanently tilted as though he were carefully weighing up whatever was said to him. He had told me that his two children were the light of his life. He looked at me as he spoke. I don't think he wanted his innocent young friend to be too influenced by all this licentious talk. 'I can't say I touch our lass that often, but when I do I've no worries. I know where she's been.'

The job I had before my first term at RADA, working as a labourer in Finsbury Park, meant an early start to the day, and I wasn't always up to it. We were supposed to start at seven and work for an hour, then have our breakfast in a small brick building, or labourers' retreat, used specially for the purpose. I often didn't arrive till the men were having their breakfast half-hour. Their retreat was presided over by an argumentative old boy, working part time in his retirement. He lit the fire and kept the place tidy. My lateness delighted him hugely. 'He's been pulling his pudden,' he offered by way of explanation, and laughed gleefully. 'Pulling his pudden.' No matter how many times I was late it was always my pudden he thought responsible. I wasn't going to disabuse him. He was very easily stirred, and the workers loved to wind him up. There was one in particular who carried a huge wad of bank notes in his pocket. He loved to pick on the old-timer. 'You talk bollocks, you silly old get.'

'I tell you what,' said the old one. 'He's the greediest facker who ever drew breath. No wonder he's got all that money. Do you know what he does for a day out? He goes to London airport and watches the planes come in. Watching facking aeroplanes. What sort of a day out is that?'

'I like watching aeroplanes,' said he of the wad. 'It doesn't cost anything.'

'Too facking right it doesn't cost anything, you greedy sod.'

I think he enjoyed getting worked up, but so enraged did he sometimes become, especially when the wad was waved under his nose, that I was quite glad he had me and my pudden about which there was no argument – an oasis of comparative calm.

There was an Irish contingent working in the park. I used to weed the American garden with them. Why American? I don't know. It was made up of leggy old shrubs. 'Oi tink we're in for a tundershtorm,' said one, to my great delight, as he leant on his spade, for the Irish were in my blood if not in Mother's. He was Harold, his friend was John, and John was married, with two lots of twins and a wife who worked in the Co-op. The Great Subject came round again.

'You'll not be married yourself?'

'No, John.'

'My wife's a foin big woman. Isn't that so?'

Harold nodded gravely, making me think that John's other half must have been monumental.

'You'll not have been to bed with a woman?'

'No, John.'

'Saturday night. Saturday night is our night. Now, let me tell you this: you mustn't go straight to it. You've got to, you know, fiddle about a bit. And I'll tell you something else.' Here he pointed at his crotch. 'On a woman,' point, point, 'On a woman, well,' point, point, 'It's not something you'd want to be lookin' at.'

It was a relief to take a spell of duty on the boating lake. For one thing I didn't have to get up so early. And I got to say those timeless words, 'Come in, number seven, your time is up.' My commandant on the boats was contented and boring. 'Um pum pum, um pum pum,' he would voice tunelessly, but even he couldn't resist telling me of his courting days. His revelations, however, were more U certificate. 'Saturday night at the pictures and a bar of Fry's chocolate cream. That's what we used to like.'

29th September [1958]

Dear Tom

I was pleased to get your letter this morning, and hear that you are full of good spirits and confidence.

It may not interest you to know but when I was quite young I was in a concert party. I loved it very much, especially the hustle and bustle behind the stage. I had interest that way even up to knowing your father even though it was only dancing and singing. I can remember it all very clearly and how much happiness it gave me. I was very keen. Thinking of all this makes me understand how much you really like what you are doing.

What do you think! Saturday after dinner I went in the front room and sat at the piano when who should walk in but Jack Stathers. He looked at me and I didn't know what sort of an expression to make. He looked full of anguish silly sod. He said he had come as he didn't want me to fall out with Alice over him.

Your father told him we didn't like him coming in full of drink and swearing. I told him I didn't like it when he mocked you. He said it was all in fun really and went on to say how daft he is with his money how hard he works and he never neglects his family and Alice always gets her wages and he is generous with Granny. I gave him a cup of tea so I suppose we are friends again. I felt a bit like a pompous prig. I have an idea his visit was planned and even Granny knew he was coming. They are a crafty lot.

It seems to me you've got to *not* think about the things you don't like in people to be able to tolerate them. You've got to come down to their level. On the other hand if you do think about what's right and wrong, no one will give you credit for intelligence but just put your moods down to physical weakness. So what has one to do?

I hope you are going to enjoy being at RADA and I am looking forward to all your news about the place. Look after yourself and be careful of the girls.

Love Mam Dad and Ann

Mother thought Aunt Alice had a lot to put up with in Jack Stathers, and she was never afraid to say so. He makes a very good fist of trying to get back in Mother's good books. It's quite cunning of him to say that he didn't want to be the cause of friction between the two loving sisters, although he generally was, because dear Aunt Alice wouldn't hear a word against him. The cornerstone of his defence, that 'Alice always gets her wages', was perfectly true, and would have appealed strongly to Mother's sense of justice. Wives getting their week's money was the number-one rule of life on Fish Dock. It didn't always happen. Bookies and beer could take quite a slice of it.

RADA TERM I
September 1958

My first term at RADA was a disappointment. Perversely, I missed the brain power that had been all around me at UCL. And I had still, among my graduate friends at the Camden Road flat, one foot in academia. Only one of our intake, Tom Kempinski, had been to a university (Cambridge). Moreover, I was having to manage on my reduced grant. You could buy a lot of food for the shortfall of £100. And I felt, as Mam and Dad must have, that my smaller grant implied I wasn't studying something entirely serious.

I had expected my fellow drama students to be more exotic. To have names like Tristram and call one another 'darling'. But John Thaw, Geoffrey Whitehead, Geoffrey Hinsliffe and Michael Blackham were from the north. Terry Rigby and Tony Douse were from the midlands, and David Lowe was a near-unintelligible cockney lad. RADA had become far less middle class than in Sir Kenneth Barnes' day.

Clifford Turner, a crucial RADA figure, and one to whom I would feel more indebted in years to come than I did at the time, taught voice production. Not young, he was tall with a very straight back and large hands which he waved gracefully as, legs crossed, he sat and made his points. Definitely of the old school, his voice was beautifully produced, supported by an enormous diaphragm, which sometimes he cradled like a baby. It was said that he could recite an entire Shakespeare sonnet on one breath. Even his laugh, though sincere, seemed very deliberate and stagey. 'Huh, huh, huh.' Ronnie Fraser remembered Mr Turner's laugh. Ronnie had a small mouth. Mr Turner asked the students to open their mouths wide. 'You, too, Fraser. Come along, get that mouth wide open.' 'It is wide open, sir,' said Ronnie as best he could with lips agape. 'Good heavens! So it is. Huh, huh, huh!'

Mr Turner gave us lots of apposite verse to work on for articulation:

> A tutor who tutored the flute
> used to tutor two tooters to toot.
> Said the two to the tutor:
> 'Is it easier to toot
> or to tutor two tooters to toot?'

And some prose:

> She is a thistle sifter. She has a sieve of sifted thistles and a sieve of unsifted thistles, because she is a thistle sifter.

For tone, Rupert Brooke:

> Oh! there the chestnuts, summer through,
> Beside the river make for you
> A tunnel of green gloom, and sleep
> Deeply above; and green and deep
> The stream mysterious glides beneath,
> Green as a dream and deep as death.

Not one of us, throughout our two years at RADA, could ever manage the 'ees' and 'oos' like he could.

He loved to correct us when we mispronounced things. He had a great time with Terry Rigby's Midlands accent. 'Oi'd like to do a piece from *Rowmeo and Juli-ette*, sir.'

' "Rowmeo, Rowmeo!" who's he? And we say Juliut, Juliut, with the accent on the first syllable. There's no "ette".' And he would wince with distaste as he said 'ette'.

Clifford Turner's voice production was perhaps stronger than his acting. In my second year we once cheered him after he did a speech from *Henry V* for us, and he left the room. He thought we were making fun of him. Perhaps we were, though without meaning to. We were all very fond of him. His criticism was always good humoured, as though he realized that we would never do things like he did. He was trying to teach us, however, to support the voice by breathing properly. Essential for a career on the stage, if not in film. On my first term's report, he had this to say: 'Your tone was very "creaky" and generally uncontrolled, but there is some improvement. Your delivery is too explosive and you need to take especial care to avoid articulatory grimaces.' I wonder if he would have found my tone so creaky had I gone straight from school and the confident Mr Knightley.

The movement class was taken by Madam Fedro. We had to have tights and ballet pumps, which made us self-conscious at first. I had worn tights only once before, in *Nightmare Abbey*. I knew I had a muscular pair of legs, they were Mother's pride and joy. But they were better when considered separately, I discovered. Together they were a bit bandy, from all that football in Harrow Street maybe. Geoffrey Whitehead had the longest, thinnest legs. Were he ever to have worn tights on the stage it would have had to be in a comedy. Madam Fedro was a legendary RADA teacher who was even then quite elderly but very energetic and lively, exhorting us to stick this bit out and that bit in. 'Open ze groin, open ze groin.' Years afterwards it was always amazing to hear from students who had just left RADA that she was still on the go. I remember her telling us about Vivien Leigh's wonderful deportment, her head facing forward, not up. 'She murdered ze ozzer actress wizz her teknick, her teknick.'

Historically speaking, our Shakespeare class is worthy of mention because it was taken by an elderly lady, Nell Carter, who had been in Beerbohm Tree's company. For our end-of-term test we did some scenes from *The Winter's Tale*. My scene began, 'Nor night nor day no rest.' The verse is tortured and difficult. In 1997 I played Leontes on the radio and loved the madness of it. For a twenty-one-year-old it was impossible. I didn't think I was any good. We were adjudicated by a professional actor, the impressive and passionate Clifford Evans. He hadn't much to say about me, but then how could he have? The play hadn't been very well chosen.

I didn't feel personal contact with any of the teachers in the first term. It took me a while to get used to performing pieces in front of my fellow students. And now, of course, I was no longer the only student hoping to become an actor. We all were.

In answer to Mother's 'be careful of the girls', let me say that at RADA they didn't cause me the heartache that the Slade girls had. But then I wasn't as miserable as I had been at college, being no longer confronted by Finals. And I wasn't that bothered. Pro tem. There was one girl I thought might make some sort of mark for herself. Sarah Miles was one of the few among us who could have been described as upper class. One of the sounds I remember from my first year at RADA was Sarah saying, 'Airw, Thomas, you're so funny.'

Thursday, 15 October 1958

Dear Tom

You will find your allowance inside don't spend it all at once. I'm struggling through my work. Yesterday my head played me up. Today I'm all aches and pains just as if someone kicked me on my backside. So instead of holding me head I'm holding the other place.

Granny has just been to tell me Jack Stathers was in their house Wednesday teatime full of beer. It appears there was hell on. Jack S. called our Jack and wanted him outside, blows were struck. I'm glad it happened, now they know all I said about him was true. He's a big barmy bugger. I thought he was quiet lately. His badness has got to come out somewhere. I think they ended up shaking hands. All this upset Granny.

Well Tom I have been thinking about you this week and wishing you didn't have to go washing up. I know you need the money but I feel you are much too intelligent to have to be washing up. I wish you would try and write a little. Don't be angry with me.

I was reading an article on Tenessee Williams. I enjoyed it. He is always full of despair and worry. He used to think he would die before he was 40 and now he thinks he will die before he is 50. He wakes up in the night and Ghouls are on his shoulder (smashing). We saw part of Cat on a Hot Tin Roof. A man with a bad leg said 'One always wants to do things one used to when one can't.' I liked that. I bet Tenessee Williams is very understanding.

All for now.

Love Mam Dad and Ann

PS. Grannie went to an Aunt's funeral the other day. She came home on a bus with Great Aunt Jane. Grannie was disgusted because Aunt Jane didn't pay her bus fare for her. Aunt Jane told Granny it was a lonely life living on her own and in a big house. Granny said to me 'She's that much bloody money she doesn't know what to do with it. If she's lonely she should have had more kids. (They don't see eye to eye.) I don't feel bothered that Aunt Jane has loads of money but I feel sympathetic she's lonely. I may visit her soon for a good talk. This would make Grannie mad. What a mixed bunch we are.

I have no recollection of ever having gone washing up to earn money, so maybe it was just something I wrote of as being a possible source of revenue – something I might do in order not to have to keep taking money from them.

Though Mother didn't like being poor, unlike Grandma she didn't resent Great-aunt Jane being well off. Not the prevailing Hessle Road way of seeing things.

We were quite used to Mother not feeling very well, but she didn't want to burden me with it. She thought I had enough to worry about. So she makes light of it.

[31st November 1958]

Dear Tom

Christmas is getting near we are starting the decorating in about two weeks. Your father distempered out the gas cupboard last night.

I have been to Grannies this afternoon – the landlord came in he was playing hell because she wouldn't pay her rent. It is only £2 16 a month. She goes in club every night of the week. It isnt in her nature to pay her way. She made a cup of tea and never turned a hair. I would have been sick and worried and ashamed. She came out of the house with me and said she had to go to doctor's for tablets for her leg.

Uncle George was at Grannies. He has got heaps of toys for the kids. More than you or Ann ever got. Yet they never have no money in the house. I was thinking the other day about last Christmas and the way I always get upset. One is supposed to enjoy it all but sometimes I feel very miserable. Just the same with other celebrations. I can't feel happy just because it's my birthday. How can one celebrate getting older? The nicest part and what makes one more happy is that one is a lot wiser and can see things more clearly.

Well Tom you can help me when you get home. We will sup heaps of tea and coffee and have a bloody good time.

Love Mam Dad and Ann

Aunt Agnes won £100, 2 weeks ago.
Ann kept telling me how good looking I am last night so I kept looking in the mirror. I can't see it.

Mother's birthday was 2 November, as she later writes, 'stuck between the smouldering remains of Hull Fairs, Armistice Days and Bonfire Nights'. After her death, wherever I was, I would always phone Dad on 2 November, and he would always say, 'I don't have to tell you what day it is today, do I, Tom?' And I would always reply, 'No, Dad, you don't.'

*

I came home for Christmas and did my stint delivering Christmas cards. I had always loved Christmas. Aged nine, I can remember my heart lifting (like in Kingston High's school hymn 'Lift up your hearts') when we sang the first Christmas carol of the year, in early December. Wordsworth said it best, though not of Christmas: 'For me it was a time of rapture.' It was the year that I set myself to learn the Latin version of 'Oh come all ye faithful', when Mr Brabbs wrote it on the blackboard. '*Adeste fideles, Laeti triumphantes, venite, venite in Bethlehem.*' I don't know why those Christmas carols moved me so. It wasn't the religious aspect. Nor was it that Ann and I got masses of presents. It was just a magical time. Perhaps the mid-winter festival is in our genes.

I have already mentioned our Christmas Eve dos with Mother at the piano and me allowed up to give them a song. It's remarkable that Father Christmas managed to fill our stockings without our ever being aware of his doing so, and that after a night of some merrymaking. Perhaps it was Mother Christmas – she was never the worse for wear. The stockings came courtesy of Grandad Quest. They were the thick white woollen ones, known as hob socks, that he wore inside his clogs on Fish Dock, knitted by Grandma. There was always an orange at the bottom and a bar of chocolate. I can feel their shape now through the thick wool. Mother used sometimes to regret that we weren't given more presents, as did I, but I really enjoyed seeing what other kids had got. Some of them had pillowcases to be filled instead of stockings. Much more roomy, of course. Mam and Dad were too clever for that. They didn't want to get into debt in order to show off their generosity to the neighbours. Christmas presents could be a matter of pride on Hessle Road. 'We're gettin' our Eric an air rifle and a toy fort and our Betty a doll and pram set and some rollerskates. She wants some like our Eric got last year.' To be paid for 'on a club', reluctantly.

For most of my childhood we had rabbit for Christmas dinner. Dad sometimes fattened one up himself in a hutch in our back yard, but he didn't like putting an end to it. Then chicken came into vogue and Fish Dock wives used to like to announce that they were no longer having the cheap and common rabbit. 'We're havin' chicken this Christmas,' was quite the thing to say, and I remember being pleased to report to my grammar school classmates after our first Christmas break that we had made the great leap forward. I wouldn't have mentioned rabbit. Dad, however, was enraged. Mother could only afford a small chicken, and there was nothing on it compared to a buck rabbit and it was twice the price. His anger put quite a damper on our festivities. Having made such a fuss, he had difficulty in praising his chicken leg, unlike his beloved rabbit, to which he gave a rave notice every year. 'By hell, in't there some meat on the back leg of a big buck rabbit,' the cheapness of the creature serving only to intensify its flavour. I didn't mind that he didn't like the chicken. I was looking forward to mentioning it at school. When the term started I slyly swung the conversation round to Christmas eating. 'I really like Christmas. We have such a lot to eat.' So eliciting, 'What did you have for Christmas dinner?' I paused, as though I had difficulty in remembering, then said simply, 'Chicken,' as modestly as I could manage. Chicken for Christmas, going south for our holidays, cousin Michael's cast-off dressing gown. I was becoming more sophisticated by the minute.

What I genuinely loved was Mother's Christmas pudding made from Grandma Quest's recipe. It was thick and gooey and fruity, with little bits of carrot in it, and it clung to your teeth and the roof of your mouth as though showing off before it was swallowed.

After the Christmas pudding had descended, so too would our spirits. We had our meal at three or four o'clock, same as Sunday, and it was like the Sunday afternoon depression only worse. Dad had to go to work on Boxing Day, and he would fall asleep in his chair after the pudding. The magic was over.

While recently looking in an old cardboard box I came across four end-of-term reports from RADA, including my first term's report. By then I'd had enough of end-of-term reports, but I showed it to Mam and Dad. It saved me having to tell them much. I no longer wanted to. RADA was mine, not theirs. But the wait to get there had been something of a sentence, and the confidence I had had at school had evaporated, making me very unsure that my hopes would be successfully realized. I didn't want to share those hopes with Mam and Dad. I would have liked them not to be interested or worried about their possible outcome. Some chance! Besides, it was hard to say in front of Dad that we had to do a class in tights and ballet pumps, that we were supposed to learn deportment. Much easier in front of Mother. 'Well, you've always had a good pair of legs on you, Tommy.' One item on the report said: 'He shows signs of being a very good actor indeed. He has a sense of character and a sense of comedy. At present he is inclined to be uncontrolled and do more than is quite necessary. Work hard in technical classes and control will come. Judith Gick.'

They didn't know what to make of that. They didn't know what to make of my being at RADA. And I hadn't got my degree.

While I was at home I went with Mother to see Grandma, who was in hospital. It took a lot to stop Grandma's trek for a Guinness. Her favourite saying was 'It's a sad heart that never rejoices.' In December 1958 she had one trek too many, slipped on a patch of ice and broke her hip. Mother, fighting her aversion to hospital visiting and trying to be positive, pointed out that, since Grandma had been off her feet for two or three weeks for the first time in her life, the ulcer on her leg was almost healed.

Mam and Dad told me that Christmas that, should the opportunity arise, they would seriously consider following Aunt Alice to the Longhill housing estate in East Hull, but I didn't believe they would ever leave Hessle Road.

My departure for London after Christmas is stuck in my memory. As I waited on the Sunday afternoon till it was time to get the bus to Paragon Station, there was a play on their newly hired television starring Clifford Evans, who had adjudicated our Shakespeare test. That would normally have been quite a talking point, but no way was it then, try as we might to appear interested, because Mother was so downcast by my imminent departure. We had to watch the play, obviously. Here was an actual RADA teacher performing. But interest in it could not permeate the gloom Mother felt as I waited to leave for the strange drama school about which, having finally got to it, I seemed so uncertain and uncommunicative.

RADA TERM II
January 1959

Dear Tom

I was taking out the vacuum cleaner this morning and I suddenly thought I would have to write you a letter. I didn't feel much inspired and wondered how I should start the letter. People generally say 'We miss you very much' – I wondered about this. Did I miss you very much? Well! I hadn't so much cooking to do and so much washing to do, is this missing people? Then I thought a bit and I felt a bit weepy and I realised that if one thought very deeply about missing people one would be in a hell of a state in no time. Mind you at the same time as all this thinking was going on I was cleaning up and I also knew I had a beef pie to make for dinner which I didn't feel like doing. It's a rather interesting subject really missing people.

Although it is not so cold now it has never stopped raining since you went on Saturday. The time passes quickly and I hope you are settled again. I liked it very much when you said before you went away 'You will show them how good you are.' Are you doing that? [That might have been the beer talking.]

We went in Subway club Saturday it was terrible, although the place has been closed a year everyone went in the same place as before. People don't like change and this is a bad thing. I hope I never lose interest in new ideas and young people and say things like 'in my day'. I know I sometimes get carried away and nobody seems to understand me. I have to come back to earth so to speak. I think the only thing that could satisfy me would be if I could write something worthwhile. I always wanted to write something.

Love Mam Dad and Ann

I am sending you some stamps with your shirt and pyjamas and then you will have *some stamps*!

Ralph Richardson's play is in Hull. Ann is going Friday night. I think I will write a letter to Ralph R and ask him to keep you in mind for future work. (No I wont). Well Tom write soon and don't take me too seriously.

'I felt a bit weepy and I realised that if one thought very deeply about missing people one would be in a hell of a state in no time.'

I think it was this letter that made me decide to keep everything else she would write to me.

While on my full grant at UCL I had saved up and bought a (just about) portable record player that I used to lug from Hull to London and back. The record player at Camden Road made it unnecessary in London, and Dad very generously offered to buy it from me, ostensibly for Mother and Ann. It was a good way of giving me money without my having to feel too indebted.

Sitting in a booth in Imhoff's record store at the corner of New Oxford Street and Tottenham Court Road with my sensitive teacher friend Mike Lunnon, I listened to an LP of Dinu Lipatti playing Chopin waltzes. It had been recorded not long before the great pianist's untimely death, and in spite of his illness, and I had to buy it for Mother. It was beautiful, and I knew she would love it.

[5th February 1959]

Dear Tom

The record came as a lovely surprise on Tuesday morning. I was
sitting in my chair planning my jobs when there was a tap tap at the
door. You know I'm a bit wary about going to the door. I don't like
canvassers. I think about Mrs West who used to live near us she
would go upstairs to work in hot weather and then would come the
knock on door. She used to be very annoyed, she's very fat. After
several knocks she would paddle downstairs open the front door
and without beating about the bush tell the man to F . . . OFF. Well
I haven't reached that point. I generally wait for two knocks and
then go with a feeling of battle. If anyone knocks more than once
they either want you or your money. Anyhow after the tapping I
heard someone fumble with the door so I went and found the
record. It took me ten minutes to take the wrapping off and I was
very touched. It's a gorgeous record and I love it. I enjoyed the
reading on the back of the cover, especially the extract from
Chopin's letter. I didn't like to think the pianist knew he was dying
but it doesn't show in the playing. Ann likes it very much, and
when your father came home Tuesday evening I tried to explain to
him how I always liked Chopin tunes but never bothered to buy
such a luxury and he said 'why not'. This surprised me. He has
been very nice and patient for a few days and I suddenly felt like a
saint and I didn't like that so I thought I must be a fraud.

Granny is still making good progress. How I hate it on Saturday
night when I am supposed to visit her. Last Saturday night I
thought to myself 'just go without thinking and worrying about
anything'. This I did. While there I caught an expression on
Granny's face of sorrowfulness and she tapped her finger. I felt a bit
ashamed. After an hour in that place it just about bowls me over.
Am I ready for a glass of beer when I get home.

Thanks again for the record. I shall get lots of pleasure from it.
I'm sure it is much nicer to receive a Christmas gift in say Feb. or
Oct. Take care of yourself.

Love Mam, Dad and Ann

PS. I had a funny feeling I didn't want to put this letter in the envelope until the last minute. Like one wouldn't want to close the lid of a coffin of a loved one until necessary. I will quickly scrub the kitchen floor.

The record expressed my feelings far more eloquently than anything I could write. For a few weeks the platitudes that came into my head didn't seem worthy of her, and she didn't get a letter.

From Dad [20th February 1959]

Dear Tom

Just in case you've forgot our address is 29 Harrow Street. Hull. Your Mother is wondering if you're ill, got married, or anything else that can occupy your time and leave none to write a few lines.

Our three teams did well yesterday. Sid Davis went to York. Hull put up a marvellous show he said. The Tigers are still winning and must have a wonderful chance of promotion. I fully intended going to see them yesterday but Uncle Pat, Stan Houghton and Subway Club held my attention for too long. Straight home next Saturday.

Ma speaking. Tom hope you havent got flu. There isnt much to report though house exchanging is in the air again. I have a for and against list. Granny can walk a few steps. Your father went to see her last night. John Stathers [my cousin and Jack's son, a chip off the old block but sweeter] was home from sea and because his father calls Granny an old battleship, John said he had been to see her and take her some fuel oil (Guinness.) Love Ma.

So long for now. Love Pop.

[26th February 1959]

Dear Tom

I do hope you had a happy birthday. I said to your father, 'We got him on a Wednesday.' I was thinking of you on Wednesday and what a Tusseling time I had when you were born. Your father likes to talk about how clever it is to get up early in a morning and get ones work done. But I bet he's never done anything in his whole life so bloody strenuous as produce a son and heir by a quarter past seven. But as your grannie would say 'It's a woman's job.'

Your father came home teatime with a parcel under his arm. It was a pair of new brown shoes he had bought off someone for a £1. They were a new Escalator type with a raised inner heel. I said if the neighbours see you in them they will say hasn't Mr Courtenay got tall or more like it isn't Mrs Courtenay shrinking. He said he thought they might fit you. Ann said 'Our Tom wouldn't wear them he prefers something like Italian suede.' After tea your father settled down to a happy hour fiddling with these shoes and found that the magic of them was a piece of cork laid under the inner sole. This he removed with a beaming face. He now has a nearly normal pair of shoes.

Love Mam Dad and Ann

[1st March 1959]

Dear Tom

I wasn't going to write, not because you hadn't wrote but because things don't seem very interesting. Then I thought it's at these times one has to leave the motley throng and start weighing things up if you understand me, hence a letter.

When I was quite young, your grandad used to borrow money from a money lender and it was me who had to go and take the repayments. I used to take a friend with me never letting her know what I was going for. After the money was paid I would join my friend and suggest we pretended we were married to rich men. My God the things our rich husbands bought us. This lasted while we got home to our back doors. We tried being married to poor men but it only lasted one week. I liked Rene she was very nice. Looking back I can remember the different times I have done this romancing. I can't think of anyone else who does it and I hope it's not a childish trick I should have lost.

Our Jack came down the street this morning. Smiling face happy mood nearly running even asked me if I was alright. I thought what the hells got into him then I remembered it was Pay day. If he had been gloomy on Pay day I would have liked him much better.

Then I was talking to Mrs Phillips she is working at Woolworths and her husband seems to do her housework and cooking. We was talking about moving and she said maybe a new district would improve my health. This made me feel a bit weak and I thought next time anyone says anything like this to me I'll remind them my brain doesn't need improving.

Well Tom that's the lot. I hope you are well and happy. We have heard no more about a house. Who wants our house? I can't even walk outside our front door but I have to be careful not to tread in someones deep spit. But by hell it's bloody interesting listening to other people's conversations.

Love Mam Dad and Ann

Wed. Washday. In fish shop some women were having a lovely conversation. One woman said she didn't want any more bairns. She had one. Another woman had eight. She wouldn't part with one. Mrs Serving said she had two and she wouldn't be without them. One takes her a cup of tea to bed every morning. The woman with one and a long face said she didn't want anymore than her one. The woman with eight laughing said 'It's not always what you want but what you get.'
I hope you don't think I'm a drip, but it's just how things strike me. I should concentrate more on the housework.
The fish was good.

Aunt Alice's move to the Longhill housing estate, built post war in East Hull, made Mother's yearning for a nicer house seem less of a day-dream. The houses there had gardens and bathrooms. The usual way to effect a move was by exchange. A family had to be found at Longhill who wanted to move back to Hessle Road. Then, once the respective landlords were happy that their rents would continue to be paid, an exchange could be organized.

[8th March 1959]

Dear Tom

I expect you wondered if we were moving house. It all seems to have fallen through. It was last Friday our Jacqueline [my cousin, daughter of Jack Stathers and Aunt Alice, sister of John – much more like her mother than her father] came to tell us that her mother and father were coming round to tell us about a house. I said Oh! Your father looked at me with suspicion. You see Jacqueline sometimes comes in and starts telling me they are building houses at Longhill near them and right away I start wanting a new house and garden. She tells me they are building shops and a school and a church and I say what about a cemetery.

Well Alice and Jack came round and it appears a man Jack was talking to in club had chance of a new house but didn't fancy it as he had 6 bairns and a grandmother to look after and he couldn't afford the rent. Well your father said he would prefer Anlaby or Hessle but there was no harm in seeing if the people would like our house and also if our landlord would agree to it all. Right away after Alice and Jack went I felt a little sad and I said to your father, 'All this talk of flitting gives me a funny feeling inside' and he said the trouble with me was I liked to have funny feelings. You see he goes about everything like he's making a cup of tea and the only time he raises any enthusiasm is when he goes on a football trip. So I tried to look at it his way and said to him 'It isn't fair to you having to go all that way to and from work' as sometimes he isn't very well. He said 'Well or not I havent had a day off work for 3 years 4 months and a day.' Hell!

Saturday passed peacefully and after tea your father said he would have a steady walk along bank to see the people about the house. My inside turned. When he came back he said the man never came to the door it was the Mrs. By the way he described her I imagine she had been in the middle of bathing the six kids. She said she had no idea when or where she was getting a house and she would come round on Mon or Tues. The man of the house was a little under the weather, she said. He had been in club.

Tues dinner. When Ann came home I said to her if we have a front garden I shall have night scented stocks in it so if I am awake at night I shall be able to smell them. I am sick of the smell of Tom cats. She said I would complain the smell made me sick. That was the thing I had against St Wilfred's Catholic Church. When I passed by the smell of incense made me shudder. It's horrible. I said to Ann I was surprised the woman hadnt been to see our house. She said she knew she wouldn't. Ann said my trouble was I didn't see things in the right perspective. I was mad and went to stand again door. It was sunny. Already the bairns are charging up and down on their bikes. I saw a young woman who has a daughter called Marylin, and I thought Hell have I to look forward to seeing her all summer passing up and down screaming Marylin. It's been bad enough this winter dodging people's spit and toffee papers and dog muck.

Love Mam Dad and Ann

The Mrs whose husband was under the weather from being in club, having found someone at Longhill who wanted to exchange with her, wasn't sure whether she wanted to make the move. Longhill estate was two bus rides eastwards from Fish Dock. Rumour had it that many families who went there from Hessle Road never got used to it. The Mrs' uncertainty might have given Mam and Dad a chance of an exchange, in her place. It certainly gave them something to think about.

[15th March 1959]

Dear Tom

I hope the 3 young men who share the flat with you don't go about with sad expressions wondering what they are going to do when one room is full up with all these letters.

Well Tom we don't seem to be any nearer a new home. I had Mrs Thomas to see me as she is due for a new house and would like our house. But I don't know anymore yet. She was looking harassed and told me how her daughter Betty was courting a very nice quiet young Merchant Navy man called Mick, but for no known reason Betty met another chap and got married to him all in six weeks. It appears Mrs Thomas doesn't like him at all. Its his manners. Mrs T said when he comes in her house instead of sitting on her settee he lounges about all over the place and props his legs up. He also feeds the gold fish. I felt sorry for her.

I think it would be a good idea if people say like my father who have the intelligence to study the habits and customs of birds and animals should try to study also the customs and habits of human animals. But the idea never strikes them. Then they would find more happiness maybe. I havent heard or seen much of Sheila Delaney, who wrote 'Taste of Honey' but I have an idea she takes life as she sees it and has no wish to alter things. Whereas someone like me is full of resentment for what goes on. I think hers is the best idea.

Love Mam Dad and Ann

Shelagh Delaney was nineteen when she wrote *A Taste of Honey*. The daughter of a bus driver in Salford, she was working in an engineering factory when she saw a play at the Opera House, Manchester, and she thought she could do as well. That story would have appealed to Mother.

During our second term a pair of middle-aged bachelors gave us make-up classes in the Vanbrugh Theatre dressing rooms. One of them did the girls and one did the boys, though the one who did the girls used to pop in to see how the boys were getting along. We had a good time in there playing with sticks of greasepaint. None of us seemed to fit the bill when it came to 'straight juvenile' – i.e. a young man capable of bursting through the french windows in white flannels. We all had to be changed. I had to obliterate my eyebrows, first with soap and then with a stick of Leichner's flesh-coloured number 5, and colour them in higher up.

Not only my eyebrows but my spirits perked up in our second term, largely because one of the new teachers didn't hide the fact that he thought I was talented. He was also keen on John Thaw. John was extremely silent when he arrived at RADA from Manchester. He wore a red-spotted neckerchief atop his dark grey jersey, and a manner that didn't invite conversation. I was the only one of us in the first term who dared speak to him. The first time I tried, standing in the queue in the RADA canteen, all I got for my pains was a grunt, but something about him made me persist and we soon became pals. He was only sixteen when he started at RADA (I was twenty-one), though he looked older than I did, and his forbidding manner was just a cover-up for his shyness.

The teacher who liked John and me was called Adam O'Riordan. We were in his class only for that one term, but he was encouraging to both of us. He wasn't very tactful and didn't teach at RADA for long. He never made any headway in the business either as actor or director, though that didn't quench his love for it, and he ended up running a pub in Devon, teaching a bit and doing amateur dramatics like crazy. He used to come and see me in shows in London and was very free with his criticism. Amateur theatrical devotees can be a bit irksome with their comments, and even if they are right one doesn't usually want to listen to them. But I always let Adam have his say because he had given me encouragement when I needed it. He made me feel I had something to offer the theatre. I didn't forget that and neither did John. For what it's worth, the part I played for Adam that so delighted him was Rorlund, in Ibsen's *Pillars of the Community*. A priest, and fussy with it, as directed. Like Adam, really.

[22nd March 1959]

Dear Tom

I am pleased for your sake you have got a job, but I was very disappointed when you wasn't coming home on Monday. I realise one has got to get used to disappointments all the time but Monday isnt a day I like and I couldn't think of one bloody thing to liven things up.

After dinner your father sat in his chair and I said 'Don't you think when people were first on the earth they relied on their natural instincts and now everything is altering so rapidly that one has to be trained to take a place.' He said Mmm. He sat on the settee and I asked something else in the same vein and he nodded his head. I said 'Are you agreeing with me on purpose so as to avoid arguing with me?' he never answered. I said 'I don't blame you at all and I think you did a good bit of thinking there.'

Just lately I have had a feeling that I am more than one me. It is very strange. There's the me that goes careering off writing thinking and playing the Piano. This me takes over completely. Then there is the ordinary me that mocks the writing me and thinks she is silly and boring and a fool. The me I like best is the one that romances and says 'Ann if you open the sideboard door you will find a box of chocolates' and to father on Sunday 'Shall we go in the garden it will be warm in the sun, open the french windows.' That's the me I like, young and gay and easy to steer. A feeling like being tossed gently about all over the place. Like a Shuttlecock and Battledore that I once won at school in juniors for being clever. If I keep the last me up too long people get suspicious.

Last night I was saying to Ann something about when I die. Ann said 'Shall you throw me a star?' I said 'No, I shall be a ghost. I shall be a wicked ghost by Hell. I shant only be wicked to wicked people but I shall be wicked to nice people as well. Because I think being nice is a weakness.' One gets fed up of being nice and having to coax people all the time.

Don't be embarrassed by the £1. It's nothing and never go without while we are here we couldn't bear it.

Love Mam, Dad and Ann

In 1963 or 1964 I made a film, *For King and Country*, directed by Joe Losey and starring Dirk Bogarde. They were very kind and I became fond of them both. Years afterwards I met Dirk at a dinner party and he greeted me with 'How's the fishwife's son?' He said it affectionately and without a trace of malice, so I smiled and didn't say what I was thinking. Some fishwife.

Of the actresses I have worked with, Celia Johnson was my favourite. I can remember telling her about Mother, and feeling sorry they never met. Not in this world certainly. They were both equally girlish, but though Mother was bright she didn't have Celia's brainpower. Few people did. Celia was unusually intelligent for a very talented actress. She used to do those awesomely difficult crosswords devised for the really brainy – the ones called Mephisto and Ximenes. She told me she used to delight in amazing David Lean by learning new pages of film script at a glance. 'I was showing orff!' Celia and Mother both had a great sense of what was true. During a rehearsal in Chichester of *The Cherry Orchard* Celia broke off while speaking and asked if she could hear music. It seemed to be interrupting her train of thought. I looked out of the rehearsal-room window for the band, but there wasn't one, and then I realized she had been saying her lines. She had completely taken me in. In the Sixties Albert Finney and I were supposed to be part of the new broom of realism sweeping through our antiquated theatre. Not so.

Neither Mother nor Celia liked pretension, including their own. Celia used to like to quote from past bad reviews. Her favourite was for a performance of Juliet she had given on the radio when she was possibly too advanced in years. A headline said, 'Old actress spoils play.'

I once bumped into Celia in the West End. 'Where are you off to?' she enquired.

'I'm going to have lunch with Alec [Guinness].'

'What fun. I'm coming with you.'

'But, Celia, you haven't been invited.'

'I'm sure Alec won't mind.'

And he didn't.

[27th March 1959]

Dear Tom

I said to Ann this morning this is the first Good Friday our Tom hasn't been at home since he was born. We had some lovely halibut and parsely sauce. You would have loved it. It's a very busy week in Hull Easter week. Aunt Al said Uncle Jack S. could be working until 10 at night. I wondered how she could still believe him after 20 years marriage.

A trawler buzzer woke me up one morning it was blowing its

head off just like a loud bugle, and I wondered if it was some
trawler hand sending a message to his 'Duckie' as John would say.
Maybe the message meant 'put the kettle on' or 'get the beer out'
'put the radiogram on' 'get up' or maybe 'stay in bed'.

I've often wished your father went to sea. Fishermen are always
sending wives flowers, falling out and making up. When I used to
tell your father this he would say 'The only time he would go to sea
was when he was skulling his boat in dock.' That was when he used
to paint ships' sides. He used to have many a yarn to tell. What
made your father mad was when someone used the ship's lavatory
and flushed it all in their boat on them. He'd shout, 'now then you
up there, can you hear me, pudding head.' A little man with a
bewildered look would put his face over the side. Your father
would shout 'Can you read?' The man would nod. 'Didn't you
know you hadn't to use the lavatory in dock.' The man would
shake his head. Then your father 'If I come up there I'll knock 7
sorts of shit out of you.' The little man would disappear and your
father would then start scheming how he could get time off work
and money for clothes for all the mess.

My favourite story was when he was working at King George
Dock in a Merchant ship. Him and his mates had rigged a stage
over the ship's side to work on and when they climbed on it with
their paint pots someone made it cockle and they all fell in dock
much to the delight of some Indian Coolies on another ship
who pointed and giggled at the struggling men. The Coolies
had a good day because the men fell in three times that day.
One man was terrified he'd get pneumonia and would get
your father to rub his back. All these yarns happened on sunny
days.

After tea your father told Ann and me he had some news to tell
us and I said I don't want to know unless its to my advantage
because it could be something like 'Ive got a ticket to see England v.
Scotland.' The news is your cousin Michael Spaven was getting
married on Easter Monday. Ann and me laughed.

Anyhow think of us on Monday morning in church at 11 o'clock.
We're having a taxi. I just asked Ann if she likes me and she said

No. I asked your father if he likes me he said No. I said only me likes me.

Love Mam Dad and Ann

Would you call my letters an anthology?

[31st March 1959]

Dear Tom

MICHAEL'S WEDDING

Snatches of conversation

AUNT DORRIE:	I have no meat in house.
AUNT IVY:	I have plenty to eat in house.
AUNT AGNES:	This wedding is all their side.
UNCLE DAN:	I've only sixteen bob.
IVY'S UNCLE ARTHUR:	I've been knocking a wall down since I came from sea.
UNCLE WILF:	I have to go on Dock.
AUNT MARIE:	Bill doesn't want me to slim.
[BILL:	Not a word.]
MICHAEL:	I'm now going to get a ship and go away for 2 year.

Love Mam Dad and Ann

Now that I was a drama student Mother decided to try her hand at writing a play. It was set at a wedding breakfast. It was not easy to read. Because it wasn't a letter, she wrote even more compactly than usual, as though not wanting to waste too much paper on it. She said it was in fun, but it expresses her preoccupations. My part in it gives them voice. Here are the selected highlights.

Act 1. By the way this young man looks like you.
Young man. The only persons in this hall that really meant the wishes they gave are mothers not even fathers but mothers. Why? Because if they thought their offspring could have all this health

wealth and happiness they would be relieved of a hell of a lot of worry.

Guests. Who is it?

Young man. I am the person who turns up uninvited and should always be provided for.

Act 2. Silver wedding day of 1st Bride and groom, also their child's wedding day. Same hall and settings, same guests, same speeches, same sameness.

Young man to mother, now very fat. Has your 25 years of marriage been a success.

Mother. Well I think so.

Young man. Do you know your sin?

Guests. (Muttering.) Sin?

Young man. You have sunk so low you have to have things like Mothering Day. You need children to bring you pathetic little bunches of flowers and grown up children to send you big ugly Mothers Day cards. If you had done your job well as a mother the result would be all the consolation you would need.

Act 3.

Young man growing a little tired. To new Bride and Groom. How awful that you have been brought up in this world of sameness. But there is just a little hope for your children. Never commit the sin of depriving them of education. Cultivate yourselves some interesting hobbies. Don't make the grave mistake of making your children your hobby. Don't fail yourself by stooping so low as having to scrub places out to pass away the time. Instead of say painting, writing, or playing the piano.

A gun is now raised and the young man is shot. Finally all the crowd starts weeping and wailing. Everyone is terribly depressed and so am I. Finis.

This morning I heard the wedding march played. Very stirring. Like a challenge.

[16th April 1959]

Dear Tom

I hope you enjoyed your weekend. You seem to have disappeared
again like the young man in the play. I liked it when you came in
unexpected on Friday teatime.

You didn't seem to have much to say when you was home. You
didn't say anything bad and you didn't say anything good. I was
saying to Ann on Monday, it's time I stopped fooling around trying
to write plays etc. I am going to put my 'Wedding' at the bottom of
a deep drawer. Ann said my play was all attack, I should have some
interesting characters in it.

I said to your father I'm going to start liking everything that goes
on around here. When I open the back door and smell cats I shall
take a deep breath and say 'Ah, cats.' And when I see the woman
with the dog with its leg cocked up I shall smile and look right at
them and say good morning afternoon or night.

We seem to be a hell of a time getting a house exchange, in fact
the card advertising our house up Longhill must by now be very
dusty. I didn't seem to want to work at all on Mon or Tues and I
said to Ann I will just collect peoples conversations and keep them
for future reference.

You may think I am getting ambitious but I have been writing
letters now for nearly four years and I used to try writing plays and
stories and poems when I was quite young about 12 and I still
couldn't write one sentence that Womans Own would want to
publish. But press on.

I was listening to R. Hoggart on radio Fri. night he was talking
about S Delaney and J Braine's play etc, he said he was suspicious of
their work. He said people should write about what they know
(truth) in the districts of Salford and Hessle Road. I was going to lie
and say he sounded like he was talking to me, but really he didn't
sound like he was talking to anybody. But for all that he said write
about your sister or brother or anyone you know. These are things
that will stand alongside any classic. When he said Hessle Road I
knew what he meant.

I said goodnight to your father last night and then later I said goodnight again. He said I'd already said goodnight. I said yes but that was a P.S.

Love Mam Dad and Ann

I looked in my pocket diary for 1959 to try to find a clue as to what the job was that kept me in London for the Easter vacation that year, but there isn't one. What it does say, on 11 April, is, 'Hull 15 Featherstone 5.' That was the reason for my weekend visit home and the prelude to Hull's 1959 appearance in the Rugby League Cup Final at Wembley.

Dad and I always had our love of sport in common. It was the one thing that connected us powerfully and excluded Mother. It was a source of regret to both Dad and myself that I was no athlete. He usually sent a copy of the Saturday *Sports Mail* with Mother's weekly letter. It carried reports on matches played by Hull City FC (black and amber), the Tigers; and the two Hull Rugby League teams: Hull (black and white), the Early Birds, so called because their ground was in Airlie Street, and Hull Kingston Rovers (red and white), the Robins. Their nickname came from the single, thick red stripe around their white shirts. Hull was the Fish Dock team, Rovers were based in east Hull, and represented the commercial docks. Though Hull was my number-one rugby team, I had an interest in Rovers because of Uncle Wilf, their chairman, and also because we had a teacher at West Dock Avenue who used to play for them. Bryn Goldswain, a Welshman. He once took us to 'field', the municipal school pitches near Pickering Park, alongside Kingston High's playing fields. When little lads play rugby or soccer they follow the ball about in a pack. Mr Goldswain tried to correct this tendency: 'Spread out, lads,' he urged. 'Don't conglomerate. Don't con-glomerate round the ball.' This appealed to me very strongly, both as a word and as a tactic, and I took it to heart. I became so skilful at non-conglomeration that in my last year at West Dock Avenue I made the soccer team because of what Mr Nicholson described as my 'outstand-ing positional sense'. There I would stand, beautifully positioned, lonely and cold.

For a season or so in the late Nineties the Hull Rugby League team adopted the horrible American-style name of the Hull Sharks, as fashion dictated. (Wigan Warriors, Leeds Rhinos, Bradford Bulls.) 'Sharks' has now, I'm happy to report, been thrown back into the sea and the team is called simply 'Hull'. Though, oddly enough, the Early Birds' song, 'Old Faithful', seems to have come from the American Wild West:

> Old Faithful, we'll roam the range together,
> Old Faithful, in every kind of weather.
> When your round-up days are over
> There'll be pastures white with clover
> For you, Old Faithful, pal of mine.

On the Saturday evening after Hull's victory over Featherstone we went in the Subway Street Working Men's Club. It was L-shaped, with snooker tables and the bar in the foot of the L, and a small stage in the corner vaguely facing both parts of the L. Not an easy house to play, I should have thought, even without the racket going on during a busy night. Saturday night was generally the big night of the week. The snooker tables were covered over and the ladies came along. I used to go with Mam and Dad when I was old enough. Mother loved me to be out with them. We always sat on benches next to the snooker tables, on which our beer could rest. Not greatly comfortable, but that seemed to be our place. The bar was handy.

The entertainment consisted of a couple of turns and, of course, housey-housey. Now called Bingo. I loved the nicknames the caller gave the numbers. 'Kelly's eye . . . number one,' 'clickety click . . . sixty six,' 'legs . . . eleven.' And the cries that went up when somebody triumphantly called out 'House!' 'Bloody hell, not them again!' or 'I couldn't win a bloody argument.' The turns would generally be a singer and a comedian. Quite a low comedian:

'A young mate of mine got married the other week. They didn't go away for their honeymoon, they stayed on Hessle Road. After their wedding night, after their wedding night, he wakes up and he hears paper lad in street. So he gets out of bed, opens the window and shouts down, "Will you save us a *Sunday Pictorial*?" "*Sunday*

Pictorial? I haven't got a *Sunday Pictorial*. It's Wednesday." '

I can see Mother's sweet little smile as she glanced at me after a rude bit.

I showed Mam and Dad my RADA report. Though this report is not among the four now in my possession, it was made lyrical, I have no doubt, by Adam O'Riordan. But I found it much easier to talk about the rugby than about RADA.

[19th April 1959]

Dear Tom

Don't worry about not being able to listen to me. I am used to it. I am pleased your report is so good. I am now beginning to realise you will be an actor and you are not the Tommy Courtenay that played down Harrow Street and used to hang out in the backyard with the pigeons. When you first went to RADA I couldn't accept it I don't work like that. I used to think about it, not think about it, laugh about it and also cry and hate it as well as romance over it and now it's finally home. I hope you know what I mean, Tom Courtenay Actor.

Love Mam Dad and Ann

It must have been painful for her that I spent the whole weekend talking about the rugby match. That I didn't talk to her about what was happening to me in London or about something she had written in a letter. Obsessed by my own search for a means of self-expression and the uncertainty of its outcome, I couldn't always respond to her longing to share her world with me, and I would shut myself off from her. Then from time to time, like when I was desperate to buy her the Chopin record, my feelings would well up and I would find myself weeping. It had been so much easier when I was little and could run her an errand to Mr Tuton's and back. Like lightning, because I loved her.

[23rd April 1959]

Dear Tom

When your father came home Monday night I told him he was late sending the Sports Mail and the letter would be stale. He said he had never heard of a stale letter. I hope you didn't find it stale.

Ann brought me a book of Chekhov's plays and I felt so friendly towards it and I thought my initials are the same as his. I have read 'The Wedding' and 'A Tragedian in Spite of Himself'. I shall read the rest and then some of his short stories.

After tea Tues Jack Stathers came in. He was in a right state crying. He said he had backed a winner or he wouldn't be in that state. It seems his sister's carrying on prays on his mind. [There was a great deal of gossip about Jack's sister's lifestyle. Whether deserved or no I am not able to judge.] I thought his face looked much better tearful and sad. Ann rang him a car and he apologised for himself and I thought people drink beer to laugh to sing to argue to be happy and to cry etc.

One of Florrie Watson's bairns came with a note for me. Aunt Phyl wanted to borrow 2/6d. A week before she won £5. Also Granny won £14 in two weeks. I lent her it. Granny had smuggled the note into Florrie's before she went in club. Phyl wanted the money to go out with. In bed I thought if I was laid deep down in my coffin they would still expect me to lend them money.

Washday. Again door a woman was saying she once knew a prostitute and when you went in her home your feet sank in the carpets. Her two children didn't know what was going on, she sent them to boarding school and they came home little ladies. The woman said she would sooner take some washing in.

After dinner I met Mrs Randall and Nita. I told Nita you was going to be in Proposal. She hadnt read Chekov much. I told her I'd got a book of his plays and I was very interested. She knew a woman who had just got to like Shakespeare. I said how when I heard Romeo and Juliet on wireless I'd said how if they had been occupied all that could have been avoided but I said things were different in those days. She said it was only fictitious and I said I think all plays are real. I asked if she knew Richard Hoggart. She said no but she'd had to read his book for an exam. I said I thought it was a wonderful book. When Mrs Randall heard it was about working class she frowned. I said it said in one part how people pay £30 for a pram. Mrs Randall said she paid £25 for Robin's pram. Nita said she means they pay £30 and don't wash the bairns faces, but I didn't mean that. I said how these large prams fill up the small houses and it's all competition. I said Richard Hoggart loves his working class. But I don't. I said we are brought up on superstitions. Nita said so are other classes. I went home to finish my washing and could have cried because I wasn't educated.

After tea I went in front room and put my record on. Ann came in and said I'd got the wrong needle. I said 'that's my trouble I think I know it all and I know nowt' and I looked through the window. The lads were all playing football in schoolyard and then I noticed a small boy sat in a perambulator on the road and he was working the wheels with his hands making the pram move along and a little boy was perched high up on the school gate watching him and I showed it to Ann and we both laughed. I hope you understand all this. The grammar is bad and next time I see anyone I shant say anything at all. But the trouble is one knows they wont say anything and it is so quiet.

Love Mam Dad and Ann

Richard Hoggart's *The Uses of Literacy* had made a great impression on me. He was a pre-Welfare-state northern working-class lad, one of the tiny few of Mam and Dad's generation who had managed to get themselves educated. He spoke unselfconsciously about the working class that I knew. I loved seeing the people I had grown up among taken seriously. (One of my excitements reading Dickens had been that some of the characters were working class.) He knew about their camaraderie and dependence on one another. About the working men's clubs, the rugby outings, the desire to keep up with the neighbours in the getting of Christmas presents or the buying of prams.

Of course my early fame as an actor was due in some measure to my background, but I never beat my chest about being either North Country or working class. There was a time during the Sixties when it was the thing to be working class, and ambitious young men in London would compete to demonstrate their credentials. Nobody's were purer than mine. I can remember the writer and critic Alan Brien being mightily impressed when I told him that we used to store newspapers under an armchair seat cushion. To be used later for lighting and drawing the fire. He knew then that I was the genuine article. But so did I. I wasn't proud of it and I wasn't ashamed of it. I certainly didn't want to make a career out of it. It's just the way it was.

I can remember when *Romeo and Juliet* was on the radio Mother said, 'If they'd both of them had a job to go to, none of that would have happened.' Something about the broadcast obviously failed to convince her. Perhaps it wasn't a very good production. She wasn't usually so down to earth. When she heard Tchaikovsky's *Romeo and Juliet* overture, which she loved, she told me happily that the composer had found his inspiration for Juliet's pretty theme by thinking of 'the lace on her dress'.

Chekhov was more her cup of tea than Shakespeare. I was going to be in one of his one-acters, *The Proposal*, and that encouraged her to take a volume of his plays out of the library. It's lovely that she could respond to the plays. Had she not, she couldn't have pretended otherwise. She also read *The Seagull*, which was soon to figure hugely in my life. The most remarkable statement in this letter is, for me, 'I said all plays are real.' Mother means both that plays, or novels come to that, in order to be any good, have to be about the way we live our lives, and also that the imaginative part of life, the search for meaning and expression of that meaning, is the most important part of life. Quite something from a Hull Fish Dock worker's wife.

'I went home to finish my washing and could have cried because I wasn't educated.' It is hardly surprising that when at UCL I found that getting a good education had become an almost intolerable burden, I felt very, very guilty.

[26th April 1959]

Dear Tom

I told your father I didn't think I would write today. I can easily lose faith in me. I imagine you getting one of my letters as you are getting ready for work, opening the envelope, glancing at the mass of writing and putting it away to read enroute, with eyes on you in the train and you laughing out or maybe crying!

I saw Mrs Randall again Thursday. When I told her I didn't seem to have much interest in housework she said I don't get out enough and I worry too much. When I got home I started doing everything automatically and I said to Ann I don't care about anything from now on. When your father said 'Did Phyl bring your 2/6?' I just said 'No.' I felt a different person and liked it but it didn't last.

Aunt Dorrie won £17. She gave the credit for winning to God, Cath picking the numbers and herself for letting her New Year in. She said last year was a very unlucky year. I said if I started talking about unlucky years Hell. Then I thought what is luck. Some people think they are lucky if they breathe alright. Some winning money. Some borrowing it. Some getting married and so on. I suppose my luck is You, Ann and Dad and more so if I could really write.

Aunt Al called and Uncle Jack. He appreciated us understanding his sorrow. The only thing bothering me is we might start seeing him too often. One has got to know when to draw the line.

You will be pleased to know I haven't got any more plays in mind.

Love Mam Dad and Ann

'I suppose my luck is You, Ann and Dad and more so if I could really write.' This letter touched me and I showed it to highly educated Arthur Brooks, one of my Camden Road flatmates. He wasn't as taken by it as I was. But why should he have been? He didn't know her.

In my next letter I told her that he hadn't reacted as I had hoped. She didn't mind. She appreciated that I thought enough of her letter to show it to an educated friend. Unlike when I came home for the rugby match, I was communicating with her and taking her seriously.

I sometimes wonder, now, whether I kept her letters thinking that I would be able to give them, and hence her, the love they deserved when I was older and less bound up in myself. I can't remember exactly how clearly I sensed that she wouldn't live for very long. I do think I had a strong feeling that I had the chance to make a life for myself in the arts, but that Mother, whose sensibilities were at least as heightened as mine, had never had that chance and never would have.

My leaving home, so painful to her, gave her the one opportunity she did have to express herself in writing. What magic if, after all these years, people read her letters and are affected by them. Or, as she called it, 'poetry'.

[30th April 1959]

Dear Tom

I've read your 'Proposal' and like it. I like the part about the trees. How an argument can soon start without any planning, something just sparks it off. Like Tuesday. Your father sent some fish home after I had bought some chops for dinner. When he came home I said 'You're not having fish it's chops.' I said I had given mother the fish. He said 'What and you can't spare her with a good name. You wish she was dead.' I said 'I wish I were dead. Alright I've done something wicked I've given the fish away.' Another time he grumbles if I don't. He said why should he get fish for her when her two sons are fish bobbers. I had a twitch in my eye that lasted all day.

I can just imagine you reading snatches of my letters to Arthur and someone else is in the room. They give an upward glance and clear out. When I get a letter from you I don't just read it and put it away, I read it scores of times. Ann might read it twice, your father once. I leave it around for long enough and play hell if someone tears a bit off to light a cig.

I kept on reading this bit at the end about what I try to express. I didn't feel very happy about it somehow. In fact it held up this letter. I know what Arthur meant and it's true. I'm artistic but not a good artist. A lazy and rather crooked artist and anyone who knows can soon spot this. Then I woke up last night and seemed to put things together. I remember how we got a piano after I was at work and my brother younger then me started to learn Piano. Well he used to play a tune, a simple sad vamping sort of tune. Well I taught myself this tune easily and used to enjoy playing it. My brother would be angry with me. Then I discovered I could also fit songs to this vamping and it sounded alright. I kept on pinching new sounds and you know I can play all sorts. The Trout, even that Rural something you hum and that Italian piece that always reminds me of Anna Karenina. [Beethoven's Sixth and Mendelssohn's Fourth.] 'I've got a large repertoire.' I somehow discover the knowhow. People say 'You have learnt to play,' and I laugh and say 'watch my fingers and you will know I'm a fraud!'

Well to continue! I read a book or two, Tolstoy and P. G. Woodhouse, and I seem to know and recognise that vamp. It's as if I know how they got their ideas. In P. G. Woodhouse I sometimes recognise a deep suffering. So I start writing these letters and suddenly find the Vamp or knowhow and what do I do I suddenly start adding conversations to this vamp and incidents. I imagine a writer feels sees and hears all his work. Well maybe I am wrong. Arthur is a scholar and he smells a rat. It isn't good art (not on the piano side). But maybe with writing one can use one's thoughts and ideas. I'm pleased I've discovered all this. It makes my 'Wedding' seem faded. Never mind.

This morning I noticed the boys in schoolyard were chanting something like Hey Dog. The Dog note lower than the Hey. They go on and on teasing someone's dog. I thought how when two boys are fighting they chant something like O.O.O.O.O. and so on until a teacher stops them. Now any musician would take these notes and compose some tune and it would be good because it's real and lively and honest. Then again no good musician would be here to hear all this, would they. Maybe I will. I don't think I meant Arthur smells a rat, I think it's me that does. Well Tom, write soon and let me know about your next play. I think it's smashing.

Love Mam Dad and Ann

I could never persuade Mother to like something that didn't appeal to her. We once went to the Langham Cinema, round the corner from us on Hessle Road, to see *The Wages of Fear*, a French film full of Fifties realism. I lapped it up, but she didn't. Especially when three sweaty Frenchmen stood in a row urinating. She went to the pictures for a bit of glamour and romance. Tyrone Power wouldn't have done that.

Her taste in music was very wide ranging, from popular to classical, from high-spirited to sad. When I was a student I loved listening to cello music – including the Bach solo cello suites. The Sarabande from the second suite, a long mournful melody, became a great favourite of hers. She asked me if I would write to *Housewives' Choice*, requesting it for her. 'Ma, you can't write to *Housewives' Choice* asking them to play the Sarabande from Bach's second solo cello suite. It doesn't sound right.' But Mother couldn't see why not. She liked it.

I have always enjoyed telling people that she taught herself to play the piano by ear. Her pride in me in reverse. I can see her now sitting at her piano in our front room. She had been greatly affected by David Lean's *Summertime* starring Katharine Hepburn, the story of a woman who went to Venice and found romance. She picked out the theme tune and accompanied it with what she thought were fitting and descriptive sounds. Then she ran her hand over the keys. 'That's the pigeons flying around in the big square, Tommy.'

'I'm going to be in a film directed by David Lean, Ma,' I could have told her. But she had gone by then.

[5th May 1959]

Dear Tom

Next week is Wembley and I shall be pleased when it's all over. There seems to be an atmosphere all the time. I would like to come to London but I don't feel like the rush of it. When you came home it was football football football. I feel out of it there is no time to talk and I am fed up of being something that comes through your letter box.

Friday night, after your father's night out bloody Wembley started again and after a lot of strong words on both sides he said all I wanted to see you in the play for was to let everyone know I was your mother and not because I was genuinely interested, I was only interested in me. I told him he only reads your letters once. Men!

Saturday. Football on TV. (FA Cup Final at Wembley.) Joe and your father sat on the settee, your father watching to pick out where his seat would be and bursting with pride to Joe about the thrill of Wembley. Me with backache.

When I went outside I saw Mr Ron Platten already dressed up for Wembley and as usual drunk. I thought next week he will be quite a sensation in London all in black and white and everybody laughing and pointing at him.

Aunt Phyl called in. She had backed three horses and won £3 for 1/-. The horses were called Cash and Courage, Better Off and My Pal. I said how do you pick these horses do you read them like a story? She nodded and said she chooses funny names.

She said she had had her teacup read. The fortune teller said 'Have you a sister who plays piano by ear?' she nodded. I said don't tell me if I'm going to die. She said no, I was going to be invited to lots of parties and will take her with me.

Saturday night in club a woman who is going to Wembley told your father she is going to sit next to him in the train. I thought how I like her somehow but I couldn't call her husband Fred. I don't make myself familiar with men. A Chopin tune on the wireless this morning. I could have cried. I read the play called 'The Seagull' and enjoyed it very much. Let us know about your new play.

Love Mam Dad and Ann

'Don't tell me if I'm going to die.' Mother often mentions her death, usually half-jokingly. Perhaps she knew far more clearly than we did that she wouldn't make 'old bones'. Ann said that one of her most-used expressions about plans for the future – a trip south, say – was 'all being well'.

From Dad [5th May 1959]

Dear Tom

I don't know if I told you before but we leave Hull on Sat. morn at 5.45, and are due at Kings Cross at 10.15. So don't be late.

I am looking forward to a real good day. Our programme will be a drink to give us an appetite then a good feed so I'm hoping you know where a good pint and a meal can be had. We shall have plenty of time. I think if we get to Wembley Stadium by 2.30 we should be in clover. But after the match we shall have to lose no time if your play starts at 6.30.

Up to now I don't know of anyone who is going who appeals to me. Sid Davis and Mr Stockton aren't going, so after the match I shall have to find someone to have a yarn with. I am sure to bump into someone from another trip.

So all we want now Tom is a fine day. It will I think be a match worth going a long way to see. Hull victorious. Till Saturday.

Love Pop

PS. 10.15 am. Don't be late.

From my point of view, Dad's keenly anticipated trip to Wembley was very badly timed. I had been prevailed upon to appear, on the evening of the match, with some former university friends in a performance of Chekhov one-act plays at Senate House, London University Students' Union. It was just across the street from RADA's Vanbrugh Theatre. This is why Mother had been reading Chekhov. I was the nervous young man in *The Proposal*, and I also performed a monologue, *The Harmfulness of Tobacco*. So I had plenty on that day. There's a photo of Dad and me on his great day out. He looks as though he's had a couple and I look like I want to be a million miles away.

In fact I left the match shortly after halftime. Hull were getting hammered and lost to Wigan by a record score. I can see the mighty Billy Boston flying towards the Hull line, knocking over anyone in his path. So no 'Old Faithful' sung to celebrate victory. Dad, I'm sure, would have bumped into plenty of Hull supporters after the game, with whom he could commiserate and reflect on the thrill of Wembley. I had to go and perform.

Quote from my pocket diary, Saturday 9 May, 1959: *Met Dad, went to Wembley. Played Chekhov in evening. Quite a day.*

[7th May 1959]

Dear Tom

I wasn't going to write but it gets the better of me.

Teatime the paper arrived and opening it I read about a man who had committed suicide and on his sweetheart's grave he had chalked 'God has called me to you Ann darling. I have not been the same since he took you away from me.' He was a paint works labourer and it wouldn't have surprised me if they had called him Mr Thomas Courtenay. It made me laugh.

After tea your father went in front room to finish the ceiling he was painting. After he had finished he went again the front door and I joined him. Coming towards us was an old man clean looking with a funny shaped large red nose. He said Hello! Your father just looked at him but the man wanted to talk. I half smiled. He said how he had just been visiting his niece. I said 'Oh.' He said how he visited one down another street and on Sun he visited one in Hessle. Your father just looked at him out the corner of his eye frowning. The old man went on he was going to visit a niece down Coronation Road. He had lots of nieces. I said 'Oh.' He said he had been carrying a sandwich board up to 4 o'clock. He still hesitated then decided to say well Goodnight smilingly. He thought he had a full life.

Then the young woman who is always shouting 'Marylin' came up the street with her husband. She wore a blue coat, blue sandals and walked along looking full of confidence and I thought sometimes people like this poor old man seem to say more likeable things than people who look full of confidence.

BEAR UP TOM

After that I thought I will find my nice nylon duster and dust out the writing desk. I've noticed I say nice duster, nice floor cloth or nice wash leather. After I climbed over the settee and got to the desk I started the dusting and found lots of your letters. I couldn't just read one or two I had to read the whole lot. One letter made me feel screwed up inside and I realised how unhappy you were last year. When I told Ann she said 'We won't go into all that again.' There was one about Romeo and Juliet and one about you could only give us your love and not your career. I haven't finished dusting yet!

Sometimes people say how praying always gets them things. I've often tried it. Sometimes I'm washing up and I go near the back door to try and find a bit of sky (drying a cup) and say O I wish we had a new house or maybe Pray for something concerning me. But it doesn't work never. Well, as I was going to say, I just said 'Oh God send Ann a nice young man.'

Your father started rummaging in the drawer for the comb. When anyone starts looking for something I instantly want to help them. I had an idea the comb was near me, it always is. I like combing my hair. I found the comb and thought how everything I like doing is handy for me. Across my chair a woolly, on my chair arm the dictionary, stuffed down the chair side a book I'm reading. I can just stretch out and reach these things. A writing pad in the cupboard, a pen plonked in the ornament. Your father on settee I can reach. Ann I can touch with my toes and aspirin handy and all just by stretching out my arm. And if I don't hurry up and finish this letter it will stretch all the way to London.

Love Mam Dad and Ann

Twenty-nine Harrow Street faced west, so, on a pleasant evening, Mother liked to go 'again door' to get a bit of sunshine and watch the world go by. Dad would sometimes join her there. The 'again door' area included the front-room window ledge, against which they would lodge themselves. The front-room window was exactly opposite West Dock Avenue Juniors schoolyard entrance. Mother was much more inclined to chat to passers-by than was Dad. 'Looked out the corner of his eye frowning', gets him perfectly.

Had my trainspotting teacher Mr W. asked for a paragraph entitled 'Home', Mother's description of having her world to hand would surely have melted his prosaic heart. Ten out of ten, I don't doubt.

RADA TERM III
May 1959

Dear Tom

Your father left work early and after his breakfast decided to mend
his boots, the rubber had bulged on the soles, so he took off the soles
and stuck them on again only to find they overlapped the leather.
There was black sticky and bits of rubber all over. He also cut some
leather off the backs of those escalator type shoes he got, and did he
enjoy it! Then he suggested a walk to Park. Granny came round
and I went in scullery and decided I was going to write you a letter.
I always do to make me feel better.

Tues. Father and Ann home to tea. They are very much alike
and can sit with frowning faces and closed eyes. A young star was
on TV. She is going to play in a picture with Alec Guinness. I said
maybe our Tom will meet her one day. [Susannah York. I did.] Ann
said 'Hmm.' I said 'Why not? He's good looking don't you think?'
Ann said 'No.' Father said 'That's all you bloody well think about,
who's good looking.' I said 'That's a lie' and went to wash up. Then
I said 'I am not mending the fire' and went to stand again the front
door.

All the kids were out playing. Two boys were using the skeleton of a pram for a bogey. The boy at the front stretched his legs out and the one at the back walked his legs backward to make it move. They had to steer their way through a gang playing rounders. One of them shouted 'The ball Rosie! Rosemary!' but Rosemary was tying her ribbon and Rosemary was fat. And a dog ran across the road and a bird came down for a last bite. A green lorry standing and on the back of it 'Hull for the Cup' is fading away and the drain is smelling. Your father had reared the steps inside the front door to measure the fan light so I had to go round the backway. Ann laughed.

A bit later as I passed your bedroom there was a noise inside so I went to investigate. I opened the door, switched on the light. The window had dropped and the wind was blowing in. The oil stove rattled and the clock ticked and I couldn't shut the window so I left it, switched off the light and closed the door.

Love Mam Dad and Ann

In the sixth form I remember reading *The Faerie Queene* in my bedroom, sitting by the smelly paraffin stove, its wick as low as possible. So there must have been a lightbulb in the socket. There wasn't when I was younger. Nor on the landing. I didn't like it when Ann first slept in the back bedroom. We'd go up the stairs together, part company on the landing and I would grope my way nervously to my bedroom, Ann telling me not to be so daft. I couldn't see my hand in front of me, but to appease the demons of the night I would look under my bed anyway. I'd lie on my back for a while, ready to repel severed hands and such like. Then sleepiness would bring its blessing. It was lovely, later, to wake for a moment as Mam and Dad came up to their bedroom, and feel too dozy to be frightened.

[28th May 1959]

Dear Tom

When I have finished a letter it's like I've finished a job and can settle down to do something without thought but last Thursday I was on the step looking for your father coming home when a big man and a big alsatian came across from club. The dog started emptying itself again Brooks' then our passage where the bairns play and right up the street. I felt raving mad. I think the dog had been drinking beer too. I felt like writing a letter to the Mail. Your father said you can do nothing about it these things have been going on all our life. I couldn't eat me tea, everytime I was going to eat I thought about this dog. So really this page belongs to last week's letter because I couldn't very well get the letter out the post box. My grandfather was supposed to do that trick with a piece of wire and ended up in prison.

I went round to Teresa's. She laughed when I said our chimney pot was leaning on next doors. I hope I arent talking queer and people will remark on it. Then I'll get put in an institution and you and your father looking weary will have to come and get me out. When you was home you said people are stupid when they are old. Maybe that is what is happening to me. Hell!

I got a sudden urge to write something. It was Mrs Rutter she called my name and said how she had been on road and her bloomers had fallen down and I thought 'Mrs Rutter dropped her bloomers in the gutter' and it finished up

> Poor Mrs Rutter – Why
> She dropped her bloomers in the gutter
> Did she frown   No
> She only laughed   Sportingly
> When they fell down.
>
> And now her basket's full of sky blue
> And her arms full of pinky flowers for Cemetary
> And they also nodding their empty heads.

I decided to go out in the sun so I should last longer. Ann and me took a bus to Aunt Als. I filled myself up with Longhill, French windows, bathroom, new furniture, garden, sitting in the sun and different atmosphere and felt sick all the way coming home on the bus. I thought hell if I lived up Longhill I'd feel sick all the time. I asked your father where he would like to live. He didn't know. I said I can't think of a single place I want to live.

Tues. Your father came home and said 'It's been a long day away from you.' I looked at him and said 'Yes it's been a long long long day.' I said to Ann 'I once heard a man on TV talking who'd written a book about Witches. He believes there are women witches and I agree with him.' I remember our forewoman at work. A young girl wanted half a day off work because her young man was home from sea. Because the girl took the time off the forewoman gave her the sack. The girl got married later on and she hadnt been married long before she died. That little woman at the bottom of our passage is a witch. She limps her dog to the terrace end early each morning and lets fly handfuls of white dog hairs and everyone closes their front doors quick so as not to let the hair land in their breakfast tea. So the hair hangs about the front door-steps and the damp holds it and it looks like a poison plant and now where the hair was is growing green grass and if the bairns eat it I'm sure they will be poisoned and along will come the big man with the big alsation.

Well Tom all that was before Ann went to library and brought home a book of Dylan Thomas letters and poems. Since then the dog hair piece has altered and one line goes 'So the hair hangs about the front door-steps and the damp holds it close like old age.' I don't mind telling you all this I'm no coward.

I hope you havent been ill or got married and if you need any clothes maybe I could lend you the money and you can pay back weekly when you get a job in summer. It's just an idea.

Love Mam Dad and Ann

PS. Isn't this a funny letter. I think it's magic if one can write something completely. Anyhow it is my ambition.
PPS. Maybe I'm a witch.

Mother's efforts at poetry embarrassed me forty years ago. I wrote and told her I felt sad for her. I knew they wouldn't have passed muster in the English Department at UCL, that they didn't do her justice. She didn't like that.

[3rd June 1959]

Dear Tom

Last week's Woman's Own has the story of the film 'Look Back in Anger'. It reads like a novelette and I was very disappointed. I just couldn't imagine Jimmy Porter having a market stall after university and why the hell he wanted his wife's temperament bringing down to his own I can't understand. Just the reverse I think. I can understand his feelings about watching his father die. I'm angry about lots of things but then again I arent clever.

We went in club where everything was about the same. Mr Stockton said after the housey was over that what with one thing and another and Mrs being poorly in bed he must be in Jesus's bad books.

We keep having a bad smell down the street, so I told your father I'm going to write a letter to some 'official'. He said 'Why don't you hold a meeting?' I said 'Oh we have and I'm in charge.'

Dear Sir

Must one have to put up with a sickly smell that hangs around Harrow Street? The general conversation for the last year has been 'One can't do anything about it we have got the main sewer down here,' or 'The sanitary say it isn't their job.' Children play down here and there is a school down here and people can't stand and talk. I am writing on behalf of the residents of Harrow Street whose signatures are on the back of this letter. (*In fun.* PS Have you a big dog?)

I have just got your letter and if something I write makes you feel like that I shan't write anymore. Hell! I wanted you to finish it. I can't remember what I put in the beginning part. Was it the house poem?

I've got a headache. I feel very sad for you too. I'm really the liveliest person in the world.

Enclosing 10/-. I can easily do without so treat yourself.

Tom, after I've written a letter I start thinking it's silly. You say after reading my letter it made you feel sad for me. I would have said 'made me feel sad' which just goes to show how much I don't know. Anyhow your father loves you very much and is also treating you 10/-. We are millionaires today we have had a £1 floated down from heaven 'that's you by me' and Tom just let that producer man know you aren't getting paid for all the hard work you are putting into his play.

PS. Didn't you like 'Arms full of Pinkee flowers for cemetary and they also nodding their empty heads.'

The 'producer man' that Mother refers to was a professional radio director working at the Tower Theatre Canonbury, an outstanding amateur dramatic company. He had asked RADA to provide him with a juvenile lead, and Mr Fernald thought it might be a good experience for me. It wasn't. I went to meet the 'producer man' at Broadcasting House. I recognized a very famous voice in the bar there. It belonged to W. Barrington Dalby, who did the inter-round summaries during the big fights that Dad and I used to listen to with such excitement. (After the legendary Randolph Turpin v. Sugar Ray Robinson fight he had failed to realize, in his summing up, that our man, Turpin, had beaten the American favourite, Robinson.) It gave me something to write home about, and would have been of interest to Dad if not to Mother.

'That producer man' was large, camp, extrovert and, I felt, barbed. I couldn't cope with his style of directing. 'Right ho, children, acting ... go! Thomas, sweetheart, I want you to flounce on from downstage right and park your bum in that chair.' Looking back, I see there was plenty of theatrical camp at RADA, but it was funny more than frightening. I met the 'producer man' years later when he was working in television and he didn't bother me at all. But at the Tower Theatre he was too much for me. The play was called *The Third Person*.

All I can remember is having to mime playing the mouth organ to a recording.

At RADA we had more classes than ever before. 'Restoration Technique', for one, was meant to teach us to strut and say 'Zounds' and wave large handkerchiefs about. These classes were gleefully conducted by owl-eyed Teddy Gray, who delighted in our resolute twentieth century-ness. Nothing barbed about Teddy. Being in a play outside RADA was a mistake. I had plenty on, trying to find the relaxation of my pre-university days, and there was a lot riding on that term's work. I had, I thought, to be seen to be blossoming. The deal was that if my progress merited it, Mr Fernald would write to the Hull Education Committee and implore them to increase my grant.

From Dad

Dear Tom

This so called producer of yours seems to have given you a hell of a time. I suppose there are all sorts of people in all walks of life like him. He has obviously got the opinion because he has worked for the BBC he knows it all and you amateurs are just tripe. Still I suppose in that profession you get a lot of that. If you are nervous, and I know you are, experience should overcome it.

You mention in your letter that you look like finishing up in debt. We at home know you must have a struggle to make ends meet. You don't get enough money to manage properly. But honestly Tom I would sooner you be in my debt than anyone else's. So if you have to owe money let it be to me. I don't want you to be asking your friends there for anything. I mean this Tom, and don't forget.

I know you don't like being on the receiving end all the time, but your turn will come. So don't get downhearted.

Love Pop

Have a pint of Worthington E. That will steady your nerves.

In my 1959 pocket diary there's the following list:

Tony £7
Michael B. 10/-
Audrey £2
John P. £1

I was hard pressed managing on my decreased grant. Without Dad's little nest egg from his compensation money things might have been even worse. Had I not kept these letters, I would have forgotten Mam and Dad's generosity. I didn't like being beholden to them. I seemed to have been a student for ever, and with nothing to show for it. I imagine I was sustained by knowing just how much my making something of myself meant to them. I may have felt guilty that I couldn't buckle down to my work at UCL, but I had also felt resentful that I was having to get educated for the three of us. Though I was being educated at RADA for myself alone, I was still aware of carrying the burden of their expectations. I must have allowed myself to think sometimes that they were happy to pay me for that burden of theirs I carried. I couldn't have coped otherwise.

The symbol of my lack of funds that year was my white nylon shirt. Drip-dry, so it didn't need ironing, and constantly worn, it clung to me possessively, crackling with annoyance when I took it off at night. It didn't want to share me with another. It must have been very happy because it had no rival. There's a fable about someone who has to find the shirt of the happiest man in the world. The happiest man in the world is found, but he doesn't have a shirt. Well, I had one.

And the student coffee bar. Handy both for UCL and RADA, where for 2/- you could get a bowl of spaghetti. Filling. For a further 6d you could get a helping of chips. Not sophisticated, I realized, to have spaghetti and chips. But even more filling.

For the record, Ann told me recently that she, employed by what had been the London and North Eastern Railway, used to contribute to the 29 Harrow Street Student Actor Fund. 'We all had a whipround.'

10 June 1959

Dear Tom

I told you about the letter I had written about the drain smelling. Well Ann took it to work and typed it very nicely for me. She said one has to be very careful when sending these letters as the Medical Officer of Health could get on to the Sanitary who may know nothing of the smell in spite of what people say. So it is resting in my handbag (it looks nice typed) and I am now waiting for a Sanitary Inspector to come round. If he and then the gas company can't do anything about the smell then out will come my letter. My trouble is I haven't learned how to 'use myself'. It's rather worrying.

The Sanitary Inspector came this afternoon. He was rather a nice young man. I asked him in front room and he sat on the piano stool with a briefcase on his knee. He didn't know there was a smell down Harrow Street. Then he tapped his head and said 'Ha! The main sewer is down here.' He said if a woman yon end of Hull put something down the drain then we get it down here three days later. Fancy living on other people's muck. He said the smell couldn't hurt the bairns. I said it couldn't do them any good. I said the other Friday I kept feeling sick. He said he felt very sorry for us living here and if we lived in Eton Street or West Dock Ave. we wouldn't get it. I said (smiling) 'That's how things work for me.' I felt like asking him if he read Dylan Thomas. He advised me to go in the back when there's a smell. Hell! When your father came in I told him and he just went on eating his tea. I feel like battle. People make me sick.

Feeling fed up with people I went in front room to play the piano and felt pleased because I can play a tune and write a line or two. Then our Phyl came in and asked to look at our morning paper. Then she asked to borrow some writing paper and a pen. I watched with curiosity while she wrote her bet. She was writing funny names again.

Yorkshire Pudding
Brandy Sauce
My Sugar

And this made up for people. I loved it. Then an idea struck me that you can never learn to use yourself while other people are using you. So the thing to do is keep knocking them off with a toffee hammer.

Your father is mad with me because the cleaner is broke and he blames me. He said I want carrying about. I said he couldn't carry me about cos he can't carry hisself about and by hell I meant it.

And I haven't said how are you and how is your play and I feel silly about my letter.

Love Mam Dad and Ann

I used to be fascinated by the sewermen when they came clumping up the middle of Harrow Street in their huge thigh boots, their hurricane lamps at the ready. They would prise open the manhole covers of the sewer with a crowbar. I can remember one of the sewermen smiling at me as he did so, which made his work seem all the more sinister. I would quickly have a peep down the hole as he descended the iron ladder, but didn't linger. Fascinating, but horrible. A hell hole, if ever there was one. Did my scarlet fever come from down there? The crowbar had a red flag attached and it was propped up on the removed manhole cover as a danger signal. Ronnie Ellerington once climbed down the steps of the hole and earned a clip from the sewerman. The admiration he got from us who stayed above ground made it worthwhile.

The woman who had the shop in Eton Street where the butter was hacked off a huge slab must have dealt in bulk because she also used a toffee hammer to break up the tablet of toffee into mouth-sized chunks. She held it on her cupped left hand as she rapped it with her right. I used to like a triangular bit, as big as possible. One that made my cheeks stick out and the saliva slosh about.

[18th June 1959]

Dear Tom

Sunday morning. Your father went to work and I thought, 'Fancy one day everything will be "Once upon a time."' I didn't like the idea although I didn't really mean for me but for everyone. Well

although I keep telling myself I will stop my silly scribbling I
thought

> How long to Once upon a time
> How long to Life Beautiful
> How long to And Then
> How long to look back and laugh
> How long to Never Mind
> You know
> How long to How Long.

Well I know its bloody daft but just an idea.

Monday I went to Teresa's we had a good natter. She said to me
'It's one of your bright days because your wedding ring is shining.' I
told her I had never heard that one before and would have to think
about it.

Tuesday. Michael a student friend of Anns came for her after
seven. I was in the dark scullery. It was odd because as he walked to
the scullery door it seemed like he had come from another world.
One I had forgotten about. Not one I particularly wanted to be in
but one I had known. Your father did not know he was coming and
he came out of the yard. He looked at M. just as his father would
have looked. M. looked at him quizzical too. When Ann had gone
out I said to your father 'The way you looked!' he said he thought it
was the joiner we was expecting.

Wed. I went to Hales [Mrs Hales' off licence and grocery].
Someone asked her what the weather was with her glass barometer.
She laughed 'It says fine.' I stopped yawning when she said her
husband's brother, who was drowned at sea, bought his mother the
barometer for a present when he was a young man. He used to pay
weekly on the barometer and one day took the present home, but
his mother thought he was buying her something like a silk blouse
and she said to someone 'What do I want with a bloody barometer.'
But after he got drowned she treasured it, and Mrs Hales daren't let
her know they had dropped it and broken the wood. Now the old
lady is dead, but I liked the story and bet he was a nice lad.

I hope you are well and write soon. Shall be thinking of you. Always am.

Love Mam Dad and Ann

PS. I told Ann about the atmosphere when M. came. M. told Ann he didn't want to come in again he said 'You can't hide atmosphere.' I told Ann M. is more sensitive than he thinks he is. Anyhow he came in for fish and chips and the atmosphere lifted, your father had gone to bed. He's shy. I'm young at heart. I love atmosphere.

I didn't write soon, I'm afraid, because I was so taken up by my engagement at the Tower Theatre. I learnt one thing there: being in plays can be torture. The large producer man cast an actor who he said was 'a pro'. Perhaps he got a paid job, because he disappeared after a week. Then the producer man took his leave. I wished I could have taken mine. Marjorie Withers took over from him, and her calm and thoughtful presence helped get the show on. She was one of the leading lights at the Tower. Not long afterwards, quite late in life, she became a professional actress and made a success of it. That hardly ever happens.

My being distracted for several weeks outside RADA made that term's work quite nervy. This surfaced most prominently in Peter Barkworth's technique classes. How to look natural on stage. How to sit, stand up, walk across the room, look at your watch, drink your tea, smoke a cigarette, use props, and all this in sync with the words you are saying or listening to. Peter was much revered among the students because his classes were so practical and he was the only teacher who was actually in regular work. He was in a long-running West End hit, *Roar like a Dove*, and always looked very dapper. One couldn't imagine him acting without a suit and tie. Well, maybe now and again a lambswool cardy. I always admired the way he was turned out. What he had to offer was a distillation of the tradition of West End naturalistic acting. I was too jumpy to achieve it that term, but it certainly gave me something to think about.

He had names for various techniques. 'Anticipation' was one of my favourites. It just means being ready for the next bit. For instance: imagine a longish speech ending with, 'So you see, George, I can't do what you ask.' If you make sure you're looking at George a line or two before you address him directly, that's anticipation. It makes things go smoothly. Doing it has given me much innocent pleasure over the years. I wasn't quite so interested in 'interrupted action'. Humphrey Bogart was a great practitioner of 'interrupted action'. About to take a slug from his whisky, he would stop in surprise, the glass held just in front of his mouth. A single, rather than a double take. I've never managed that one. In fact Humphrey B. is welcome to it.

I think Peter's favourite technique was known as 'Look, move, speak'. Former students of his are very fond of recalling 'Look, move, speak' when they work together, though they are prone, for the hell of it, to do it either backwards or inside out. It does make sense, though. If you were going to say something important to someone, like, for example, 'Will you marry me?' you would look first, either at the person or the ground, then you would kneel, then you would clear your throat, which really counts as speaking, then you would speak. You wouldn't speak then kneel, then look at the ground. Having spoken you might then take another look, to see how your words had gone down, and then the process would start again: another move, say getting up off your knees or scratching your chin, then speaking again: 'Did you hear what I said?' It is all perfectly logical, and Peter was simply trying to help us get organized. He was teaching technique, after all, not how to emote. But, distracted at the Tower, it was a struggle for me that term.

Here's what Peter said in my end-of-term report: 'A gifted boy who makes grave mistakes: a) there is a restlessness about his acting. Feet and hands work too hard; b) he does not discover enough the true meaning of what he is putting over and let his invention spring from that rather than from a desire for cheap theatrical effect; c) he does not think enough in performance; d) he gets into bad positions. He must re-think, over the holidays, the whole business of playing out front. He is too obvious at the moment. Harsh words these: but Thomas, who is such a delightful and talented student, could be so much better than he is. He must raise his own standards about himself.'

In other words, I shouldn't have got into that play at the Tower Theatre with a large, camp, showbizzy director I wasn't ready for. I had plenty to think about at RADA. Especially when I was hoping that Mr

Fernald would write to the Hull Education Committee telling them of the serenity of my progress, and assuring them that if they increased my grant they would be putting money on a certainty.

[25th June 1959]

Dear Tom

I didn't think much of last weeks letter. I like to collect a letter together. Sometimes I think over things I have written and enjoy it. Sometimes I want to crawl into a shell. To be a professional writer must be suffering work. But I suppose it is something real writers can't help doing or they could easily spit instead. Maybe that's what writing is, a big spit. Poor me. Not poor me.

Tuesday was very warm. We watched the play later on. Leslie Caron in 'Wild Bird'. I liked it best when the friend of the rich family said how the little kitchen girl would creep round to the drawing room window after her work was done just to gaze at the lady of the house because she was so beautiful, and how maybe someone even a dog got the same pleasure from looking at the kitchen girl. I tried to explain all this to your father but he shut me up. I wouldn't let him though and I said 'I wonder who I like to look at' not your father just then sat in singlet. Poor me not Poor me and no poem this week and arnt you glad.

Wed washday and we went out after tea where there was a juke-box playing. I felt like showing my legs and rock and rolling. I noticed a man when he drank his beer he nearly devoured the whole glass so when your father said hurry up I did this trick and he laughed. I felt about sixteen. Today sixty.

Well Tom it's Thursday and although I sneezed 3 times I never got a letter and I don't care if you come home and your four years in London were a bad dream because I always have a feeling when you don't write it is because you are unhappy. I hope this is not so.

Love Mam Dad and Ann

PS. I could understand in the play how the unsuccessful pianist felt. He cried because the happy rich unhurt successful pianist

played so beautiful. He couldn't understand it and neither can I.
Good play.

[2nd July 1959]

Dear Tom

Monday was and always is and a letter from you. I said to Ann
'There isn't much in it' but Ann said everything is something. I
thought not like my letters full of nowt. After tea I went upstairs to
dust your bookshelf and I found a lot of my letters to you on the
floor so I read them. So short and not so miserable as sometimes
now. I have certainly altered my style. I laughed at some of them I
seemed very concerned about your health and said 'you should wear
vests'. One letter said 'don't read books on the irony of life'. I
remember when my letters altered it was when you was so unhappy
at College and doing exams. I was very concerned and it made me
think very hard indeed. I wanted to know where I had gone wrong
hence the change.

Tues. and Langham Club old age pensioners trip. Granny came
in early and I gave her 5/-. She asked me if I would see her off. The
dustmen were in street and one of them shouted 'Ger out the
bleeding road we want to tip the bins' and the bairns in school was
singing 'God is in my head' and the pensioners were coming down
the street. Old Pop Waddy with his trousers rolled up at the
bottoms had just been buying his grandbairns large ice cream
cornets and he said it would make no difference to him if it rained.
One old woman went for her pension but the queue was so big she
decided not to draw it and Mrs Hales lent her 2/6. I went to wave
the bus off and I thought how one wants the bus waving off when
young and old.

Your father was home early for tea. He had been an errand about
a new electric stove. This makes him so virtuous and after tea he
cleared a drawer out after sitting in the understairs gas cupboard
amongst his tools for half an hour. He suggested I use the drawer
for knives and forks. He may be right but I didn't care if they went
in the bloody coal house. Tonight while I have been writing he has

washed and dried the pots all on his own. Granny came in this morning and while watching me get something tangled in the wringer she told me about someone dying and how my clothes wouldn't dry today because it was miserable.

> I know a place near Arundel
> Theres crossroads and a pub perched high
> It's never dowly, I wish we were there, you and I
>
> There's a road close by
> And it leads to a beach
> It's private and a Lord lives there
> How I wish we were there
> You and I
>
> I'm telling a lie, I've never been
> But I heard someone say Perched high
> But never mind it doesn't matter
> Cos we can't go there you and I.

And don't say 'Hell I don't wish I was there.' Isn't it beautiful. I know it's faulty but it's an idea. How many marks!

Love Mam Dad and Ann

Mother has Arundel on her mind because the annual visit south, via London, is approaching.

I'm happy that even though I told her I didn't much care for her poems she didn't stop having a go at them. As she wrote, 'I'm no coward.'

[9th July 1959]

Dear Tom

Some forms and things came today and your father asked me to send them to you. Shall you ask for any further help or shall I write to them!

A woman told me how when she was young a coalman would take all the bairns down Harrow St. for a ride round the country-side on his coal cart charging 3d each one. She said he had them out all day and they had a marvellous time. The horse knew every pub as they came to them. The coalman had always had enough by the time they reached home in the evening. Intelligent horse.

Wed. And very pleased with your letter and photos. I'm sure you look more poised now. I'm pleased you have got a job, but sometimes I think London is greedy and when I come I shall pass through with closed eyes and a hurt feeling but I do realise it has to be. Maybe you can be home for Christmas weeks. Our holidays are 2 weeks on Saturday and we arrive in London teatime.

That piece of rhyme I sent you – the word was dowley. It was about 2 yr ago. I said to the woman in the pub 'I bet it's never dowley here.'

I was making my pie and it just seemed as if the words cascaded around and fell together.

Tom don't forget to fill in forms.

Love Mam Dad and Ann

The forms were from the Hull Education Committee concerning the following year's grant. Mr Fernald did in fact write to them, encouraging further investment in me, though I'm sure he didn't send them a copy of my end-of-term report. He must have known that my Tower Theatre adventure, his idea, had got me in a bit of a state and had checked the smoothness of my progress. When I sensed at my RADA audition that he was on my side, my instinct had been working at full throttle. The Education Committee responded favourably to his pleadings and awarded me what they called a Supplementary Grant for my second year at RADA, in addition to the Intermediate Grant I got from them in my first year. So I would be back to my undergraduate income level. Nonetheless, I still needed a vacation job, and I returned to labouring in Finsbury Park. My duties again included a fortnight's idyll on the boating lake while the boating commandant went on his holidays. This job of mine kept me away from Mother for most of the summer, which can't have pleased her. But she must have been relieved that I was going to be less short of money.

[14th July 1959]

Dear Tom

All my writing has disappeared. Not one sentence has come to light. Monday dinner time I said to Ann 'Ive an ache in my neck and a boil on my arse. I don't think there's one inch of me that's any good' and she said 'What about your tongue.'

It will be nice seeing you in London. Isn't it funny you have been in London 4 years and Ive never seen where you lay your head. It's the rummest bloody world. And a bit of brightness has just floated through the door. Ann has managed to get 'Portrait of an Artist'.

Aunt Alice has been in with little Susan. Alice minds her while her mother is at work. Susan now calls me Aunt Ann. I told Alice how on Saturday some bairns were playing in next doors yard and one called Ellerington started climbing up and looking over the wall. I surprised myself by looking through the window and saying loudly 'Get down you horrible looking little sod.' Also much to your father's surprise. Ann said 'Were me and Tom horrible looking' and I said no. If the bairn's mother had heard me the air would have been purple red. It made me laugh a lot.

I went with Ann shopping on Friday for holidays. I got a grey pleated skirt. Ann got a two piece striped in green yellow lilac and white. She felt she was really going to Italy when she tried it on. Susan asked was it a table cloth. I hope the £1 helped you and you didn't feel embarrassed and while I remember I think in the play photos you look kind of James Mason Laurence Olivierish. I used to think your voice sounded like James Masons.

Love Mam Dad and Ann

Ann's 'What about your tongue' was to make Mother laugh, to get her to stop feeling sorry for herself. It worked, and she couldn't resist passing the joke on to me. But neither Ann nor I knew that Mother wasn't just off-colour.

Reading having been *de rigueur* for so long in my life, I didn't do it so much once it wasn't compulsory. Occasionally, though, a book took my fancy. John Berger's *Portrait of an Artist* had, and I recommended it to Mother. 'An artist' was something we both wanted to be.

Ann's trip to Italy, her first holiday abroad, with a girlfriend from work, wasn't going to be that much more expensive for her than staying put in England, because her rail fare to Florence and Alassio was paid for by her employers, the former London and North Eastern Railway Company. One of the perks of the job.

[23rd July 1959]

Dear Tom

We leave Hull 1.20 Saturday lunch time and every time I think about it my inside goes up and down anybody would think I was going to a bloody funeral. We should arrive in London about 6 o'clock tea time. I expect you'll be there to meet us.

I hope you will be happy in your new room. A set designer should have some grand decorating ideas. I wish I was a set designer. Poor me. I'll never alter. My writing is flagging and I havent wrote 1 word in a week.

Aunt Dorrie came yesterday and is as contented as hell because she is working at a cleaning job and earning about 30/- a week. Cath is 21 next week and is having a party.

I was thinking the other day. Maybe an Eastern retinue should be meeting me in London with one of these carrier chairs and large straw fans working and then I would be carried off to a tranquil place or wherever Eastern retinues carry off their Princesses.

To better off people luxuries are taken for granted. Sometimes I can't understand things at all.

Can one get used to a thing and then not get used to it again? I wrote and told you I was used to the idea of you being an actor, now I cant get used to the idea. Arent I a fool.

Dogs are fighting in street and a little boy has peed against a wall, a man's talking on wireless, people's walking backwards and forwards, outside voices are shouting and sparrows are chirping and dogs are barking and a young woman is pushing a pram and I havent moved an inch out the front room chair and I love to write movement. And your father has just popped his head in the room to say 'Don't think I'm washing up the pots every night.' Pots! A lad on a bike with a seaside cap on and the fire brigade just whizzed by street end and I said to Ann, 'Have you found what you're looking for?' and she said 'I'll never find what I'm looking for' and I can hear your father and Ann laughing. Pots. Your father has bought a new lock for the front door and I bet he has to cut a piece out the door before it fits. Pots and I think it will rain. Washing on the line, a trawler buzzer, coming or going. Pots. Bat and ball outside, mind the windows and little bursts of life exploding all around and I'm a poet.

Your father said have you seen to the forms.

What's that song Lovely Blushing Rose. Bairns keep singing it.

Love Mam Dad and Ann

'Bairns', incidentally, though written with a Scottish accent, was pronounced 'banes' on Hessle Road, with a long, flat northern 'a'. As in 'the bane of my life'.

My 'new room' was at 9 Highbury Crescent, a huge maisonette overlooking Highbury Fields. Vic Symonds, a set designer with ITV, who had designed the set for the Tower Theatre play, invited me to join him there. He was sharing with an ITV cameraman called Terry Bicknell (who later married Rita Tushingham). They had a spare bedroom. Vic did indeed have some grand decorating ideas. Very simple paintwork, greenish, I think, which he and Terry had done themselves, and bare floorboards. And over the fireplace a huge, circular blow-up of a photograph of the young Ellen Terry, beautiful and pensive, in profile, her hand below her chin. He'd got it from one of the ITV sets he'd designed. The large windows overlooked trees and grass. It was considerably smarter and more pleasant than the dank and gloomy basement in Camden Road. And the atmosphere was less intellectual. I had been very fond of my graduate pals in their basement, but shared their love of music more than their love of Goethe and Schiller. I had once been told I had a butterfly mind. Highbury Crescent was less Goethe and Schiller and more Morecambe and Wise. Vic, thin, quick and nervily jaunty, constantly pushing his horn-rimmed glasses back up the bridge of his nose, was a livewire from north London, with funny sayings. 'From arsehole to breakfast time' comes to mind. One of his stories was about an actor, out of work for ages, who eventually got a job standing in for one of the chimps during the chimps' tea party at the zoo. The unfortunate actor, very hot in his chimp's costume, was mortified when one of the proper chimps threw tea at him, and he cried out in anger, 'Do you fucking mind!' A giraffe, hearing this from close by, leant over and whispered conspiratorially, 'Do be careful, laddie, you'll get us all the sack!' I loved it. It was a good parable of the resourcefulness required in the profession I was hoping to enter.

So I moved a further step from academia towards showbiz. And from basement to ground floor. 'More light.' As Goethe put it.

My improved living conditions brought with them an onerous duty. I had to help with the cleaning. At Camden Road I can't remember who went round with a hoover. I certainly didn't. But at Highbury it was expected of me and I had little flair for it. Obviously I had to do the floor, but then what? Skirting board? Door panels? Coffee table? The top of Terry's specially designed record player? Windowframes? There seemed no end to it.

I met Mam and Dad at King's Cross on their way to Portchester, escorting them across London, and I spent a Sunday at Portchester with them. I hadn't been to Portchester for a holiday with them for some years. It wasn't the same as when I was younger, and Ann, saving up for Italy, wasn't there. Aunt Hilda and Uncle Bill were just as bemused about my intended career as Mam and Dad, though they tried hard to be positive. Uncle Bill reminded us all of when I asked him 'Am I registering terror?' aged eleven, so demonstrating that even then the writing had been on the wall.

15 Lonsdale Avenue
[30th July 1959]

Portchester

Dear Tom

I hope you had a nice day Sunday. I didn't like it when you had to go.

It's a monkey's birthday, today. Not Goodwood weather. So a ride to Lee on Solent. I saw in a little furniture shop a brass French clock, a shield shaped mirror but not the reading lamp with cut glass drops all round. We went for a beer and your father talked about when you and Ann were small and we used to go to Withernsea. He said you loved playing on the sands until you discovered donkey rides and amusements and then the sand hurt your feet.

Then on to Gosport with unfamiliar street names like Willow Lane, Seahorse Street and Cobden Street. We went to watch the boats, saw the Vanguard and Uncle Bill's crane in the distance and your father watching a painter said 'He'd make a bloody painter cry.' I liked the sea smell but not the unfriendly buses. We all fell in the car with creaking bones.

Riding along I saw a house with large open windows and a chair in view. I thought I'd like to climb in the window sit in the chair and then the lady of the house would open the room door start to say something then I would disappear.

A storm came up and there was only us on the downs and it may be heaven. The storm was stimulating, lightening thunder rain and lost in a lane of blackberries, and your father humming and Aunt Hilda getting splashed and Uncle Bill finding the way home on a Monkey's birthday.

Well Tom write a few lines. I'm eating well and hope you are.

So lots of love
Mam and Dad

PS. What's a monkey's birthday, ask me.

When their holiday was over I accompanied them back across London from Waterloo to King's Cross.

[14th August 1959]

Dear Tom

Friday and I am feeling more settled. Why settled I don't know but one is supposed to settle. When we left you at Kings Cross I felt happy, thinking how when you came home you was going to have a look at my 'Wedding' etc. this made me feel clever, but it only lasted about an hour and I started thinking you'll come home and it won't even be mentioned, but it doesn't matter because I'm a bloody fool.

I can't say I felt well when I got home. I had a wuzzy head and the weather has been drizzley and gloomy and when I heard on the wireless how storms have been raging down South I felt responsible for the storms as if I had left some electric current charging all over the place, funny isnt it.

Monday I tried sorting myself out a bit. Annie next door told me a young woman opposite had been bashed by her husband and had to have stitches in her face. She had him up in court and now he's got 6 months in jail. Settled. I heard a woman telling a small boy she couldn't lend his mother any money because she'd just come off her holidays and she hadnt any money and I saw a girl who I think is very nice going in pawn shop for her mother. Settled. These things make me really mad also cats keep scenting up the place.

Ann was at Manor Club with Jean when we were away and went to talk to Florrie Barker. She wasn't a bit surprised you going on the stage as she remembers how I would go in the scullery when I was at their house, put a towel over my head, close my hands together and come out looking like a nun, never smiling. I was always doing this trick and others too with a hairnet over my face acting French and traipsing like a mannequin in someone's coat and on entering their house I would announce I had left me plane outside.

Some bright woman in 'Woman's Own' said a good decorating

idea is paper the chimney breast with a brick wallpaper and this gives a country house style effect. Seeing I did this nearly a year ago I feel like writing and saying another idea is to use a wrought iron pattern paper on a dividing wall between two rooms, or a staircase wall you ask your designer friend. I like modern ideas but I like a touch of the old styles, like a shield shape mirror, a French clock (real) and a lamp for the table with glass drops round that glitter when the light is on.

Well Tom hope this letter doesn't bore you. By the way a Monkey's birthday is a day of sunshine and showers. Bill said when he was a lad people always called April showers a 'monkey's birthday'.

I shall be pleased when you come home again and I'll play you that tune I composed called Hey Dog. All for now.

Love Mam Dad and Ann

RADA TERM IV
September 1959

The most significant thing about the start of our second year at RADA, our fourth term, was that we would get to perform in the Vanbrugh, RADA's public theatre. It meant the outside world could take a look at us. Even more significant would be our fifth and sixth terms, when theatrical agents were invited to the shows.

[20th August 1959]

Dear Tom

The postman on his bike he looked at me and I looked at him and he only had official envelopes and I said to our Ann at dinner time I arent writing to our Tom this week. We have been home nearly 2 weeks and not a word and I thought it makes my letters look a bit cheap.

Your father when he was out last Friday night met a couple who we have known years so he arranged for us to meet them Saturday night and he said to me you can have two and a half hours talking. Hell! The couple called Finals have no family and she bought you your first pair of white shoes a little too big but you grew into them and she always calls you Thos because that was the name on your clinic card. I didn't feel as smart as her she has her hair tinted. We talked all the time and I didn't seem to notice my surroundings. They were interested in you and Ann and seemed to let one know how wrapped up they are in each other. This seems to me to be impossible that two people can have a world of their own. I think it's a hard task to practise this life and I wouldn't like it.

Wednesday a big race day and a woman in Annie's was having a bet. She is a single woman and seems to have things pretty rough, nursing her sick mother and her also not well. She said two years ago she went to York races and every horse she bet won. Some man near her was also betting all her horses. Then the last race so she said to her friend I'm having 5/- each way this time shit or bust. She meant she was being rash with her money. Anyhow this man said to a bookie he wanted to bet Shit or Bust. This nearly killed everybody on this most perfect day. She bought her mother a bird in a cage out of her winnings.

Now this might not seem much of a story but to me it is that woman's poetry. I'm sure everyone has got poetry and it is interesting finding and recognising that something. I told your father this is the thing I like writing down.

Mrs Jenneson was telling me one day about Patrick Firth do you remember him he was at Kingston. He passed for some University and his people have bought him a new car and he has his shirts made for him costing over £3 each. Just think nice looking clever lad loaded with money but not feeling superstitious about it but all taken for granted in a Sunshiny World. Some people get it handed to them on a silver tray and others my God should never have been born. I wonder what his poetry is and I bet he's a nice lad he looks it. Hell it all puzzles me and I wouldn't curtsy to Royalty would I Hell.

Scullery tidied half hearted soon your father will be home. He'll say isn't it bloody warm then Ann will come home. She will say 'How's Dad and you, Ma. Isn't it hot.' They're very nice and I'm your father's poetry.

Love Mam Dad and Ann

[24th August 1959]

Dear Tom

PEACHES AND PEARS

Saturday. I'm reading a book about Louis Armstrong's life it's a good book and he is a fine honest person full of reaching out.

Sat. night we went in club all the women in summer dresses and before ten o clock I noticed a young man put his face on a girls bare neck teasingly and I saw how she tapped her fingers on the table showing an engagement ring and a girl was singing 'A very precious love'.

Granny came in and told how someone's daughter had got a baby girl and had we heard about a trawler disaster. NO! A trawler coming home full of fish has sunk. Joe out for a paper met a woman who had had a wire. Her husband was safe.

We sat having our egg and bacon and on the wireless 'Alice where art thou'. This tune always touches me. Fancy a trawler disaster this time of year your father said and him on it up street whose wife is always trying to borrow money.

Love Mam Dad and Ann

If you took all my letters of the last year corrected them and made them into a book and all the pages with gold edging and everyone would say what a beautiful book. Am I conceited?

This is the first of Mother's letters to carry a title. She often doesn't explain the reason behind her titles and it is sometimes difficult to divine it, but as her editor and chronicler I feel duty bound to include them.

Deep-sea trawling was hard and dangerous work. For the deckhands especially, gutting the catch in the bitter cold in heavy seas was un-imaginably arduous. No wonder they liked their beer in between trips.

Trawlers usually went down in the winter. The community really felt the loss. Uncle Bernard, Dad's kid brother, had a friend, Dennis, an engineer like him, who was lost at sea one winter. He had given me a bicycle. We used to see a lot of him, and Uncle Bernard was very upset. We all were. Uncle Bernard told me his ship ran aground once and he had thought his number was up, but they all got safely ashore.

Uncle Bernard loved his engines and didn't want to stop going to sea. 'Did you stop going to sea because we lost the Cod War?' I asked him. There were three Cod Wars, he told me, and Hull lost them all. As the exclusion zones around Iceland and Norway were extended ever further, so the Hull trawlers lost more and more of their fishing grounds. It was a political thing, said Uncle Bernard. On account of the American naval bases in Norway and Iceland.

[1st September 1959]

Dear Tom

BUTTER BEANS

I had a restless nights sleep. The warm weather woke me up and once awake I started thinking about a programme we saw Tues on BBC TV. It was about nuns who enter a convent and never leave all their life. When two nuns opened the gate to let the TV people in they pulled hoods over their faces so as not to see outside. Fancy living within a high wall and not wanting to look over the top. The head nun was interviewed and with her a giggly happy little nun. When they showed us how a nun gets dressed up in a brides gown and a veil to marry the Lord with all the other married nuns following on and a little girl attendant holding the brides veil I felt disgusted. I think I am intelligent enough to talk about these things. The interviewer asked the head nun why they shut themselves in the convent. She said 'We don't we lock the world out.' Surely this is the same thing.

Then the man interviewed a young nun aged 19. He said 'You are here for say 50 year' and she said with an untouched lovely voice and face 'Lovely Lovely.' She said she loves her Lord more than a young girl loves her husband. Now with all seriousness and respect I say how does she know that. A young bride has the worry of being pregnant every month and it is a worry to lots of people. The young nun has chosen the easy way, her love is all imaginary. I think these nuns are earthly ghosts. Their job is praying for our good, they say, so their imprint is in the clouds of prayer that float about all over the place, but I didn't notice any prayer clouds settle over Hessle Road on Sunday after the trawler accident which always leaves a gloom and depression. The nuns holidays is 10 days alone in a hut at the bottom of the garden. Do they love it? 'Oh yes.' It was a good programme because it got me going. But I felt something disgusting and sinister about it. No wonder I couldn't sleep.

Then I thought how the day before your father had that car accident I was half dozing in bed and thought I saw two nuns stood against the wardrobe and one walked round to my side of the bed. Hell was I frightened. Last night I suddenly thought 'Has the nuns won?' Then I thought I could smell peppermint and thought one doesn't know who the Hell's walking about when one's asleep. Then I started doubting all this and I knew my thinking had finished and I fell asleep.

Honestly I don't think I like women much, you can't trust their make up. I'm watching one now who's just married a young fisherman who is also paying to some other girl for his child. I knew one like her years ago. She put on airs and graces, walking about like a mannequin in royal blue and a big white hat. Then I remember she had a sale, selling frocks and beach wear and her big hat and now she is like the rest, 2 or 3 bairns, ordinary husband and glamour gone.

I remember when I got married I had some nice tailor suits made, they lasted me for years. They always looked smart. We hadn't money for clothes.

Thanks for nice news letter which gives me something to think about. Like you I had that Monday morning hangover and at dinnertime I said to Ann 'I've had aspirin Rennies and mints. If I swallow any more dope my inside will be leaning on its elbow.' I liked that and wrote it down.

Tuesday and we all ended up narky by bedtime. I think Ann made me mad when she said my life was too sheltered. Later your father told me not to give orders. 'I didn't know I was.' I told them they are a good pair. They went to bed. I didn't mind.

Well Tom don't take all my letters without a grain of salt. I bet if I end this letter something will want writing.

Love Mam Dad and Ann

There's a sweet picture in my mind's eye of Mam, Ann and me visiting Dad in hospital after his accident. I must have been sixteen or seventeen. Mother in her best grey coat holding his hand. His face swollen and his lip trembling. She was a very good comforter. How could someone who was so fragile be so strong?

I am very fond of Mother's description of the programme about the convent. Yet another example of her antipathy towards organized religion. And not the last.

She had such compassion, though, for those around her. No Christian could hope to have half the amount. Of all the people I have known, she, more than any other, makes me feel that there might be a life after the present one. Perhaps it's the power and sweetness of her presence in my mind. Or is it that I can't abide the thought of never seeing her again?

[5th September 1959]

Dear Tom

Thursday night your father and me went for a drink in Halfway. There was a pianist and drummer and a young man singing. A blonde woman came in who I knew before she led a loose life. She would insist on buying us a drink and she got merry and kept saying 'Sing up Annie' and when a photographer came in she begged me to have my photograph taken with her which I laughingly did.

Ann had left two cardigans airing on two chair backs and they reminded me of two Anns. One was bright and one was pale. I cleared Anns bedroom in the afternoon and could have cried washing the windows because the job didn't make me feel happy. But near teatime I thought, after hearing the paper lads shouting, the change from summer to autumn can be heard in the voices of the paper lads, and that made me happy.

I thought how two days before I said to your father 'Is it the anniversary of the war starting?' he said 'Yes.' I never remember dates. I thought how I was evacuated with you and Ann. And the first morning I could hear the landlady Mrs Orange gossiping to the woman next door. I looked out the bedroom window, saw the miserable looking little garden and Mrs Orange saying 'Everyone is always crying.' It was true. I cried a lot and so did you, you wouldn't leave go of my pinny, you kept on crying and pulling my pinny. I remember I got up really early to help Mrs Orange and it made me think I could face the world but the world couldn't face me. Mrs Oranges grandaughter came with me you and Ann for a walk and she liked my shoes, they were my best and it worried me wearing them a lot. Then Uncle Jack came it was before he was called up. I think it was Grannie's idea to help me home with you. It was lovely weather we went on the sands and Ann kept dipping her ice cream cornet in the sand and eating it. She's like that now. I can remember Hessle Road seemed a lot scruffier than it does now. Your father said 'Hello' to us. We were really newly married 3 year and he said what a terrible job he had had drowning a little dog he never sweated so much, it wouldn't die he would never do it again. So on through 6 year of wicked war.

I am writing this Thursday and just before tea I was sweeping the front and an elderly man stopped to talk. He said don't waste your time sweeping Mrs, it'll be no better. I agreed. 'The old man sweeping the road doesn't make much of a job of it but he gets paid which is the main job.' He went on it wasn't right stopping prostitution. Any woman could be attacked. He knew one woman, poor old bugger, she only had 3/6 in her bag, some teddy boy raped her. 'When my old woman goes out' he said, 'I give her a shillalagh I brought home from Ireland.' But his wife refused it and says she can use her knee. He enjoyed his talk. I didn't mind it finished my letter. 'God bless you lass' he said.

Love Mam Dad and Ann

Ann leaves for Italy a week on Monday.

Mother, Ann and I were evacuated up the coast to Bridlington at the beginning of the war to escape the air raids on Hull. Dad stayed at work, painting either trawlers or warships. I have little recollection of Mrs Orange's house. I once asked Mother if it had a pit in the garden and she said it did, so maybe that's my earliest memory. I was two or three. Ann, even younger, remembers nothing, though Mother told her Mrs Orange was religious and used to thank the Lord when the All Clear sirens sounded. Mother would have been more inclined to ask Him why He'd started the air raid in the first place. No wonder we didn't stay for long.

[18th September 1959]

Dear Tom

BOUQUET

Hope you got the check OK. [From Hull Education Committee.]

Annie Brooks in shop told me that Granny was selling raffle tickets. She was raffling a bedspread she had made. I knew she was needing the money as usual. I then washed the floor and went in your bedroom, found a poetry book, and sat on the bed with it. I don't like some poetry, flowery stuff, but I read two verses from 'A Ballad upon a Wedding'. I liked them. 'Her feet beneath her petticoat like little mice stole in and out' then at the end after saying her cheeks were white – 'For streaks of red were mingled there, Such as are on a Katherine pear, The side that's next the sun.' Bonnie.

After that I went downstairs to clean the kitchen. I put a light to the waste in the fireplace and was kneeling taking bits off the hearth rug. A funny tune was playing on the wireless and I just felt as if I was in India. It was peculiar the heat from the fireplace and the music and it just seemed like blue skies and white buildings. It lasted 2 seconds.

After tea your father painted inside the bath pale blue very nice. I did no night thinking that night and today there is a new student teacher at school. Looks like an Indian with a white turban on. It's after tea now, your father is examining the bath, I'm awaiting Ann and outside it's India. People's skins have darkened. One woman has twins, another one is in labour and plenty more are pregnant.

Street is full of girls playing with balls, lads with bikes and waving arms, gossiping women and dogs. The bath's full of blue water and cut up onions decorate the scullery. [To take away the smell of paint.] My head aches a little. This writing is like magic and full of adventure. When I felt I was in India I didn't know I would see the Indian student next day. It's really wonderful to me.

Ann has gone to bank. I'm lending her some money for her holiday just in case. When Ann came back I said let's take our coffee in front room and watch the bairns going to school. I went in sunny room with the Italian labels and looking through the window I saw the Indian teacher. 'Hurry up Ann' I shouted but he had just disappeared in school with his turban and whiskers but passing our window was another live Indian one who is often seen around here hawking silk scarves etc in a case. Ann recognised him. She then went back to work with Italy and I stayed home with India.

It seems to me I have without realising it likened granny selling her raffle tickets to the Indian selling his case full of silk junk. It's really wonderful how it all works out.

What can I call this letter? Bouquet. Because twice I have seen a woman with a bouquet. She lost her son suddenly last year.

Don't think I'll forget India while that student is in school.

Love Mam Dad and Ann

In this term, my fourth at RADA, we did a class in mime, run by a former actress, Mary Phillips. If one can be soft yet steely, then she was. She was elegant and still, her grey hair swept back and up – not close to her head like a ballet dancer. Her class started auspiciously for me because I was the only one of us who correctly mimed stirring a cup of tea. Everyone else moved their imaginary spoon round and round as though stirring soup. I just wiggled my spoon daintily in my imaginary cup, my saucer represented by my cupped left hand. (I wasn't having tea in Harrow Street, clearly.) I don't think I reported this small triumph to Mother, but I was beginning to think that my hope of becoming an actor might be realized.

I remember Mary Phillips saying how wonderful it was to be an artist. As artists we would always have something to learn and our lives would always have meaning. I can remember hoping against hope that I might possibly become one of these artists. It was the only thing that would give my life meaning. That's what I had long thought. I remember picking on the word 'arts' when it came up at Kingston High as the alternative to science. The arts side or the science side? The arts side, please. No contest. When Mother and I were excitedly discussing the composition for Mr Nicholson and the essay for Mr W., we were both doing what meant most to us – we were expressing ourselves, making little stories out of our lives. That I chose to give voice to other people's words, rather than my own, hardly matters. Good acting always tells a story.

Later Mother writes 'it's just a normal function of the human brain to try and make patterns of things'. She calls so urgently for Ann to come and see the Indian student teacher in West Dock Avenue school yard because suddenly her inner life and her everyday life seem to be connected. If that's not a story, what is?

[9th October 1959]

Dear Tom

LAVENDER

Monday was very lonely. After tea your father started boot repairing. He had to scrape glue off the soles of his boots so he could reglue the rubber soles on again. He said he didn't like me watching him.

Granny comes in after dinner and watches every move I make it nearly drives me mad and I start thinking about that house Aunt Alice was talking about the other side of the shops near her. I ironed and put my curtains up and covers on and washed the front door. At 4 o clock Michael [Uncle George's son] came in to see if I wanted any errands going. I told him if he could borrow a pram he could go to Teresa's for 2 round tables she was giving me. He went and I gave him 2/-. When your father came home he soon let me see he thought the tables were no good. One wanted the legs glueing. After tea he messed about glueing his boots then glued the round table legs. I said to him 'Why do you act mean when you're not?'

I decided to wash my hair. When I opened the scullery door the smell of cats nearly drove me daft. I said to your father 'One dripping tap, one gug-gugging and cat smell!' he only laughed as he sat there in singlet watching TV.

Wed. Your father at tea reminded me he couldn't understand how the smell of cats upsets me so much. He made me feel as if I was a bit tapped. I told him later that a visitor to our house didn't bother me like him and I felt sane again.

Thursday. What a quiet voting day. I haven't heard one loud speaker van. Your father voted before going to work.

Aunt Al called in for 5 minutes. Her and Jack for first time voted Conservative and then went for a drink. I feel very sorry for the labour people, mainly Welsh and Scottish and I'm sure they will hate clever buggers English mainly non-industrial South. Why can't the parties compromise? I think some people could help themselves more and I think unions are ugly but I couldn't vote conservative.

Love Mam Dad and Ann

Dad had long wanted to get a job with the Transport and General Workers' Union. When I was at UCL a vacancy came up. He did a lot of homework, though when I caught him with the union rule book he would pretend he wasn't studying it. He didn't like to appear too keen. He would have been a good union man. Sensitive to the needs of the men, yet sensible and responsible. The very best kind of old-fashioned socialist. Not hot-headed like dear Uncle Pat. The choice ended up between him and a seaman. Uncle Bernard assured me it was no contest, and I was excited that he might have an outlet for his intelligence.

The seaman got the job. Dad was very disappointed. His rival had been suspected of being . . . 'Well, Tom, I don't have to tell you what some men get up to at sea.' His pride was hurt.

[16th October 1959]

Dear Tom

RED ROSE

Am calling this letter 'Red Rose' because in Rayners, before going
to Hull Fair last week, the barmaid was wearing a red rose given to
her by a man in a wedding party who said to her 'Your husband
will love you more than ever tonight with that rose on.' But the
man didn't know her husband had been dead just one year and she
didn't tell him.

Fair was crowded the weather being fine. We ambled down
Walton Street enjoying it. I had some mussels and we had a hot dog
with onions. New shows was on. 'Lolla the Rat girl who wears only
a smile'. 'Come and see the beautiful girl alive in Dante's Inferno!'
also Black Magic and always some object with two heads. We
played housey-housey and tried to win an ironing board. Then we
felt tired and went for the bus buying a pomegranite and some
brandy snap on the way. While waiting at the worst bloody bus
service a smart young woman shouted 'I simply love toffee apples'
and we laughed. On the bus behind me a woman said it would
drive her mad to live alone and in front the little boy who wouldn't
wear his duffle coat hood but liked to carry his coconut in it and
didn't want kissing for doing so.

After tea Monday Ann went to library for books and records,
some Mozart Symphony, but she wont tidy her clothes nicely. I
think she must have seen Ricky because she didn't arrive home till
10.30. Ricky goes to library to study where he left off at fifteen. I
can't make up my mind about him. He saw a picture of Florence
and called it fabulous then I heard him talking in front room and
something else was fabulous. I heard Ann say fabulous and I said to
her 'I've heard that word before.'

Wed. and in Annie Brooks next door, Jean Phillips started saying
what a Treasure her husband was. He never gets ruffled, he does
everything for her and he never stops talking to her. She wishes she
was like him. I wasnt prepared for all this and just said I didn't
think it was natural not to quarrel. I like time to think these things

out. I told your father after tea I was going to let everyone know what a marvellous husband I had. 'He gives me a £5 note every now and again, worships me and will do anything for me.' He said 'What about Friday night?' [Dad's night out without her.]

I wouldn't like a perfect husband. Though to be quite honest I've always thought I had a perfect husband. I was really surprised when told a young girl down street was having to get married. Your father said what worried me was no one told me sooner. He said people have been getting married at 14, 15, 16, all the time. Which seems to echo Romeo and Juliet.

I thought I would wash the front room windows. All through me in and out with bucket and chair father slept even to fire going out. Perfect husband!

Love Mam Dad and Ann

For much of my time at RADA, Mother's letters say little about my life in London because I didn't tell her much. She wanted assurance and information and most of the time I offered neither.

'Does Alan Plater think you're doing well at RADA?' she once asked me tentatively. 'How the hell does he know, Ma? Nobody knows. And what does it matter anyway?' 'Don't talk like that to your mother,' said Dad. Quite rightly.

Mother got her chance to ask Alan directly when he called on her with a message for me. At the time he was working in an architect's office in Hull, having been ejected prematurely from his architectural course at Durham University. It didn't matter greatly because he wanted to be a writer, and it made him one of two former members of the Old Kingston Society of Genii who fared a sight better in show business than they did in academia. Mother couldn't resist asking Alan if he thought I would do well at RADA. He had no idea, of course, but sensing her longing for reassurance he said, 'There's no question about it, he's absolutely brilliant.' Which was kind of him if less than truthful.

'One can't help but worry,' said Mother.

I was right when I told Mother nobody knew. About any student's prospects. But what a good time we had of it guessing! Sitting in

Olivelli's, just off the Tottenham Court Road, making a sixpenny cup of coffee last for ever, surrounded by surmise. 'He'll come into his own when he's older.' 'He'll never be a star but he'll always be in work.' 'Films will suit her better than stage.' 'Milo Sperber says he could become a great actor one day.'

Phillip Madoc told me recently that Thaw and I had seen him in RADA's Little Theatre in a feeble late Shaw, *The Shewing Up of Blanco Posnet*. It seems we were far from impressed with the piece, though I had been the spokesman for the two of us: 'He just stood there. What a pair! But after you'd finished demolishing the play you said, "I'll say one thing. You can act." And you turned and went.' I was surprised that I sounded so sure in my opinions. I don't remember being much of a surmiser. Not vocally, at any rate. My record for spotting talent wasn't good. I remember congratulating one student on his performance in the Little Theatre at the end of his first year, having been very impressed by his stillness – not my strong suit at the time. Mr Fernald didn't agree with me, and the unfortunate lad never made it to the second year.

If I could be wrong, so too could our teachers. There was a handsome Irish lad who did a piece, sitting solidly on a chair, that thrilled Peter Barkworth to his marrow. 'You're going to have the most marvellous career, James. You have looks, presence, talent and technique.' James worked for a time, but he didn't have a marvellous career. In the same session he told my pal John Thaw, unable to control his arms in his excitement, that he was unemployable. Maybe he was, that day. I'm not wanting to apportion blame. Difficult always to know the difference between those who were as good as they were ever going to get, and those, with far more to offer, who hadn't yet discovered the way to offer it.

[23rd October 1959]

Dear Tom

The only thing that came through the letter box today was 2 vouchers to save 6d on Campbells soups. I can't expect a letter regular but what worries me is I may have put something in a letter that you don't like, or something silly. Not much has happened today. Granny in as usual. After tea there was a programme on TV about Goya the painter. Watching and listening I realised an artist paints all he thinks and feels about people and life so I didn't worry any more about what I may have written, and thought I can go to bed and think about things.

Tuesday. On Hessle Road who should be shouting and waving at me but Aunt Alice. She had lost her charge, little Susan, and wondered if I had seen her. She had wandered off with her doll and pram. Al went to the police and Susan was eventually brought back to her by a policeman. She had been missing two and a half hours. The policeman said Susan insisted when he found her that it was Alice who was lost. Alice shook her fist and shouted at the bairn who was none the worse and waved me ta ta. When I was quite small I was missing with my doll and pram and when I turned up doll and pram were missing and I had been hit by girls and was very tear stained. I always found girls very cruel.

Thurs. I saw Mrs Randall in Hanneman's this morning with her pedigree dog on a lead. She was telling someone her dog didn't like the traffic. 'You'll have to take him to a psychoanalyst' I said. 'What and make him as daft as people.'

I couldn't get to sleep I am wondering how things are with you. I often think it's a shame after a long day at work you have to cook yourself a meal when you get home. I wish I could be helping you more. I was saying to your father we ought to have a phone it's not a luxury. Then I thought it might mean I hadnt to write a letter and I should hate that.

Love Mam Dad and Ann

Mother was overestimating my abilities when she thought of me as having to cook myself a meal, though I did graduate from the fried-egg sandwiches of Camden Road. In Highbury Crescent's roomier and better-equipped kitchen I became capable of scrambled eggs on toast and beans on toast. There may well not have been a toaster at Camden Road, and if there was a saucepan I never found it. Vic thought it was funny when I had toast with my beans on toast, but I thought I was taking advantage of the improved facilities, and it was a good way of filling myself up. The only addition I brought to the Highbury kitchen was my unbreakable mug. It was made of thick red plastic-like stuff that could have resisted a sledgehammer. I used to like dropping it on the kitchen floor to demonstrate its strength, and I was proprietorial about it. I needn't have been. Nobody else went near it.

Our first show in the Vanbrugh Theatre was Harold Brighouse's Lancashire comedy *Hobson's Choice*. It was the first time we did not excerpts but an entire play. I was to play Willie Mossop, the shoemaker, one of the three leads.

Mr Fernald, aware perhaps that after my first year at RADA I still hadn't managed to get into the black, very thoughtfully put a little job my way. It involved my reading to someone who was partially sighted. He lived in a white-fronted house in a terrace somewhere quite smart. I can't remember exactly where. The room I read in had dark walls and heavy furnishings, and there was a reading lamp on a table piled with books. It was some kind of poetry that I read, but strange and not familiar to me. I felt sorry for the poor man, who was very erudite, and didn't think I was doing him proud. My couple of hours of trying seemed so little light to bring to him. But I got ten bob and it was something to write to Mam and Dad about.

[29th October 1959]

Dear Tom

STRAWBERRIES ROSES AND APPLES

First things first and here's answering your letter. Your reading must be a bit of a touchy job, but should be very good practice for you. Ann couldnt get the Hobson's Choice book. I think one reason I never wanted to get it is its title as it is or was the name of corn plasters.

Ann came home at dinner and the conversation was making Christmas cakes and no mention of R and was I glad. When your father came home the conversation was your letter. He read it twice. I said 'It's the first money he has earned doing something

using his voice.' And then hoping to encourage him from his
depression 'You used to read to your grandmother didn't you?'
'Yes,' he said 'she could neither read nor write.' He used to read
Andrew Marvel and all the weekly papers – for coppers and with
an urge to be out in the street playing with the lads. 'What a pity
you had to leave school at 14. You might have had a better place
than Fish Dock.' But I had said the wrong thing. 'You're always
thinking what might have been.' He said him being good at figures
could have got him in prison if he had been in a position handling
money. He really means things could be worse for him. I took my
egg and bacon to my chair and felt a very upright and stately feeling
like a queen. 'I can have an opinion' I said. 'I don't think one should
have to be thankful for a piece of bread and wear second hand shoes
and like pawn shops.'

Ann came in and said 'Stop bickering.' Father went to bed. Ann
went to library. She was very late home. 'You're very late from
library' I said not wanting to. Ann muttered something and then a
long silence. 'While you were out' I said 'they played "Buena Sera"
on wireless.' Then a door banged upstairs. It was the wireless too
loud. Everything I do is wrong. I can't help it if people come to the
house and I don't care for them. There's Ricky sits there talking
about their head rep [representative]. Hell. 'He's going to Plymouth,'
she said. I went to bed and couldn't sleep if Ann was feeling
hurt at R going. My inside ached. The rain pelted down and the
wind shook the drain pipe. Then trawler buzzers blew cosily not
caring about the rain and all blew different notes. Someone would
be putting the kettle on and bobbers clogs walked by and Ricky's
father's 4 berth launch was tossing about in the weather.

Tues. Could you sleep last night I asked Ann. Yes she said. You
havent got a broken heart. Laughter. Who should arrive at 7.30 but
Ricky to take Ann to see 'Room at the Top'. I shan't mention him
any more because I can't understand people.

Wed washday. Ann comes home and she's on the defensive for
nothing. I'm in scullery with my washing. 'What are you sighing
for?' she asks. 'It's your drip dry blouse.'

Hope you are well Tom and I hope 'Hobson's Choice' is a huge success. Think I'll make your father a bread and butter pudding for tea. Write soon.

Love Mam Dad and Ann

Dad didn't really believe that his lot could have been worse. It might have suited him to say it could have been worse and to argue with Mother, but, like her, he knew that it could have been a lot better.

'I always wanted a son, Tom, so I could give him the chances I never had.' That's what he really thought. He said that to me when I was thirteen or fourteen. Mother was in hospital after her third operation. He had just combed his hair in front of the mirror before going for a pint with Uncle Pat. I think her absence made him wonder what his life meant, and he spoke with a simple directness that I never forgot. I felt the responsibility of what he said, and, strangely enough, the honour, and I was stuck for a reply.

[6th November 1959]

Dear Tom

LADY IN A WHITE DRESS

Last Sunday I was up first and took your father a cup of tea. Later I was peeling apples and thought how things go on and on like peeling skin off an apple. I was wondering if Ann or your father was going to get up it was nearly 12 o'clock. I had been wondering whether to tell Ann how I thought Ricky was to put it plainly not much of a man, and I am very surprised at her even wanting to go out with him. Anyhow I thought I would put Ann's Italian records on loud and this would wake the two sleepers upstairs. After the second record your father arrived downstairs looking like Courtenay. 'If that's your idea of a joke it's not bloody funny.' He nearly threw the record player out. 'You poor bugger' I said feeling squashed 'it was only in fun and you didn't complain in club at the noise last night.' Granny came in then wiping her nose and wanting to sell your father raffle tickets. She soon went. While making tea I said 'I feel I ought to have a cap and apron on.' I realise though I do things which are young for my age and I shouldn't have played the records so loud but I didn't expect a row. Ann got up and even scrubbed the front step.

I went an errand to Hales and she (Mrs) told me about a relation who spent 5 year in a Japanese prison camp and never got over the cruelty of the place. He was hung up by his thumbs. All this affected his nerves and he didn't get married until he was 40 because he wasn't fit. Anyhow after one year being happily married he died. Well we all had a nice dinner and watched the Dorsey Story and I thought writing should be like music running up and down and all over the place.

This Saturday Granny brought me some nylons for my birthday and did I want to buy the eiderdown she had won the other week in club. She wanted £2 for it she said it was worth nearly £4. I said I didn't want it but would give her £1 for a Christmas box. And I really would sooner give her it now than at Christmas when everything gets too sentimental. Hell and watching the rugby match, the announcer said 'Presenting the cup a lady in a white dress' and it was Aunt Agnes and she would love the job and she is very nice.

Monday Nov 2nd. And your letter and record came along with the cards. Thanks very much it's a nice letter and record. I like all your letters. I always liked the other Louis Armstrong record you bought Ann. Your father bought me some chocs and Ann some underneath gear. I don't like birthdays much. When I was young I always had something like chilblains or cold spots. We had a nice evening your father making us laugh. Ann didn't go to library. Your father tells me I measure more round my hips than him so we got out the steel tape measure and started measuring. It made me laugh a lot.

Love Mam Dad and Ann

I went to see Aunt Agnes in the summer of 1997, a few weeks after Uncle Pat had died. Aunt Agnes whose cake I ate. She was the eldest of Dad's sisters, four years younger than Dad, two years younger than Uncle Pat. Quite by chance I saw her on her eighty-fifth birthday, so the flowers I bore were apposite, and she was delighted by the coincidence. She also enjoyed being reminded of the day I ate the cake. She still looked very bonnie and complained only gently that her legs wouldn't let her go dancing any longer. I asked her about their childhood on Hessle Road.

'There were six of us then. [One girl, Mary, the eldest of them all, died young. Uncle Bernard, the baby of the family, arrived much later.] Us four girls slept in one bedroom with Mother; your Dad and Uncle Pat in the other bedroom with Father.'

'Dad and Uncle Pat would have liked a lot more education than they got. They were very intelligent, weren't they, Aunt Agnes?'

'Oh yes, they were. They helped a girl at school get a scholarship to Marist [i.e. Roman Catholic] College.'

'But why couldn't they have sat for a scholarship?'

'Our mother couldn't have afforded it on what your Grandad Courtenay earned. We couldn't have afforded the bus fares, never mind the clothes. It didn't matter how scruffy you were on Hessle Road, but it did at Marist College. And Mother wouldn't have favoured one without the others. There was no question of a scholarship.

'I used to hate it that our house was so scruffy [as did I] which was wrong of me, I suppose. I managed to get a job in service for a while, Cottingham way. I loved being in a nice house, with nice furniture and the food all nicely served up. Not like in our house. I wanted to be a little lady. Wrong of me, I suppose.'

Her honesty and self-knowledge were impressive. Mother had always known how formidable she was.

[13th November 1959]

Dear Tom

MONDAY (Didn't intend that as a title but shall leave it.)

Two weeks is a long time when we don't have a letter. It seems you have gone to London and that's that.

Fri. During cleaning up I read how an American novelist

Sinclair Lewis asked a University audience 'Hands up all you who want to write.' Everyone put their hands up. 'Well why the hell arent you at home writing.' Somerset Maugham has said 'Only amateurs fall in love with their own words.'

Sunday. Your father thought he would try to stick the sole on his boot again, using one last, one razor blade, a tube of glue, a piece of wood and 3 screwdrivers. I said to him 'You look like a cobbler. Our Tom's a cobbler in his play. Do you remember how he was always hammering nails in the steps. How old would he have been then?' 'About one' said your father 'and I taught him to hammer with his left hand too.' Grandad had noticed this. And we laughed about it.

I read in 'the People' about a girl of 15 who poets think is writing good poetry so Hell I shall start reading my efforts.

I really enjoyed seeing Colin Davis at work on TV Monitor programme. I could soon understand good music through him.

What is Pre-Dada and simultaneity? You must tell me sometimes when you are at home and in the humour. I think it's some kind of artistic expression. Well Tom I hope you are well and enjoying the play or is it over?

Love Mam Dad and Ann

Ann's been home for dinner and we avoided any clashes. I have adopted a singing and laughing mood and wonder if I shall keep it up.

Two of my university friends thought they'd come and see *Hobson's Choice*. They were both hankering after a life in showbiz, and they did achieve it. Roy Battersby, one of my best friends at UCL, directs in television, and Tony Garnet is a producer. Roy was by then studying for a Ph.D. in economics. Something to do with the price of potatoes in some century or other. I know it didn't make him happy. Maybe he thought my failure to get a degree was a much better statement of intent. Tony Garnet didn't appear till my last year. At that time he wanted to be an actor and was reading psychology, believing it might help. He had been in weekly rep and terrified me with stories of its arduousness, and its inevitability for any aspiring actor.

I thought Roy's and Tony's visit to the Vanbrugh might give an indication of my progress so far. However, when Tony heard I was playing Willie Mossop, the timid little cobbler, he said it was the perfect part for me and if I couldn't play that I couldn't play anything, negating, at a stroke, any success I might have. I don't think it was the perfect part for me, it's too straightforward, but what Tony said went home. I always felt there wasn't the brain power at RADA that there had been at UCL.

The casting of our production didn't help with authenticity. The only student with the necessary bulk for Hobson was a large, genial American lad from the deep south; and Ada Figgins, Willie's betrothed at the play's outset, was played by a Greek girl. She tried her best with the Lancashire accent, and in the cool of the rehearsal room she was at least as authentic as the American, though that's not saying much. In the heat of the performance, however, her words were all Greek – to me and everyone else. And the big American lad's ee baa gum delivery was absurd. It would have been better had my pal Thaw played Hobson. After the performance, Roy and Tony both wore faces as long as a wet week. I can still feel their gloom. They told me that Joan Littlewood had seen the show. She ran the Theatre Workshop at Stratford East and was a huge influence on the realism then taking hold. I had seen her production of *Edward II* and been mightily impressed by its directness. It made our efforts seem all the more pitiful.

I couldn't help seeing my progress through the eyes of my intelligent university friends: which is to say there wasn't any. But that was soon to change, and there'd be news worth writing home about.

[20th November 1959]

Dear Tom

ORANGE BALLOON

Was pleased as always to get your letter. I'm sure your 'Hobson's Choice' was very good. I've heard of Theatre Workshop and would like you to be in the company. I remember seeing Alfred Lynch and I thought he was very good. [Joan Littlewood was about to do Brendan Behan's *The Hostage* with A. Lynch.] I said to Ann 'Fancy a play can be about one night's leave.'

Weekend was comfortable your father kept calling me Mother. Ann was quite amiable and told me Ricky had rung up. I would like him to keep off the scene. I didn't sleep very good maybe I should do more work in the house instead of dreaming about. Often I think when I'm going to write a letter it's going to be a most marvellous letter with all ups and downs and I find out I write just the same bad grammar.

Alice has been with news of a house near them, so I said I'll see what father says. Alice had her little charge with her. She laughed, Susan I mean. It seemed a long time since I'd heard a child laughing. I told your father all about the house and he said wait and see what Alice has to say tomorrow. He doesn't mind a new house and I want to do what's best.

Friday. Aunt Al came before dinner and announced the woman who wants an exchange is coming to see our house after dinner. HELL! The young son of the house (he works in a fish shop near Al) wants to know if pigeons could be kept in our yard. Alice and Jack think I'm a fool if I don't take this house. I said I can't imagine why this woman wants to flit around Christmas and imagined us flitting on Christmas day in a decorated van.

The woman is called Mrs Hotham. She came at nearly 2 o'clock. She looked over our house and thinks it's alright. She has two lads at sea. I said 'Why this flitting at Christmas?' She wants to be down Hessle Road for Christmas and it seems she's used to flitting. I only want to do what's best. Well Tom what do you think about all this. What will you be doing at Christmas? Looks like we may want your help or am I just being selfish.

Love Mam Dad and Ann

Towards the end of the RADA autumn term a notice went up on the board in the entrance hall to the effect that the following term there would be a musical production in the Vanbrugh theatre. Students eligible to be chosen for it (i.e. those who would then be in their last or next to last term, like me) were invited to do a singing audition. There were some, including John Thaw and Geoffrey Whitehead, who scorned this invitation.

Two Billies, 1961. *Express Newspapers*

School prefects, Kingston High School, 1954.
Front row, fourth from left: me; centre, Dr Walker; third from right,
Jack Barnaby; extreme right, Mr Large.

Ian Hamilton and Arab (me),
The Stars Bow Down, Kingston
High, 1953.

Mr Knightley, Kingston High, 1954.

Sixth-form trip to Stratford, 1955. Me and the girls.

As Scythrop
Glowry in
Nightmare Abbey,
with Tony
Davenport, UCL
Dramsoc, 1957.
'I was always glad
you had a good
pair of legs on
you, Tommy.'

God's teeth. 1957.

BELOW: Thaw,
scaffolding and me.
Faust, RADA, 1960.

With seagull and lovely
Ann Bell, Old Vic, 1960.

Angus McBean/© Harvard Theatre Collection

The result of Mother's interview
with the *Hull and Yorkshire Times.*

RIGHT: Cartoon by Ronald Searle.

© *Ronald Searle*

Alec McCowen, me and ears. *Midsummer's Night's Dream*, Old Vic, 1961.

Billy enters, Act I.

A moment of reflection, Cambridge Theatre, 1961.

Running...

The opening of *The Loneliness of the Long Distance Runner* in Hull,
December 1962. My smart suit is courtesy of the *Tatler.*
From left: Grandma Quest, me, Dad, Aunt Agnes, Ann. *Hull Daily Mail*

Dad.

I thought I would have a go at getting into the musical. I didn't mind the prospect of having to sing. Hadn't my showbiz career started musically in Harrow Street when I was four? The show was rumoured to be set in the East End and featured a young tearaway or two. I thought it might be a chance to appear in the Vanbrugh playing someone of my own age. We set great store by appearing undisguised in front of the agents who came to the Vanbrugh shows looking for young talent. I sped off to get a copy of Schubert's 'Who Is Sylvia?' I knew the tune and wouldn't have to read the music.

The room where the audition took place had a glass-panelled door and as I got to 'That all our swains commend her' who should I spy through the glass but Thaw and Whitehead laughing at me and, I presumed, taking the piss. I carried on undaunted, not wishing to waste the money I had spent on the music – and, besides, I liked the piano accompaniment.

The following week the cast list went up on the noticeboard for the next term's shows in the Vanbrugh theatre. T. Courtenay was to play Bernie, the leader of a gang of teddy boys, in a musical called *Shut Up and Sing*. For Thaw and Whitehead? A dramatization of *Paradise Lost*.

I got myself a job on St Pancras Station, sorting the mailbags during the Christmas rush. Better-paid than postal work in Hull because it involved working through the night. It also meant that I wouldn't be helping Mother with the flitting. And that by the time I got home, though I could hardly believe it, they would have left Harrow Street.

[26th November 1959]

Dear Tom

ORANGE BALLOON (CONTINUED)

It's nice or not nice for you that you have got a job, but what I'm wondering is when shall you sleep. I hope you are not having any more colds. When will the schools programme of RADA be on TV? Let me know.

Sunday and me and your father got ready to go and see the house on Longhill Estate. We had a drink in Rayners before going. At Longhill we called in Aunt Alice's house first and she came with us.

The house is about a couple of bus stops from Aunt Al. I was quite surprised at how nice the grove was and so was father. It is a semi circle and there are eleven houses in it. In the centre is a patch of grass and leading down to it is about 3 or 4 stone steps and a pavement is all the way round and just outside the front garden are 2 trees, just like a stage setting for a Chekov play. I thought someone had said the back garden was small so as we walked down the side passage I hoped there was enough garden and there was, well enough to make pleasant with grass and flowers. What a lovely kitchenette or scullery and a lovely room large and square and through the window 2 trees and steps. I went to see the upstairs – 3 bedrooms bathroom and lav, Oh and a small hallway. One bedroom is smallish but big enough for a single bed and writing desk etc. Your father was very pleased with all this and said it was a better house than Aunt Als. He told the woman he would see our landlord about exchanging and so you can imagine when we got home telling Ann all the news and your father seemed restless after tea and we went out in Rayners. I didn't sleep very well that night and all I could see was 2 trees and these steps, and all Monday the thoughts of them made me feel sick and I didn't like them. I told Ann at dinner time and she said 'Any excuse.' No one understands me. Barbara and Granny came in after dinner, Granny saying 'Our Alice is always cold living up there.'

Monday teatime your father came home after seeing the landlord and said we can exchange But. 'But what?' I said. Our rents will go up and is this woman, Mrs Hotham, willing to pay another £1 a month. So he said he would go and see her himself and work his charm. Anyhow the woman and her three sons want to come back to Hessle Road so much they don't mind the extra rent and in bed Monday night your father couldn't sleep and said 'What a nice brick shed there is and it has a window in. He had thought of paying a few pounds for a shed.

Father didn't like it when I said I can't alter being like I am because I go in another house. What I mean is sometimes I shall like it, sometimes I won't. I've got to remember that at the liking and not liking times.

Jack Stathers called at teatime to ask how we were getting on about the house. 'Don't let people kid you it's too far' he said. 'Springtime is the time you'll appreciate living at Longhill.' So now we are waiting the Corporations consent and maybe a man will come to our house and ask why we want this Corporation house. And I could say lots and lots of very good and intelligent reasons but I daren't say how I liked the look of the two trees and the steps because I might not. It's a tricky business liking and not liking isn't it. Well, it looks like 'Orange Balloon' is nearly ended.

Love Mam Dad and Ann

Helping with the mail bags on St Pancras Station was my last vacation job outside the profession. I was happy doing it because I was so excited about my part in the musical, and I felt very fortunate not to have to appear in *Paradise Lost*. Not many laughs there. It was as though a hole had opened up in the road beside me engulfing my pals Thaw and Whitehead and leaving me dancing and singing merrily on my way.

[14th December 1959]

Dear Tom

Sorry about not writing but I was in bed nearly all last week with tonsilitis and my brush nylon nightie and did not like the aches and pains and misery of it. We was in Club Sat night before last and I won a duck but hadnt been feeling so good. I started shivering when we arrived home and when I got to bed with hot water bottle and stove lit I was sick and felt horrible. All Sunday I sat in my chair while Ann tidied up and cooked dinner and I was surprised to see colour in my cheeks. Monday my throat was hurting and I decided to have the doctor. Ann stayed off work until dinner time. During the morning she said she would play 'Buena Sera' and I would think I was in Italy. Doctor Dunn came near dinner time and said I had a temperature and tonsilitis and must go to bed for three days. Hell.

Ann was very kind and thoughtful and left everything she thought I would need before going to work, including wireless on loud and then when Granny came in she would turn it off. Doctor Dunn came on Wednesday and I said I feel worse than before I was in bed and so bloody miserable. He said he felt miserable too even bloody fed up. I said I bet he did. He examined me and decided my cold was much better but I was very run down and had to keep under him for Iron Tablets. I told him we were going to flit and he said 'don't you want a new house.' 'Yes I said honestly but its everything' and words stopped.

I was glad to get your letter Saturday morning and you can imagine how I'm going to need some of this singing and dancing you are talking about. Along with your letter came one from the housing to say we had got the house. So we will be moving on Saturday. We will be busy packing this week but have lots of volunteer helpers, and already a duck towards Christmas dinner.

Love Mam Dad and Ann

Having completed my duties at St Pancras I said farewell to a friendly porter. He wished me luck. 'It's a funny fackin' business you're goin' into.' But I was buoyant as I got the train to Hull on Christmas Eve. I had a lot to think about. I had my list of agents to whom I could write, and the dates of the performances at RADA when they would have the chance of seeing me. Had I not been so excited and pre-occupied, I would have been overwhelmed by not going home to Harrow Street. As it was, it just seemed strange. Fancy getting a bus going east from the centre of Hull and not west towards Fish Dock. Along Holderness, not Hessle Road. Past East Park and Rovers' old ground, Craven Park, to the very edge of the city, and the Longhill housing estate. Two or three stops on the main road through the estate, and I got off and found my way to Duddon Grove. A semicircular row of houses punctuated by passages to the rear. Mother hadn't been wrong about the tall old trees. The estate had been built around them, and they didn't seem at home with it. Number 20 had a bit of garden at the front, brown and bleak. No fencing. I went back way, along the passage between number 20 and next door. A short passage, not shitty and gloomy, and there was the back garden – not claustrophobic like our previous back yard – and also the brick shed Dad had hankered for.

I went through the back door and into the kitchen. It was much bigger than its Harrow Street equivalent, the scullery of number 29. Likewise the sitting room, which doubled as the front room. It had a small square hallway rather than a passage, and upstairs were three bedrooms and, glory of glories, a bathroom. Mine was the smallest bedroom and one of Mother's letters tells me it was papered with nursery paper, which Dad eventually removed, but I don't remember. I only have an impression of 20 Duddon Grove. I was hardly ever there. Ann tells me our old sideboard lived opposite the fireplace and Mother's piano stood between the fireplace and the front window.

What an upheaval it must have been for Mother. Flitting at Christmas. No wonder she was poorly. But it was a chance and they grabbed it. Ann told me that the road was up outside number 29 because the main sewer was being dealt with, making Harrow Street even less attractive than usual. And they thought the fresher air at Longhill would do Mother good.

The last time Mam and Dad flitted I had been four and we only went from one end of Harrow Street to the other. Mother put butter on the cat's paws. It was supposed to ensure that she would stay at number 29 and not run back down Harrow Street to Fern Grove. My beloved Tiddles' precursor (I was too young to be really attached to her), she was black and white and I can remember her skulking beneath the couch, before licking the butter off. The trick seemed to work because she stayed at number 29.

The move from Hessle Road was a hell of a step to take. The Fish Dock area was like a large village within the city and leaving it was really leaving home. I had always intended to leave it, but looking back I can see how fortunate I was to grow up there. It had such a powerful sense of community and common purpose. All the men worked 'on Dock'. People were direct and good humoured. They worked hard and they liked a good time. There were more pubs to the square inch on Hessle Road than anywhere else in the world, it was said, and I bet it was true. And fish and chip shops, I should think. There was no crime to speak of. It was hard for me sometimes when I was little, among the lads in street, who were not so clever as me and a lot rougher, and I had to learn to curb my tongue so as not to get my head thumped. But I managed it. They used to grin at me when I came down Harrow Street in my maroon grammar-school cap. 'How're yuh doin', professor?'

I think I had a tremendous background for an actor. It was the directness of it.

Middle class: 'How lovely to see you.'

Hessle Road: 'What the 'ell's up with you, you look bloody terrible.'

Not that one need use it all the time, of course.

I can remember that there was a lot of bare floor at Duddon Grove. Quite a bit of lino (canvas they used to call it) to be laid. Mam and Dad had let themselves be rushed by Mrs Hotham, and their Christmas was shot to hell.

It was easier now to talk about RADA, because I was excited about the part I had got and the timing of my getting it. All those agents coming to see me! And there was the additional curiosity of not being in Harrow Street. The houses at Longhill were not so jammed together, there was more light and it was cleaner. But it wasn't so homely and it wasn't what Mother had been used to all her life. And two bus rides for Dad to get to work. He would sometimes come home at lunchtime in Harrow Street, but not any more. Nor Ann: Longhill was too far from her office in the city centre. Aunt Alice was there, true. But she was the only one. No kindly Mrs Hinchcliffe next door, or Annie Brooks' shop alongside us. No Mrs Hales' beer off shop for a natter. No Aunt Phyllis calling in for a sub till Friday, and no Grandma Quest to sit there and get on her nerves. Full though I was of my coming opportunity, I had the ominous feeling that she would be very lonely out at Longhill. And I didn't like to think about it.

RADA TERM V
January 1960

[20 Duddon Grove, 18th January 1960]

Dear Tom

WHEN SPRING COMES
AND SO WE CAME TO LONGHILL

It's Sunday. Ann has gone to Hessle with her friend Jeannie. Your
father and me are by the fire and it's *Sunday Night at the Palladium*.
Aunt Al said she had seen a yellow bird in their garden and I
thought hell another story is starting and I haven't wrote last weeks
yet and I was itching to get started but after I had started some
knitting and washed a load of pots writing disappeared. So I am
trying very hard now for it to come back again from wherever it
goes.

I never enjoy it when you go back to London and I said to Ann
'Never mind he'll soon settle down again' and Ann reminded me
that it's here where you find it hard to settle down as you are in
London about 50 weeks in a year and only in Hull about 6 weeks.
People say lovely things. After you had gone I thought it looked
very dull through the window then lights started popping on and
the moon was between the two trees. Someone drew our curtains

but left an opening down the centre and I saw the sky had turned a deep blue and the moon was a pale turquoise. Who should arrive then but Granny and Aunt Al. Aunt Al drew the curtains together. To tell the truth I didn't feel very amiable. Granny had a new coat on and it wasn't on a club she said.

Monday and I don't feel happy but unsettled. Snow had been falling. Ann came home for dinner. 'Where's Geneva?' she asked. 'How the hell should I know' I said. She said she was thinking of writing after a job there. 'Geneva can be anywhere' I said. 'Talk sense' she said, but I felt angry with her. Ann started writing her letter Monday night and your father was painting our bedroom. He has all the house to decorate himself. He went first to bed and when I went up I told him what Ann was doing. 'What about it' he said. 'It's just the way she does things' I said. 'You was married at her age.' I wasn't. It's not that but Hell Geneva. But I got no sympathy.

Wed. washday and my usual walk to shops and I asked Alice when does Spring come. I cooked neck of mutton for tea and baked a cake. Your father was in awkward mood stove in scullery too high and fire too low and he didn't talk all night but went upstairs to paint. Ann's friend Jeannie came after tea with writing paper to write to Geneva. Her family are angry with her she told me. 'Don't let Ann persuade you to go away' I said to Jeannie and I told her I thought Ann could at least have waited till we got settled in this new house. 'It's just the way she does things.' 'Bad wicked Ann' said Ann. 'I wouldn't have bought the new bed either' I said. 'Would I hell. I don't pick £5 notes up in the street.' Father painting the house and then two empty bedrooms, I thought I would take in a lodger. Ann laughed and I didn't want to see the photo she was sending to Geneva. I said to Al next day 'Let Ann skate off to Geneva if she wants why should I care.'

Thursday. I did a good clean up and made a beef pie for tea and put yours away in the dish in pantry. The weather was very cold and the old man tree now has snow in his eye. Your father came home in better mood, weekend was drawing near. After tea Ann and me went upstairs to help your father and Ann planned a colour scheme for her bedroom. All was harmony and Geneva was in the distance.

Fri. Aunt Al and little Susan and her doll carricot came for me to go to Hessle Road. The weather was milder and little Susan liked the bus ride. We stopped off at Ann's office. I wanted her to let your father know I may be home late as I was going to doctors. I was surprised how big Ann's office was. She was taking down shorthand for her boss. Ann was surprised to see me and introduced me to Pauline. I thanked Pauline for sending me flowers when I was ill. 'Won't it be nice for Ann going to Geneva' she said. 'She isn't going' I answered. 'But it's just the thing for her.' 'It isn't that' I said. I felt mad even though Pauline must be a kind person, and thought 'It's a pity Pauline didn't go to Geneva when she met the married man she's living with.' I'm no fool and Pauline mentioned Geneva at the wrong time. One can't be interested in people for 20 year and then drop all thoughts of them.

We continued on to Granny's. I laughed a lot when little Susan started singing in a wobbly high pitched voice 'Torchy' on the bus. Everything was much the same on Hessle Road. Gossip and scandal. 'Fancy Irene So-and-so turned prostitute.' 'No!' Well I felt proud of Ann and how nice she looked taking down shorthand.

Hope you are well and your musical is going well too.

PS. Does my arm ache! Next week I shall write a little each day.

All the two weeks you was home I was looking for the right time to tell you how I got the 'Orange Balloon' title. It was when Alice came to tell me about this house. The first thing that entered the kitchen was little Susan's orange balloon which she had on a stick. And before we moved one of Watson's had an orange balloon in Hales.

Love Mam Dad and Ann

I recently asked Ann how serious she had been about getting a job in Geneva. 'Geneva was only a dream to escape a dull office routine,' she said. 'My initial resentment at Mother's swift discouragement was also about being made to feel guilty for needing a new bed. It soon left me, and I didn't even bother to attend the interview in London. Hessle Road women might have to get used to sons and husbands going away, but not daughters. I went everywhere with her, shared the gossip, visited friends, was even an arm to lean on going to the doctor. As she became more depressed and ill, where else would I be? Geneva? No.

'My real ambition was to become a teacher and this was received with immediate support. "We'll manage," said Mother, "if you want to go to college." But I couldn't then. I didn't have the heart. My wage made such a difference to them.

'I can't remember a time I didn't feel the supporter in the team. I was never expected to bring home trophies or to be the star at the top of the tree. But during her last years I shared her day-to-day struggle, saw Hessle Road through her sharp focus – the actual experience that you only knew, Tom, through her letters. I even got to spend many an hour by the piano with no one to mind if I sang. I shall never forget those years. You missed a lot, Tom.'

Ann went to college as an adult, after she had married Ken and produced two lads, Peter and John. She became a remarkable teacher of young children.

[22nd January 1960]

Dear Tom

WHEN SPRING COMES
CANVAS LAYING

I hope you don't mind me sending back the £1 you sent me, but I arent in need of it and you have lots to do with it. So give it me when you're rich.

Tues. Your father came home in a canvas-laying mood. I went upstairs to help him. Hell! After him measuring wrong and me making suggestions I came downstairs and when he came down to ask was I putting the carpet down I didn't answer I couldn't so he went back up to put the bed up. When I went up later with Ann we both laughed quietly. He had put it up the wrong way round. Ann said what shall you do. But I thought why should I worry about which way the bed is and the wind was blowing and did your father grumble when I couldn't get in the bedroom because the canvas stopped me so he had to get out of bed to let me in. I looked through the bedroom window and thought how tall the trees are when it's windy. I lay awake a long while listening to the wind and thinking how far your father has to go to work.

A lovely bright day, cold, and I didn't mind as I hung out my washing. The sun looked in the front way and it looked in the back way. After tea your father went upstairs to put canvas in the cupboard. I sat on the settee my face was red my chilblains itched and the fire crackled. Then your father came down. 'About this carpet. It's like a shit house this house.' 'I thought you was going to turn the bed round' I said 'and don't shout.' I held my head like an actress. 'You're always at me. I've worked today.' I went on 'The minute you open the door you're looking for something to chew at.' 'Hell I'm working every night' he said. 'Well you shouldn't' I said and wished he could have a week off.

Thurs. Ann went to Aunt Dorries for tea. After tea your father and me went upstairs to lay the carpet, turn the bed round, and the bedroom looks nice. Your father went up to bed first and then came down again. 'I forgot to shave' he said. 'Oh I thought I'd done something' I said. We all laughed. Ann had returned from Aunt Dorries who is coming to see us when the snow goes.

Love Mam Dad and Ann

Don't be angry at me sending the money back.
I hope you meet Paul Scofield.

I love the way Mother deals with Dad's rage, meeting it head on then lancing it. '"Hell I'm working every night" he said. "Well you shouldn't" I said and wished he could have a week off.'

The actor who promised to introduce me to Paul Scofield was called James Maxwell. He had been working with Pat Keene, who was going to play Scofield's daughter in Robert Bolt's *A Man for All Seasons*, due to open in London later in the year. He said he would do his best to introduce me to the Great Man when we went backstage after the show.

I had met James, or Max, as we used to call him, in the previous term when he came to the Vanbrugh theatre to see a production, by John Fernald, of *The Seagull*. He was far more intelligent than anyone teaching at RADA, yet he was a professional actor, not a university professor. He had a wide and effortless knowledge of music, literature and the theatre, and when he talked about acting his approach was perceptive without being intellectual. He wouldn't have liked being thought of as an intellectual, though he couldn't help, by dint of grey matter, being one. He was American, though you would never have thought it. As a youth he had seen Edith Evans acting in New York and realized he had to come to England and become an actor here. He became a huge influence on my life. My favourite of his sayings concerned a shrub he had planted. He felt it didn't have enough light but he knew that, having a tap root, it would not take kindly to being moved. 'It will have to stay where it is,' he said. 'It may have to have a less than perfect life.'

[7th February 1960]

Dear Tom

WHEN SPRING COMES
MOSAIC

Thanks for cheerful letter. It makes me laugh. Ann got a reply from the Geneva job. I've noticed with Ann it's always a case of who's winning. Sometimes it's her (unpleasant) and sometimes it's me by hell.

I minded Susan for Aunt Al for an hour. I took her to Carlines and she wanted some spangles. I didn't buy any because she'd had some sweets. She wouldn't hold my hand to cross the road. I suppose its hard for children to understand why grown ups sometimes give them money and sometimes refuse. So they find out that it isnt always pleasure poor kids.

Sunday. I was wearing my new blouse Ann bought me for Christmas. I'm a bit silly really because I said to your father 'Look at that.' 'What?' I pointed to the cuff of my blouse. 'Doesn't it look nice.' He just looked at me a bit puzzled and no wonder.

Thursday. We had a man Mr Scott call about making us a fender in marble. He brought with him his young son Tom who is deaf and dumb. He is a dark eyed dark haired boy and when Ann offered him an apple he shook his head and made a nasty expression.

Mr Scott seems a nice person and likes his work tiling floors and fireplaces. He also does mosaic work and I told him I would like a fender made of small pieces like mosaic and he said it costs so many pounds a foot. 'I know' I said 'I get such grand ideas.' We are now awaiting the marble fender.

Love Mam Dad and Ann

Shut Up and Sing, set in the East End of London, was written by Caryl Brahms and Ned Sherrin. The music, as I recall, consisted of some traditional folk tunes and some original pieces. Little, thin, squeaky-voiced Ant Bowles was musical director and very good too: disciplined but charming with it, like a clever and authoritative little doll. Everybody loved Ant. He knew we weren't musicians. He made sure we knew when to come in, when to start singing.

> There ain't no flies on Bernie
> Them flies all flies away.
> They flies to all the other blokes
> That Bernie's making pay.

It transpired that Bernie didn't have to do any dancing, for which I was glad. He either sauntered about meaningfully or just stood, and his gang of teddy boys and girls danced round him. Recently incarcerated for his misdeeds, he had returned to rule the roost. It was crucial that I stand still in order to appear powerful, and here I was indebted to our director, Michael Ashton. He didn't equivocate: 'Stand fucking still.' I got the message, and I shall always be grateful to him. He was very sharp, but not frightening. Over a gap of almost forty years, he seems in my memory a bit like a steely version of Larry Grayson. He had been a student at RADA some years before. He told us that the fencing teacher, Mr Froeschlen, used always to refer to him as 'that boy over there in pink'. He used to like to send me up. 'Smile!' he commanded at one moment in rehearsal. I thought for a second or two, then said, 'I don't think I can.' 'Don't think you can. Don't think you can! Wait till you're in Southport rep and the director asks you to do something and you tell him you don't think you can. You might find yourself out of a job.' But he didn't press the point and later on he got his smile.

As Bernie I had my hair in a duck's arse, teddy-boy style, and I combed it a lot. Bernie was proud of his appearance. It was a good part because being the gang leader he was the focus of attention while he was on. Derek Fowlds had the longest part but he had to spend a lot of time commenting on the action and strumming a guitar. (He bore me no grudge.) As the first night approached, I couldn't stifle the feeling that something good was going to happen to me. I can remember a pretty, slender stick of an American girl who played one of Bernie's gang say-ing excitedly, 'Isn't he frightening? Isn't he frightening?' It had never occurred to me that I was, but I didn't argue with her, I just basked. Here we were, putting on a show in the Vanbrugh theatre for the out-side world to see, and I found myself at the heart of it, having a good time. It was like enjoying the excitement of the school play all over again.

Michael Ashton, already in the business, was a great source of inside information. All the theatrical agencies would be sending someone to the show, he told us. We had all written to the better-known ones. One or two sent an acknowledgement, but just to say that they had all the clients they could deal with. Names like Fraser & Dunlop, Peter Crouch, Eric Glass, Essanay Management, Christopher Mann, John Redway, Al Parker and the biggest of all, MCA. 'And there'll be plenty of people from the business.' He found a moment to say quietly in my ear: 'Ian Dallas is coming to the opening.'

'Who's he?'

'He's a playwright. He wrote a play that Albert Finney was in at RADA. He thinks he discovered him.' Then, a bit tartly: 'Don't let him think he's discovered you.'

And I could have been in *Paradise Lost*! I mightn't have been able to stand still in that.

[19th February 1960]

Dear Tom

MOSAIC CONTINUED

After tea Tuesday night there was a knock at the door. It was the man with the fender. Your father jumped off the settee and started hopping about. The man stood with the new fender and your father struggled with the old one. 'We'll get rid of that' he said and stood it in the corner. 'Isn't it nice' Ann said as Mr Scott unwrapped the new one and I rescued your father's piece of orange he'd been eating off the settee cushion. The moment came to place the fender on the hearth. I could see it was a bit short. Mr Scott said 'It's contemporary really.' We all said it was nice and how heavy. Mr Scott said we could fit canvas up to it when we got some. 'How much?' I asked and your father said he'd have to go upstairs. Hell! '£2' Mr Scott said. I paid him and he said there's a lot of work in them fenders and he'd brought it in the firm's car but he shouldn't have. Mr Scott went. 'Fancy going to lavatory just then' I said to your father. 'I can't help it if I have to go,' he said. We all sat looking at the fender. 'He's made a blob' I said. 'He measured it wrong' said your father. Ann said 'I like it. Besides he's got a deaf and dumb son and a wife with asthma and he likes his job' and she propped her feet on the fender. Ann! 'I'd sooner have paid him £2 10s for the right size' I said 'and I bet he could make tomb curbs. I bet he measures the next one right.' Your father said when we get a canvas it will fit up to it, but in the meantime he'd get some brown paint and paint the hearth that shows. I gazed at the fender and felt myself growing depressed and I looked up at the new light shade like a sun shade upside down. 'Ann make a cup of tea will you please. My head aches.'

We shall be thinking of you in your show. It really sounds as though you love it. Can't wait to hear how it goes.

Love Mam Dad and Ann

From Dad [19th February 1960]

Dear Tom

So Hull got through to the second round. Only just by the score, but by all accounts that wasn't a fair reflection of the play. The next round, Keighley away, is no walkover, but if the pack is in form all should be well. Do you fancy Wembley again? [Did I buggery.] Rovers don't seem able to get the lucky breaks that's needed on the field or is it bad management.

Wednesday seems to be a very important day for you and you seem to be very much on edge. I certainly would be and I'm sure I don't seem to worry over things as much as you. At least I don't bite my nails. You cant really with false teeth.

I'm sure if hard work and concentration is any guide you will be a success. But don't forget Tom this is only your first chance, don't expect too much.

As a small boy you could sing and I've always thought you still could if you liked to try. Maybe this is a chance to prove me right. So try and relax. Confidence in yourself I know you've got. Do your best. In my opinion, and I'm sure in others that matter, your best is good.

Love Pop. Would a pint of bitter help.

Dad, remembering how I used to wow them when I was little, was right to seem confident. The opening of *Shut Up and Sing* passed off without any hitches. I sauntered and stood meaningfully and sang my little songs on cue. Mr Fernald was pleased, Caryl Brahms and Ned Sherrin were pleased and Michael Ashton was pleased. Ian Dallas, as predicted, came backstage. He was a charming and loquacious Scot and he didn't beat about the bush: 'You're fantastic. You're going to be the next Albert Finney.'

Within a day or so the 'C' pigeonhole was filled with letters from all the leading agencies wanting to sign me up, even though I still had another term and a half at RADA. They all said how impressed they had been and would I like to go and see them for a chat. They would very much like to help me. One letter went so far as to say I was the fortunate possessor of something called 'natural timing'. I quietly asked Thaw what he thought it meant. 'Well, kid, I think it means that you've got a good sense of timing – you know – getting laughs and that, and it's . . . er . . . natural.'

I have always thought of that little musical at RADA as the greatest success I have ever had. Up till then my progress at RADA had not been serene. I had arrived there in a nervous state after my last grim year at UCL and hadn't generally been considered West End material. Too fidgety, too emotional, too uncontrolled. But suddenly I was discovered. For the first time I felt certain that I had been right all along in wanting to become an actor. That I would become one. That my dream of being an artist was going to be fulfilled. And it was a wonderful feeling. I couldn't wait to write to Mother.

[2nd March 1960]

Dear Tom

PATHS

Sunday your father was laying a path and I was thinking changes seem to be in the air. First you and I'm so pleased your musical was a success. You have worked so hard I think for so many years since you were 11. Then Ann has got herself a job at Reckitts where she will be a secretary. The money is more I think and the firm look after the employees. Your father is also having his stores re-organised for him. He came home one day last week he had hit his head on a nail and a policeman had stopped him as he was getting off the bus near Osborne St. He wanted to examine his little sail cloth bag but all that was in it was his overalls because he had to take them to Stoneferry the next day to find out how their stores are run. (Your father put lot of bricks underneath some concrete slabs so the path is rather high. Never mind.)

Then Monday morning! All your talk of films and someone with an interest in you. You thought it was going to be difficult to get someone interested in you and it seems to be in reverse. I am very impatient to hear how you go on.

I went round to Alice's Tuesday morning. We had a bus ride to town to go to the gas offices. I had to find out who was paying a gas bill in Mrs Hothams name. Remember it was her we exchanged houses with. We was trying not to pay it although we did want the gas fire fitting and Mrs Hotham didn't intend to pay as she had left the house. What a lot of underhand thoughts and goings on over a bloody £1 bill. Your father didn't seem at all happy on Tuesday night and he kept looking at me with a frown. 'Stop looking at me like that' I said 'you wrinkle faced bugger.' I felt mad.

Thursday came. The weather was very cold and sullen as if we was living in a sunless world. Your father came home from work with a pile of comics for Mrs Sole's (next door) little boy who has been in hospital. 'The man rom the gas board has been and I've signed for the gas fitting' I said. Hell! 'You've too much money paying Mrs Hotham's bill,' he said. 'She'll be laughing at you.' 'No she won't' I answered 'because she can't laugh.' We had our tea in silence. Fish patties. Then Ann came home with a lovely red suitcase they had bought her at work because she's leaving. She gave your father an ounce of bacca and me some chocolate and she starts her new job on Monday.

Well Tom I do hope you are keeping well and often wish I could get you a meal ready or something. We are all very pleased about you being a success. I suppose you have signed on with good agents and I hope they look after you well. Don't forget to write us all the news because we seem so far from all that is happening to you.

Love Mam Dad and Ann

From Dad [2nd March 1960]

Dear Tom

We are all pleased with the contents of your letter re your successful show. Anyone can talk after the event but I knew you could and would prove a hit.

I can well imagine your feelings when you say 7 or 8 agents

would like to sign you up. That producer must also like your style.

But the fact remains the same Tom luck must play a big part in your future success, and I think my head would be in a whirl wondering what to do for the best. But I think you have now got your foot on the first rung. Don't you?

Love Pop

After asking around among the staff and students at RADA I elected to go and see three of the agents who had written to me. It was quite a thing to have to ask 'Which agent shall I choose?' We all felt it would be a terrific thing to get an agent, yet here was I, still at RADA, and spoilt for choice.

The leading agency was then called MCA. Something Creative Something. Initials rather than names were, I thought, imposing but impersonal. Albert Finney was with them, I discovered. I went to see Julian Belfrage, their theatre man, at the Hyde Park Corner end of Piccadilly. I also went to Soho to the offices of Fraser & Dunlop. Jimmy Fraser was white-haired and very Scottish, perched on the corner of his desk and smilingly telling me that I mustn't take too much notice of the fuss being made of me and that I should be packed off to a theatre in the provinces to learn my trade. That's what Albert had done. He was quite right, of course, but I didn't take it on board – for a reason that will shortly become clear.

And I went to see John Cadell (Simon's father) of the Christopher Mann agency in a large and impressive office overlooking Hyde Park. He introduced me to Brian Maller, who was very genial and looked after the film side of things, and a jolly, round lady whose name I don't recall who dealt with television jobs. Three of them to dance attendance on me.

Ian Dallas, the king maker, invited me to a cocktail party somewhere in Chelsea with sophisticated-looking people. I had never been to a cocktail party before. Many a bottle party but never a cocktail party. No bottle required, just turn up. He introduced me to the people holding their cocktails. 'He's going to have a huge impact, just like Albert before him.' And nobody said, 'Pull the other one.'

My pal Thaw christened me Golden Bollocks. But then he was stuck in *Paradise Lost*.

[20th March 1960]

Dear Tom

It's Sunday morning 5 and 20 past 8 and I'm on my first cup of tea. (I shall back 'Tea's Fund' in the Grand National next week.) I'm sorry I'm late answering your letter but sometimes I feel I can't write for some reason, maybe I'm lazy. Maybe all your news is rather bewildering and I can't keep up with it. I mean one can't very well tell people Our Tom may be in a film with Dirk Bogarde because they look at one suspiciously. People always want lots of proof and take a lot of convincing. I feel I have a hell of a job making people understand me and I think they need glasses on or a hearing aid. I honestly can't imagine you getting the part, not because I don't think you're good enough because I think you're on equal terms with anyone else who may be after the part. You're highly intelligent, young and very good looking we think. I would love you to get the part so you can buy yourself some good clothes Saville Row. I've been wondering about you every day, wondering if you would send a quick letter if you were successful.

Your father has had to go to work today. He had to get the 5 to 7 bus. But he doesn't mind, he said he felt so fit he could walk. Hell! He didn't sound so good on Thursday teatime when he came in from work. He opened the door. 'Couldn't you sweep them bloody cinders up off that path' he said as he entered. Was I surprised. I admit I had been with Aunt Al visiting in the morning but I made up for it when I returned. I cleaned the front place and finished the other half of the scullery (I do one half on washday). I made a beef pie, apple pie, spring cabbage and everything. He didn't speak all night. I swept up the cinders in the dark even though Ann said 'Don't you.' What made him in this humour I puzzled. Was it because I was going to have a bath and he wanted one, was it because he hadn't got a ticket for the match or was it because he is having a hell of a job taking the nursery paper off in your bedroom.

I said to Ann if he talks on Friday I shall tell him to sod off. (Third cup.)

Fri. Al and me and little Susan went down Hessle Road. It was Aunt Barbara's birthday, 30. Granny had bought her a large scented card in a box. There was a houseful. Aunt Barbara, Granny, Aunt Al, me and little Susan and John came, and the dog. There was plenty of high spirits. Barbara was going out to Continental in the evening. Bill had bought her a marvellous birthday card which said things like he couldn't believe his luck. Alice said it was Jack's birthday in the week. Granny bought him a packet of Park Drive she couldn't afford. Granny is always hard up. She had bought the magazine 'She' to see if your photo was in it so I gave her 1/- for it. Your photo was in although I was a bit doubtful about it being you, but I could tell it was your hand holding a cigarette. You looked annoyed. It was an article about RADA. I went on road with Granny and in Woolworths I noticed her admiring mother's day gifts and I felt a headache coming on. Your father said Granny thinks the world owes her something. He doesn't think it owes him anything. I aren't sure about me but I'm sure I don't begrudge you or Ann anything. (Tea cold.)

Ann and me went in town. I got a coat from Bladons. I hate buying things, I'm never sure and even when the assistant was telling me how nice the coat fit me I didn't know if I liked it and I didn't like her very much. But I did need a coat that looks like a bloody coat your father said. It's grey. I didn't fancy oatmeal or blue or large check. Anyhow it isn't ugly. [I had told her the garish blue coat she got cheap from Jack Stathers' sister was ugly.] It's fine worsted. We looked at carpets in Bladons and I always feel I take up too much of the assistants time looking at beautiful carpets I aren't going to buy such as Wilton £40 in a traditional pattern. Anyhow the young man wrote and gave me some prices on his card which are still high. I said to him 'I hear you are having an open night tonight.' He didn't know whose idea it was, Saturday night and all. Ann bought some curtaining for her bedroom from Shenkers. It's heavy contemporary. Isnt it dear I kept on saying. I always find myself wondering how much the article's really worth after everyone has been paid wages and the rent's paid. There are so many assistants in shops like Hammonds doing nothing and haven't they got queer figures I said to Ann and believe me some have faces made up like clowns – eye shadow and colours round their eyes and even pink hair. I'm not old fashioned but I don't like it. Screwed up faces, eyes like cats. Loads of leg showing and not much honesty, too much posing. Maybe I am old fashioned and matronly and I don't like it. Me I mean. Well Tom I think the sun is trying ever so hard to break through. But all week it's been a cold stare. I thought how your letter last week was like the orange balloon the rag man held in his hand 'Not blown up' and when the little girl held her hand out for it the rag man said 'You can't have it until you fetch some rags.' I wrote this in a letter I started on Monday, but I burnt it. Well Tom I'm finishing the first chapter called 'When Spring Comes' because spring comes tomorrow on your father's birthday, bless him.

Love Mam Dad and Ann

After taking advice from John Fernald and Ellen Pollock, one of our teachers, I joined the Christopher Mann agency. John Cadell's mother Jean had been a distinguished actress, and this was thought to be a good thing. The theatre was in his blood. The biggest agency, MCA, was rejected as being 'too big'.

When I went to the swanky office to sign on the dotted line, John Cadell suggested a suit would be useful for interviews and auditions. Peter Barkworth had also told us that if we were ever fortunate enough to get a West End job we would need a suit for rehearsals. Since I didn't have one, I asked Thaw and Whitehead if they would mind coming with me to help me get one. We went to Burton's in Tottenham Court Road and I tried one on. After considerable reassurance from them as to its merits, I came away eleven quid the poorer. Looking at my new acquisition back at Highbury Crescent I wasn't at all sure that the tweedy grey thing either fitted or suited me. I felt it wasn't a patch on the donkey jacket that had by then replaced my duffel coat as my look, and that Thaw and Whitehead, their minds filled with *Paradise Lost*, hadn't been concentrating.

After the thrill of the musical it wasn't at all easy to concern myself with our next production at RADA, a Greek comedy called *Alcestis* in which I played Admetus – or was it the other way round? I had got a bit ahead of myself.

There was too much excitement outside RADA for me to be able to concentrate properly on an incomprehensible Greek play. Tina Currie and I did a scene from it for Peter Barkworth – and he didn't know what to make of it either. He congratulated me on my success in the musical, however, and I think he was pleased that I had finally managed to stand still on the stage.

Brian Maller sent me off for two interviews. Dirk Bogarde was to star in a film in Spain that summer, called *The Singer not the Song*, and Brian arranged for me to meet the director, Roy Ward Baker. Since the part was of a young Spanish lad, I didn't think it was really right for me, but I was thrilled to have something to tell Mother that I thought would excite her. Roy Ward Baker was very amiable and I was pretty full of myself in spite of my new suit. I pointed out to him that I looked young for my age, which he can't have failed to notice, and that if he used me he would get someone who looked very young but was in fact a comparatively old hand. Suddenly I had become confident. Anyway, I was tickled to be going to offices in Wardour Street to see a film director.

My second interview was with either Basil Dearden or Michael Relph, who were a very successful British producer/director combination. Looking back, I don't know which of them I saw, and the name of the film eludes me, but it was a contemporary subject and I therefore resolved to go unsuited, as myself. I wore my faithful drip-dry shirt, its collar peeping out over my crewneck pullover, and my donkey jacket. This was my look. Pretty cool, I thought.

Basil Dearden or Michael Relph didn't. I can't remember a word that was said during the interview, but it wasn't as lively as the first one. Whichever one of them it was, he was unimpressed by my scheme of being myself. 'I do think he might have worn a suit,' he told Brian Maller. 'Who does he think he is?'

I don't know whether I told Mother about this interview, but I certainly told her about the first one. And about another possibility I had heard of.

[31st March 1960]

Dear Tom

IT'S NEARLY APRIL

I wonder if you know anything definite yet. It would be nice to get
the film part and go to Spain for 5 weeks. I have seen in the papers
a photo of a girl age 23 taking the part of a 15 year old girl in the
same film. French I think she is and married. I can understand you
are in a muddle and that Mr Fernald can be of help to you. The
thing I haven't to breathe a word about sounds great. No one would
understand if I told them things like 'The Seagull' and The Old
Vic. I have read 'The Seagull' once. There is a young man who
wants to write and shoots himself at the end. I bet that's your part. I
am sure you would play it beautifully. I remember the stage setting
and there is a lake. I will ask Ann to get the play out of the library
again. I'm glad the Greek Plays went well. Why should the Vic
Company's actors object to you? You won't be a RADA student in
the summer you know. If the film part falls through and there
doesn't seem to be any quick TV work you must come home. But I
know you must make your own arrangements. Money is a problem.
Maybe your agents will understand this and get you a job, but we
would like you to come home as well.

There's a bird outside singing beautifully. The weather is more
spring like but it keeps cold. Your father isnt at work today (Sunday
Morning). He wasn't very well in the week. He would love a 5 day
week. I still wonder if the journey is too much for him. The bird
isnt singing now. Easter is less than 2 weeks away.

Thursday who should arrive but Uncle George and Aunt Joan.
She said she wouldn't like to live up here. I said 'I know what you
mean but one doesn't have to have a light on all day and it's
cleaner.' They went about four and I continued my work. I noticed
when I talked to them I didn't seem to have time to drink my coffee
and had to say 'let me have a drink before I go on'. I bet I'm a bore.
Although your father wasn't at work Saturday morning he still had
to find a job to do, such as tidying out the shed. When I looked
through the window at him he was somewhere near the rooftop.

Then he thought he ought to do the gas cupboard out but I put my foot down. We want a bit of peace I said. We went out for a drink Saturday night. First at The Dart then we walked to the Ganstead (between The Dart and the Ganstead that's us.) Was it windy! But very fresh. Later I played hell because your father left me downstairs falling asleep in the chair. I wouldn't leave anybody falling asleep in a chair downstairs at night I told him. But he just laughed. Was I mad. So when I took him a cup of tea in the morning I left it where he'd have to get out of bed to get it and he looked at me with one eye.

I'm looking forward to all your news and I'm daring the bird to start singing again so I can write it down but it wont. The stoves gug gugging and your father's singing 'Why because I love you' but no bird.

We saw the play 'The Birthday Party'. I think the author is very clever. I read in the paper he has two plays on in London. Royal Court Theatre.

Love Mam Dad and Ann

I wasn't offered the part in *The Singer not the Song*. I had known it wasn't for me, just nice to write to Mother about it. I have since glimpsed it on television. Dirk was clad in black leather from top to bottom.

It was *The Seagull* that was for me. I knew it the moment I heard about it, even before it was certain that the Old Vic were going to do it. It's the only prescience I've ever experienced in the theatre. When I had been to see Julian Belfrage at MCA he had asked me what parts I would like to play. I told him I would love to play Constantin in *The Seagull*. 'The Old Vic might be doing it later this year,' he said. 'It'll either be that or *The Cherry Orchard*.' I guessed which one it would be, and for some unknown reason I thought I'd be in it. What I didn't learn then, because he didn't know, was that it would be directed by John Fernald, RADA principal and my great supporter.

My reward at RADA for the success I had enjoyed in the musical, if it was a reward, was that in my final term I would get to play the part of Faust, in Goethe's version, part one. Part one was plenty long enough.

In the last week of my penultimate term the jolly, round lady from Christopher Mann took me in her car to be checked out for the part of a van driver's mate in an episode of a series called *Inside Story*, about the various residents of a block of flats. The episode was called 'A Present for Penny'. I can't remember who did the checking, but I got the job. My last-ever vacation job, and my first engagement as a professional actor. The plot involved something having to be delivered to a girl called Penny, played by Joanna Dunham, with whom I had acted some years before in *Dark of the Moon* at UCL while she was still at RADA. Small world, we agreed, and she gave me more of her lovely smile than she had before. I assumed that was out of respect for my having got the part of Faust, but maybe I was just getting easier to smile at.

I was surprised at how humdrum professional rehearsals were. It wasn't much of a script, and the actors didn't appear to be greatly bothering themselves. The director had to tell them off because they didn't know their lines. I was word perfect. I only had two. I was the mate of the van driver delivering the present, whatever it was, and the van driver was Arthur Lowe. I spent most of the time in the rehearsal hall with him. He seemed a canny old thing. Very much a pro. Television had transformed his life, he told me. No more traipsing round the provinces for next to nothing, and all the work he wanted.

I met him again many years later after his huge success in *Dad's Army*. Did he remember that I had played mate to his van driver? He did. Perhaps because I had had plenty to say for myself. I was keen that the cast of 'Present for Penny' should know that van drivers' mates were not my usual line of work, and that I was about to play Faust. By Goethe. Part one.

After 'Present for Penny' was recorded at Granada studios in Manchester I had time before the start of my last term at RADA to go home to Hull. The show was aired a couple of days later on a Sunday, and we all watched it. There was not much to be said about it. My appearance was little more than a walk-on but paid me a few pounds. More than I would have got helping with the mail. We all laughed at what I thought was my gauche appearance, and Mother cut out the cast list from the *TV Times* and put it in her purse.

In my pocket diary for 1960 there's an entry for Monday 2 May. 'With Mother all day.'

That was a lovely time to share with her. I had had my great success at RADA, I already had an agent, there was a great deal of interest in me from the profession outside RADA, I had done my little job on the telly, and I still had another term as a student actor. I felt unconditionally happy for the first time since leaving school and she loved it. It took her mind off being unhappy at having moved house. I tried to reassure her that they had been right to move, especially with summer coming. But I wasn't at all convinced. It just wasn't as homely as mucky, scruffy Harrow Street. She was so worried that it was too far for Dad to go to work, and she longed for him to get Saturday mornings off.

'With Mother all day.' Hardly fulsome, but I wouldn't have written it if the day hadn't meant a great deal to me. I sang her some of the songs from *Shut Up and Sing*, and her face lit up with pleasure. It felt like days we had spent together in Harrow Street years before. When I left the following day to get the bus to Paragon Station my eyes filled with tears. I wasn't aware that she was ill, but she looked so lost and lonely waving from the front door of 20 Duddon Grove.

RADA TERM VI
May 1960

Dear Tom

THE TREE

I hope you are well and Faust is coming along alright. As I said to Aunt Al if it wasn't for an ache in my back and my arm has gone a bit queer I think Ive overreached it and my head goes a bit funny I arnt so bad really. On my way back from Als I met two women who live near us. One I call 'The woman who smiles' and the other 'The woman with a nice garden'. The woman with the nice garden said she could hear you singing when you was home and both of them felt sorry for me when I looked through the window because I had no one to talk to. I said 'Oh I'm alright I go to Alice's and Ive plenty to do.'

I was sweeping outside back way when her with all the bairns told me some one was at the door. I went. Two strapping young men stood there dressed in new style overcoats and very healthy looking and tall. 'We're ministers can we step inside' they said. 'I'm sorry, I'm busy.' I felt mad. 'We know' they went on 'but . . .' 'Not today, I'm sorry' I said feeling angry. Ministers. A pity they hadn't nothing else to do.

Believe it or not our back garden is looking quite neat and tidy. The potatoes are coming up in rows also the onions cauliflowers and lettuce. Uncle Jack Stathers sent us 8 outdoor tomato plants and we have 4 climbing strawberry plants with two poles and wire to encourage them up. Then we have a very small lawn big enough for a bit of sun bathing, also some sweet peas are struggling along one side as well as the brave grass. Your father likes being outside though he wont admit it he says it has to be done. The leaning tree has got one eye covered up now and reminds me of a lady's feathered fan swaying about and the other tree is looking greener. We seem to do a lot of falling asleep I think it's the air.

A letter has just arrived from Hilda and Bill. They saw you in 'Present for Penny' and enjoyed it. You had a lot more camera than they thought youd have or they would have told a lot more people. On Hessle Road a few told me about seeing you on TV including Florrie Watson Annie Brooks Mrs Randall, Mrs Jenneson.

I have seen three orange balloons this week the rag man had one on his cart yesterday. His cart has motor wheels and the little man wears his cap on an angle and his small horse is very quiet and I like to see it. I don't think orange balloons is very clever but its just a normal function of the human brain to make patterns of things. Your father is relaying the concrete path to keep him busy and when he waters the garden he nearly floods the house out.

I want you to know that we realise you have plenty on. So look after yourself and don't worry too much.

Love Mam Dad and Ann

One of the reasons for the move to Longhill was the garden with its 'brave grass'. Our claustrophobic, north-facing back yard in Harrow Street hardly ever saw the sun. Its tiny patch of earth was never home to any plants, was just a tip. Not one single occupant of Harrow Street ever grew anything at home. One or two, including Grandad Quest, had an allotment out near Gypsyville. Gladioli were his speciality. I can remember them being proudly brandished around their living quarters. Massive, I thought they were. Not at all delicate. Mother didn't like them very much.

[29th May 1960]

Dear Tom

RED GERANIUMS

It's Sunday morning and your father has had to go to work. [Dad sometimes had to work Sunday mornings when the paint store needed to be open.] I hope you are still coping. It's a lovely sunny day. Ann is going to plant some red geraniums today. She bought them for your father because he likes them.

I was trying to compare Longhill to Hessle Road this morning laid in bed. People on Hessle Road talk all the time about people. Everybody you meet talks about somebody else. I suppose it's because they have nothing else to occupy their minds. In Longhill, although I suppose this talk goes on, people have their gardens to attend to and look at.

Fri. on Hessle Road and the weather being fine I heard heaps of yarns. One woman said how a young woman down Harrow Street was having her husband up for rape. I remember when that young woman got married she acted in this strange getting all glamoured up way and I said 'Now I'll wait and see what happens in this story' and so the next part is 'She's having her husband up for rape.' They have one baby. And that's Hessle Road, stories all the time. Longhill isn't so alive as Hessle Road. But there's more sunlight and fresh air and gardens. One discovers where 'I drank in the air' came from and 'sunwashed' and things like that.

Sometimes after tea and the sun is disappearing, the sky has the most beautiful colours. I looked through Ann's bedroom window one day last week. The sky looked marvellous over to the fields and I noticed a row of houses coloured pale blue, in front of the houses was a green grass square, then the dark roofs on the pale blue houses and over the tops of the roofs green trees popped up of different shapes and sizes and then the sky in a grey violet blue pattern, behind the grey violet blue flame colours sprang up and a man was digging one of the gardens of the pale blue houses. I thought it was a pretty picture really. But I aren't good at describing things like this but would sooner write things like the little boy would insist on carrying his coconut in his duffle coat hood and didn't want kissing for doing so.

The Sunday papers has just come through the letter box and I forgot to steep the peas. I've been wondering this week if as an artist one has to learn to appreciate feelings other than those of say security and comfort. I should say one has to recognise all sorts of feelings including not nice ones as part of living. Well Tom, your father will soon be home. I thought I would just send you a bit of Sunday morning.

Love Mam Dad and Ann

[16th June 1960]
Dear Tom

Tues. No letter and so on until Fri. Al and me went down Hessle Road to the Council House Office to pay Als rent. They write it down in red ink. I don't go near the counter with Alice as I'm afraid I may say 'Why do you use red ink when the rent is paid early – Friday instead of Monday?' and the man would be very surprised also everyone else, or the man behind the desk would say something sensible like 'We use red ink all the time and every day.' That's the trouble, sometimes I think I'm very clever and then I find I'm not so clever as someone who I think is stupid. It's very puzzling.

While waiting for Al not too near the counter an old lady started talking to me. Hell, they pick me out and I'm glued. She said her daughters were scattered all over Hull and she would like a pensioners bungalow near one daughter and there is one empty. She said she was more lonely than she had ever been all her life. A week ago she had to have her cat taken away and she missed it terribly.

She had had the cat 10 years. It was like a friend to her and used to warm its hands near the fire resting them on the fireguard and it talked to her. Her voice sounded trembly and I kept on nodding my head and picturing the scene with this cat resting on the fireguard and her walking in the room out of the back kitchen to talk to it. I knew she wouldn't get that bungalow from them using red ink, but I didn't say she wouldn't.

I shall certainly be thinking of you Saturday and I hope you feel strong enough for Faust. I'm sure you will put as much into Faust as anyone else is capable of.

Love Mam Dad and Ann

Mother must have wondered what on earth 'Faust' was. She knew it was very long. I definitely told her that much. John Thaw was one of my Mephistopheles, Geoffrey Hinsliffe the other. I had Faust to myself, such a favourite had I become. John and I were both very fond of our director, Milo Sperber. He was tiny, mid-European and very enthusiastic. He loved wagging his finger. We liked to talk about acting with him. He said that when I didn't know what to do I brooded, like Paul Scofield. It was meant as a criticism, but being compared to my hero, even negatively, was, I thought, praise indeed. And Milo, who played bits and pieces on television, would sermonize on how much film stars used to get for doing next to nothing. 'Remember that,' and he wagged his finger at me. He thought I might be discovered sooner than was good for me. He wasn't far out.

Fortunately I had Clifford Turner, our voice teacher, to keep things in proportion. Once when I had him to myself I did a bit of Faust. He wasn't impressed. 'You don't breathe, Thomas.' I was taken aback. Hadn't every agent in London wanted to sign me up? Hadn't I been described as the next Albert Finney – at a cocktail party? 'Mr Turner, if I don't breathe why have I been given this enormous part?' I thought that would take some answering. But no. 'I'm not saying you're not an interesting boy, Thomas. I'm saying you don't breathe.'

[27th June 1960]

Dear Tom

SMALL-CAPS-HEADER

GUARDIAN OF THE SAND

Have been wondering about you all the week and how the play is
going because I realise that a lot depends on all this 'Faust'. Maybe
when I hear from you again and how you're doing I shall feel more
settled because I'm buggered if I've felt settled all week. I was going
to write about when your father made the path the day you started
'Faust'. I thought how hot you must have been that Saturday
afternoon.

The man who brought the concrete mixture left the sand on the
roadside near the steps. So you can just imagine me as Ann would
say 'Guardian of the Sand' until your father came home an hour
later. He borrowed a barrow to move the sand and by the time he
started this job with Ann following with the red sweeping brush on
her shoulder there were about 20 bairns playing with the sand.
Your father worked and sweated all the afternoon and I was
handing him buckets of water to mix the stuff with. Was it hot.
Anyhow your father made a success of it.

Monday I couldn't open your letter quick enough and felt very
impatient for still more news but I think you must have been very
good if the producer and Mr Fernald thought you were.

Ive had the idea gardens should be watered every night and Ann
was shirking it and going out. Of course I was wrong. Its been a
long time since we had a weekly climax.

Sometimes there is too much trying not to tread on each others
toes among all of us. Anyhow this week we all gave each other a big
piece of our minds and cleared the air. I hope you are well Tom and
will be home before the sweet peas are finished.

Love Mam Dad and Ann

From Dad

Dear Tom

At last I've got round to writing a few lines. What about. Well I've been pretty busy in the garden and it now looks neat and tidy. I've laid a concrete path. Was it hard work. Practically everything we have planted has been a success up to now. I'm hoping to be eating our own potatoes next week.

I think you'll remember that for many years I've been trying to get a five day week at work. Every other trade on the Dock had it but us. When the working week was reduced from 44 to 42 hours I thought it was time we saw about it for us. I, as always, did the spade work, saw the Union Official and arranged a meeting which only 3 men and myself attended. But anyhow our application for a 42 hour 5 day week was granted. Beautiful. But wait a minute. Our manager said it didn't affect the staff and tried to make out I was on the staff and the store must be open on a Saturday. Of course when I told him I didn't get paid when I was off work, I couldn't be regarded as staff, my hours and conditions were the same as the outside workmen, our words heated up. So I had to get the managing Director's view on the matter.

So now the position is I work a 44 hour week, turn out Saturdays, and am put on a weekly wage. Which means I shall get an increase of 15/- per week and be paid for time off. About 2 months ago I asked for a raise only for myself and got 2/- per day. So in 2 month my wages have increased from £9. 4s. to £10. 10s. Not bad but I would love to be off Saturdays. A bit ironical but what can you do.

Enough of my troubles. By now you must be fed up with doing Faust. It must be a long tedious job, and if the weather is like it is here, bloody hot. Still it's got to be done and I'm sure you are making a success of it. Anyhow hoping to see you and hear all about it soon.

Love Pop

Their move to Longhill, with the bus rides that it involved, made Dad's longing for a five-day week more intense. But he ended up having to work even longer hours. Typical of him to try to be stoical about it. Mother wasn't. It didn't help with her unsettled feeling. Just as well that she had all that was happening to me to take her mind off it.

Faust was the main event of my last term at RADA, and I have to say I found it a bit of a traipse. The weather was warm and the text impenetrable. We did it for only a week or so, but it seemed longer. I think John had a jollier time as Mephistopheles and, moreover, his load was shared with Geoffrey Hinsliffe.

The scenery consisted mainly of scaffolding on a revolve, which we had to push round by hand. There was quite a bit of pushing, but I always thought one setting on the revolve looked pretty much like another. Scaffolding. Milo and Mr Fernald were pleased enough, and here we get back to the main plot. For not only was the Old Vic Company going to do *The Seagull*, which I had guessed, but I discovered that John Fernald was going to direct it. This encouraged me even more in my conviction that Constantin was for me, and I awaited the summons. It didn't come, and I kept bumping into former students on their way to audition for the part. I thought this was odd, so powerful had been my premonition. I was, however, invited to a general audition at the Old Vic, and along I went.

Michael Benthall, who ran the Vic, asked me what I would like to perform. 'How all occasions do inform against me,' I told him. It was my favourite speech. Though I seemed to have kissed goodbye to Constantin I was excited at being allowed on the stage of the Old Vic. At school I had got Harcourt-Williams' *Old Vic Saga* from the library, and loved reading about the demigods who had performed there. Gielgud, Olivier, Richardson, Guinness. It was the first theatre I went to in London. One and sixpence in the gallery. After I had spoken my soliloquy Michael Benthall asked me to follow him to his office. He invited me to sit in the chair across the desk from him and after a preamble during which he said he'd been to see me in *Faust* he uttered the immortal words: 'You can play Constantin in *The Seagull*. But not with those teeth.'

The Lord He giveth and the Lord He taketh away.

My head spun. I had been right all along! As for my teeth, so what? I knew they were irregular. I had been told so often enough. I straight away assured him that I would get something done about them, and he told me John Fernald knew of a suitable dentist. I imagine that my playing Constantin was John Fernald's idea and that Benthall had agreed to it provided I was tidied up a bit. I was too excited to care and anyway I rather fancied the idea of being improved upon. I didn't know what I was in for.

Michael Benthall went on to explain the nature of my contract. After four weeks' rehearsal, *The Seagull* would play for a week at the Edinburgh Festival and then for four weeks at the Old Vic. Thereafter I would become a junior member of the company. I would 'play and understudy as cast'. I wasn't guaranteed any more parts, but he said that several parts in the season had yet to be cast and there was every chance I would get one or two of them. And I would be paid fifteen pounds a week. Good money. I wrote and told Mam, Dad and Ann of my triumph as soon as I could get hold of some paper, an envelope and a stamp.

[29th June 1960]

Dear Tom

31459

Received your news Tuesday and was very pleased indeed. You have worked very hard and deserve what you have got. Your contract came today so your father is posting it in morning. I do hope you will be very happy with the Old Vic Company. You really wanted this part and I'm sure you will do it very well.

As you will see by the number at the top we have now got a phone, at least Ann has. [Ann organized and paid for the installation of the phone.] The first person she rang was Wendy. [She's still ringing her.] Wendy has been ill. She told Wendy about your news and how very much you wanted this part. She said you had had an audition at the Old Vic and the director came to see you in Faust and that clinched it.

I remember Ann Bell in a French play. She is very pretty and a good actress. Tony Britton I have heard of but not Dame Judith Anderson. All this sounds very interesting but I hope having a phone wont be the end of writing a letter. Although I take a while lately to get started writing. I'm sure there are heaps of things all the time waiting to be written down. I've felt a lot better this week, more settled, but somehow can feel angry about my surroundings. I'm like you say, temperamental.

Your father is quite cheered about you and told Uncle Dan and a few friends. I don't feel as if anyone really understands how well you have done, even us. I'm now an actors mother and when Ann was talking to Wendy on the phone sat on stairs she told Wendy we, your father and me, wasn't really having any holidays but your news had altered this and we would be visiting you. Me sat near the fire suddenly felt as if she was talking about someone elses parents, say some of those that used to go to Kingston when I first went and all had fashionable hats on and in the front row VIP. I don't like the feeling but I think I can live with it.

Love Mam Dad and Ann

I was pleased to find out about the phone. I didn't have to write home any more. It had so often been a struggle to find something to say that was worthy of her. I'm glad one of the last letters I wrote had such good news for them.

Back at RADA in Mr Fernald's office, he said he was delighted that I was going to play Constantin for him, and that Arkadina, Constantin's mum, would be played by Dame Judith Anderson, who was coming over from America where she now lived. 'She's one of the best actresses in the world, so you'll have something to live up to, won't you?' he said with a smile. She was best-known as Laurence Olivier's housekeeper in *Rebecca*. Ann Bell, who had played Nina a year before at RADA, was to do so again, and Tony Britton was Trigorin.

Mr Fernald arranged for me to see his dentist in Wimpole Street and said RADA would pay half the cost and lend me the other half. The going rate turned out to be £80.

The teeth alongside my eye teeth (known, I was to learn, as laterals) were set back, which isolated my eye teeth and made them seem very prominent. Like a little wolf. That was the main effect. In fact all my front teeth were a bit of a jumble, having formed themselves into two rows at the top and two at the bottom, cleverly intertwined.

It cannot be said that I gave my eye teeth in order to get my beloved part, though they were greatly reduced in size, but, on Thursday, 30th June 1960, I did give my laterals. I hadn't had a tooth pulled since childhood and the hated Coltman Street Clinic. I was astonished at the force required to yank them out. They were deeply embedded in that ridge that figured so much in Mr Turner's diction tuition. No going back now, and the sweat broke out on my forehead. I felt sick. The dentist's next coup was to remove the nerves from my central teeth, pink they were, and cut them down to gum level. Then he drilled away at my eye teeth, though he left them alive. He made considerable inroads into my lower front teeth, too, took his impressions, declared himself satisfied, and sent me packing with two huge plastic caps filled with white stuff to protect my now reduced eye teeth from the elements. To protect *me* from the elements there was nothing. I looked grotesque. Dazed, I staggered back to RADA. We were rehearsing *The Knight of the Burning Pestle*, by Beaumont and Fletcher, the last show I did there. Ellen Pollock was directing us. 'You poor child,' she said when she saw me, and I fled home to Mother.

I was stunned by what had happened. I was about to start work at the Old Vic, in a leading role, and a butcher had removed my front teeth. Any dentist properly qualified to do the work wouldn't have sent me packing without some temporary replacement for what he had removed. Wouldn't have made me feel so shocked. I felt as though I had let him cut off my hand. Back at home Mam and Dad did what they could to alleviate my distress. They reminisced about when Dad had had all, yes all, his teeth removed when he was nineteen, but I was hardly listening.

'Hope dies last,' say the Russians. The butcher had removed or reduced my six upper front teeth. On my return visit he replaced three of them with his handiwork. Though he was to stick in the other three two days later, I couldn't wait to ask my fellow students what they thought of the new me. Anyway, I was supposed to be rehearsing. The job being only half completed, aesthetic judgement cannot have been easy. Thaw got the worst of it. He was very sweet and patient. 'Those three look great, kid. You get the other three tomorrow? Terrific. They're going to be great.'

Ellen Pollock couldn't restrain herself when she saw the full complement of my new gnashers, for teeth they were not. 'What have they done to you? You had such a wicked little smile.'

I sometimes dream about those teeth and am always relieved when I wake up. Not only did they look awful, their bulk made diction tricky. Like bad engineering, they were bigger than they need have been and coming when they did they were a bugger.

I have a photo of myself with my God-given front teeth, which I occasionally show to people. Was I right to have them changed? I don't know. Isabel thinks they needed to be fixed. I am sure, though, that 30 June 1960 was not the time to have it done, and the butcher of Wimpole Street was not the man to do it.

We performed *The Knight of the Burning Pestle* at Stratford in an open-air venue on the banks of the Avon. I was supposed to have read it at UCL, along with many other Elizabethan dramas, though it doesn't make much sense. My part was Jasper, a sort of juvenile. What fun it would have been there had it had not been for those sodding teeth. We stayed in some sort of Nissen hut, and my pal Thaw was in the bed next to me. (Thanks to John Fernald's know-how and consideration, he had got a job with the Liverpool Rep.) He had a lot of encouraging to do. 'They look great, kid, they look great. And you've got plenty of time to get your diction right. Don't worry.'

At Stratford we saw Peter O'Toole in *The Merchant* and *The Shrew*. He was, we thought, just marvellous. As Shylock he wore a false nose. Yet he had just had his own nose altered. He was with the Christopher Mann agency like me, and I had heard all about it. Had the first part I played after having had a nose reduction involved my sticking on a false nose I would have gone crazy.

Word had got round that I was off to the Old Vic, to appear in their production of *The Seagull* at the Edinburgh Festival. Thaw and I met O'Toole sitting on a wall outside the Dirty Duck. (He was sitting on the wall, not us. We were standing, awe-struck.)

'You're playing Constantin?' he asked me. I managed to nod, my lips tightly closed. 'He's a loser. He doesn't get the girl. Still, it's a nice part. Do it well and they'll be round you like flies round shit.'

[28th July 1960]

Dear Tom

It's nearly August Bank Holiday. Your father should be home Sunday and Monday. The weather here is showery. Although I aren't expecting a letter from you it seems as if the postman has fell out with me. Anyhow what about those Faust photos. I hope you are going to like being with the Old Vic Company. Try not to worry about things. When you are on the phone you sound rather agitated. I was in a worrying mood last weekend and was ache and painy and I wasn't well. Your father doesn't sympathise but treats me in a laughing at me humour and I don't like it. I am rather trying I am sure.

How are you for money? Your father is willing to help you out and isn't in a hurry for repayment. It is very nice having a phone in the house but one can't ask enough questions. What was the medal you won? You don't seem to want to tell us anything. I have an idea you feel you may not be good in 'The Seagull' and so you worry. But you are always the same, you will be good I'm sure and what the hell if you aren't. I wish we wasn't so far away, but maybe it suits you better. I don't know, I always seem to be wrong lately. Your father says things like 'No news is good news' silly bugger and Ann knows it all now and says 'Our Tom won't write now you know' and 'Our Tom doesn't really care whether you go to London or not.' And I say 'Of course he does.' Anyhow it is nice having a phone so I shall keep a list of questions ready such as 'Are you eating well?' and 'Are you happy?' and 'When shall you be home?' etc. Let us know what the cast of 'The Seagull' is like.

Love Mam Dad and Ann

PS. I am getting to know people round here but arnt keen on my near neighbours. But they cant help it poor buggers. I hope your teeth are no trouble. I can imagine you hating them at times. I heard P. O'Toole being interviewed at Stratford. He said he had been there while he was at RADA.

It must sometimes have been trying for Dad to listen to Mother complaining about her health. Or, were she to have borrowed Larkin's memorable expression, 'what passes with me for health'. On this occasion she was in no mood to be snapped out of feeling 'ache and painy'. It's remarkable that she complained as little as she did, and that she lived out at Longhill for eleven months before she went to see a doctor.

For what it's worth, I won something called the Special Medal. Research over the years tells me that it was also won by Richard Attenborough. And I had thought by A. Finney. But he assures me he won the Emile Littler Prize for Professional Aptitude, of much more use because £50 went with it. Neither Attenborough, Finney nor Courtenay won the Ivor Novello Prize for Grace and Charm of Movement.

The top prize for the last term was known as the Kendal Medal. Geoff Whitehead and I bumped into our pal John Thaw in Gower Street, shortly before we left RADA.

THAW: 'Guess who's won the Kendal?'
WHITEHEAD (indicating me): 'Him.'
THAW: 'No.'
ME (my interest immediately flagging): 'Pamela Ann Davy.'
THAW: 'No.'
WHITEHEAD: 'Sarah Miles.'
THAW: 'No.'
ME (just to be polite): 'David Burke.'
THAW: 'No.'
WHITEHEAD: 'Jimmy Munnally.'
THAW: 'No.'
ME (bored): 'We give up.'
THAW (sheepishly): 'Me.'

The week before I started rehearsing *The Seagull* I got to meet Paul Scofield, as promised, in his dressing room after *A Man for All Seasons*. He was very gracious as he took off his make-up, and I was very silent, scarcely able to believe where I was.

'When I played Constantin,' he said, 'I didn't keep his feet on the ground. Remember to keep his feet on the ground.'

Afterwards, when I had calmed down, I thought to myself that since I came from Harrow Street and had just had my front teeth buggered up that shouldn't be too difficult. I wasn't likely to fly up into the air.

THE OLD VIC
1960

[16th August 1960]

Dear Tom

I thought I would write you a few lines before you left for
Edinburgh. I have felt very unsettled lately. It's the most awful
feeling of wanting to go home. Aunt Al can't understand me. She
has been decorating her scullery and bowing to Uncle Jack Stathers'
whims.

I hope 'The Seagull' is going well. I can understand how odd you
have felt since you had your teeth altered. But if you had not had
them altered you would never have stopped worrying about them.
I see in this mornings paper how Julia Lockwood has had a new
nose built in Harley Street. I do hope you are talking better. Your
teeth may look more like mine used to. They were rather showy,
large, and like a film stars people used to say. We watched Tony
Britton in his play on Sunday night 'A Dream of Treason'. I
suppose he is rather good looking and smart and has a nice voice.
He seems sure of himself. You must be well thought of to have got
the part of Constantin and I hope you don't feel too nervous.

Think how young and good looking you are to the rest.
Well Tom all for now. Look after yourself.

Love Mam Dad and Ann

PS. Don't forget to thank your father for the money.

Of course Mother wanted to go home. I wrote earlier that she had
been posted to the wrong address. Hessle Road may have been the
wrong address but it was her address and she was never going to find
another one in this life.

Hull Daily Mail, Monday, 5 September 1960

HUMBERSIDE ECHOES
Hull actor

Glowing press notices received by 23-year-old RADA student Tom
Courtenay when he made his debut with the Old Vic Company at the
Edinburgh Festival, have been read with pleasure by his friends in Hull.

Tom, son of Mr and Mrs T. Courtenay, of Longhill Estate, Hull,
first acquired a taste for acting when he was a member of Kingston
High School dramatic society. He took leading parts in the school's
productions of 'Emma' and 'The Stars Bow Down'.

Leaving school, he went to London University, then on to the
Royal Academy of Dramatic Art. He is at present appearing in 'The
Seagull' by Chekhov, and will remain with the Old Vic during their
coming London season.

[9th September 1960]

Dear Tom

I am trying very hard to keep up with all the news that keeps crop-
ping up about you. It was Wednesday morning a week ago. I was
hanging out the washing when the phone rang. I notice I always
seem to be in the backway when it rings. It was Aunt Ivy letting me

know how the Hull Daily Mail was trying to get in touch with us. Aunt Ivy was worried in case we would be annoyed because she had rung enquiries to find out our telephone number and had contacted Daily Mail herself. Me being understanding realised how one gets excited and I said I didn't mind. She said Hull Daily Mail would ring us or call on us. Well expecting reporters and washing don't mix I changed into my pleated skirt and best sandals and tried to concentrate on household jobs. No reporter came and your father and Ann made a joke of me with my best skirt on. So from then on I was wondering if anyone would call. Thursday I was wondering about Daily Mail and shaking a mat outside when the phone rang and it was you. Of course I was pleased and you seemed in a happy mood about what Punch had said. I bought Punch on Friday and thought the drawing marvellous, also the write up. I'm going to start a scrap book of all the cuttings etc. Alice and me went to Grannies along with Punch and it rained all the day and I never heard anything from Mail and thought maybe I had dreamed about it. Just after Ann had gone to work Friday I heard a review on the wireless about the 'Seagull'. I don't know if you heard it. The man with a rather posh voice said you was a Hamlet of a new school. He mentioned your name two or three times and said of you 'With the twitching shoulders and the curious flat voice, the funny trousers and the strange haircut.' He said you was more like a coffee bar intellectual.

Saturday and Sunday was quiet and I began to forget about Daily Mail. Monday teatime I opened the Daily Mail and there was a piece about you in Humberside Echoes and headed 'Hull Actor' and was very correct. It mentioned you was the son of Mr and Mrs Courtenay and I thought hell I'm still living. Tuesday teatime I was busy with dinner when the phone rang. '31459' I stumbled. 'This is John Rogers of the Yorkshire Times.' Hell! This was the day I used to joke about. 'Where shall I sit when you are famous and I am being interviewed' but I used to mean it. There I was at the foot of the stairs the lavatory at the top and my nose keeping the dinner to mind. (Hell it's hard work writing.) We had a conversation and once I had to rescue the chops. This young man with the nice voice wanted a photo of you. Well I said we would slip some photos in

Mail letter box. 'We go to press Wednesday, you see, it's a busy day,' he said in a worried voice. But that wasn't the end because your father came home and I was telling him. 'Tell 'em nowt' he said. I had made a grave mistake because I had said about a film producer being interested in you. Your father called me a big gob. I feel all the guilt in the world like after I've written a story letter with title. But this was worse I couldn't eat my tea and felt awful. Ann said 'What matter Ma?' I said 'I feel like Lucy in "I Love Lucy". Always doing the wrong thing.' 'Never mind.' Ann said she would write a note in with the photos and explain that they should not mention about film producers as the Vic might not like it. So I worried like hell with a few hours sleep in between. Your father said let them come for a photo and tell them all about it. Next time anyone wants any news I'll send them to you, I told your father, the clever bugger.

Next morning came, I put my pleated skirt on. The phone rang. John Rogers, and had we sent the photo. 'No' and I told him how worried I had been so he came to see me. He ran up the path from the red Daily Mail van and looked much as I had expected and about your age, smallish and dark with glasses on. He was very nice. He explained that he didn't think it would be harmful to you to mention that a film producer was interested in you and I agreed and said I didn't want to say anything Tom wouldn't like. We talked a lot, and I said there's such a lot to all this there's yards and yards of it. He didn't take anything down only a quote from the 'Edinburgh Evening News' (he said). Your father said 'Ay but they have a good memory.' (Christ.) We got very friendly, his home is near Highbury Crescent and he wanted to be an actor but he likes his job. I said I'm new to all this and I don't want to make a mess of it and I'd been all muddled about it. He said you was in the public eye and would get publicity. He had read Punch. It seems it's a big thing you being an actor and it's not in the family. I shall be glad when it's next week. Al and me ordered Yorkshire Times. I daren't look inside. I think he liked that large photo of you where you look sad. Anyway he ran away with 4 photos. And the day dragged on. Ann said I'm sacked as publicity manager. Am I glad – no one has faith in me. Uncle Georges daughter Margaret rang up at teatime.

Had we read about you in Mail last Monday and her father didn't like the drawing in Punch, it wasn't like you. She shouted through the phone because outside the phone box the kids were making a hell of a row. Can you hear them she said. She shouted at them. She had waited half an hour to ring. I could just imagine her in the phone box at the corner of Boulevard and all the bairns larking around outside and you wouldn't believe it but I felt a bit jealous. I could just picture Hessle Road.

Love Mam Dad and Ann

PS. I sincerely hope I haven't said anything I shouldn't have. I'm sure I haven't.

Hull and Yorkshire Times, 10 September 1960

Even the Russians applaud him
Young Hull Actor On Way To Stardom

To the names of Dickie Henderson, David Whitfield, Ian Carmichael, Brian Rix, Kenny Baker, Ronnie Hilton and Bob Wallis, Hull will soon be able to add another of her sons to have reached the top of his profession in show business.

He is 23-year-old actor Tom Courtenay whom Britain's finest drama critics have been acclaiming as an exciting new stage star, after his debut with the Old Vic Company at the Edinburgh Arts Festival.

His performance as the suicidal youth in 'The Seagull' by the Russian playwright Chekhov, was greeted in the newspapers as 'beautifully calculated', 'totally unexpected', 'played superbly', 'exhibits extraordinary power'.

In agony

Cartoonist and illustrator Ronald Searle said that Tom Courtenay's angular face was the most interesting he has drawn in the theatre for years.

A party of Russians who saw the production said Tom's interpretation of the role was outstandingly modern.

What few people realised was that this young Hull actor stepped onto the threshold of stardom while suffering agony from his teeth.

His parents who have recently moved from Harrow St., Hessle Rd., to Duddon Gr., Longhill Estate, told how their son had to undergo a major dental operation only a few days before the start of the play.

'He had to have two teeth pulled out and two more evened off, and his front teeth screwed back straight in his gums' said Mrs Courtenay.

This expensive dental operation caused him severe discomfort, besides making his means of speech – an actor's treasured possession – feel strange.

School roles

When he was a boy at West Dock Ave. Primary School no one thought Tom Courtenay was bound for fame.

Sure enough, his father's cousin, Jim, was a well-known three-quarter playing for Hull RL, but no one in the Courtenay family thought they had acting ability.

However, young Tom's first step up was when he won a scholarship to Kingston High School. There he acquired a taste for acting, and took leading parts in the school productions of 'Emma' and 'The Stars Bow Down'.

Leaving as head boy, he went to London University to study English.

Mrs Courtenay hoped her son was going to be a teacher, but Tom spent more and more of his time on the university stage.

The result was that he failed his degree after three years, but he did not waste his time since as Tom says himself, 'You go to university to find out what you want to be.'

He had found that he wanted to be an actor and he was accepted for RADA. The academy were so impressed by his ability that they awarded him a Bernard Shaw Scholarship, which enabled him to live while he studied for two more years.

Paying way

If this is not exactly a rags-to-riches story, it has its fair share of hardship.

Tom's father did not earn enough at his job at a paint

manufacturer's to be in a position to support a grown-up son away from home, so Tom had to find some spare-time occupations.

He has worked as a porter on Paragon Station, a postman, a clerk in an insurance office, a park labourer and a waiter at Bridlington. While he was at RADA he had a small part in a television film, 'Inside Story', but Konstantin in 'The Seagull' is his first big professional role.

David Deutsch, executive producer of Anglo-Amalgamated Films, has promised Tom that he will be a star in three years.

In a letter to his family, which also includes his 22-year-old sister Ann, Tom Courtenay expresses just one fear. 'I hope I don't spend the rest of the season disappearing into oblivion.'

So does everyone in Hull.

Mother had such fun writing about being interviewed. But the resulting article made her very unhappy. She couldn't have known what I have learned over the years about interviews with journalists: don't read the bloody things. Though the Quests revelled in the publicity, the Courtenays thought Mother had been shooting her mouth off. Fancy telling a reporter I was going to become a star. Dad hated that his poverty was discussed publicly. She had the curtains drawn for a week, in shame.

David Deutsch had seen me at the Edinburgh Festival and had written me a generous letter, which I had sent on to Mother, thinking it would please her, and not knowing that she would innocently show it to a reporter as evidence of the truth of what she had told him. Anglo-Amalgamated Films had their name on the credits of *Billy Liar*. Whether his letter was the start of the process whereby I got to be in the film I can't say.

It was the details of my dental treatment made even more horrific by my mother's sense of drama that embarrassed me the most.

[12th September 1960]

Dear Tom

I've felt so bloody miserable about all this newspaper business and told you a deliberate lie over the phone about no names were mentioned because I didn't want you to have a couple of days worry and wondering before you got this cutting. This must surely have all started when Mr Large told the Hull Daily Mail about you. [My old English master had provided *Humberside Echoes* with details of my Kingston High acting career.] It seems strangers know better than me. Funny isn't it?

The beginning of the Yorkshire Times article was all their idea. The reporter knew all about the Punch article and also other write ups. When I explained to him over the phone how worried I was because I had mentioned about the film producer and thought it best not to mention his name, the reporter decided to come down here. Of course to prove I wasn't lying I showed him the letter. My God he didn't take a note of it and of what I said about you but he has a bloody good memory hence other bits. I hope you are not too mad with me and by hell I'll never talk to another reporter about you. I saw the interview at Grannies Friday dinner. Everyone but me was delighted. I've been going about with a permanently sad face like you in the photo. Your father was raving mad. Friday we all ended up rowing including Ann. Your father said it was all bull-shit and I said the only thing he didn't think was bullshit was Worthington E. I don't think many people read a tuppenny hapenny bloody paper like Yorkshire Times and hope not.

Well Tom I hope you are well because over the phone you sounded like you were a bit short of breath which gave me something else to worry about. It's Monday morning and I'm trying to get some sheets washed. I didn't get much done last week. I didn't hope you would be a teacher I said I thought you might be one. I never said your father didn't earn enough I never mentioned it but told them how you did various jobs. Because they seemed to wonder how we had managed and I'm bloody fed up. All for now.

Love Ma

I finished with RADA on Friday, 22 July 1960 and started work, in the big rehearsal room above the dressing rooms at the Old Vic, the Monday immediately following. The established members of the company, who were doing the understudying, caused me the most unease. After a year or so in the job they were hoping for promotion themselves. I fancied that they didn't appreciate watching a kid with strange teeth, who had just stepped out of RADA, in one of the main parts. I felt like a novice and an intruder. The guest artistes were no problem. Dame Judith Anderson, Arkadina, couldn't have been nicer. She had her own worries: she was concerned that she was a bit old for the part of my mum. Tony Britton was charming and friendly. Lovely Ann Bell, playing Nina, had done the part a year earlier while still at RADA. In the meantime she had been at the Nottingham Rep, which made me think her vastly more experienced than me. Ralph Michael played Dr Dorn. His acting was so natural and unforced. He provided my favourite moment in the show: after Constantin's play has been ridiculed, he is consoled by the Doctor.

'I liked your play . . . it's a bit strange . . . you've got talent. You must carry on.'

He was so true that all I had to do was stand there and listen to him. No need for acting. Or rather, that was acting. I also have a fond memory of Sylvia Coleridge, playing Paulina, laughing when she wasn't supposed to because I pronounced 'Masha' like something you use on potatoes.

John Fernald blocked the entire play on the first day of rehearsal. That is to say he gave us all our moves from the beginning of the play to the end. Such a way of proceeding would be thought crude nowadays. Before taking over from Sir Kenneth Barnes as the Principal of RADA, John had been one of the West End's most successful directors. He had a broad chest, natural authority and a kindly air. His support for me was obviously crucial to my early career, and though I had little to do with him after *The Seagull* I didn't forget. Thirty years later Rachel Gurney told me he was very ill in University College Hospital. I went to see him. I was surprised at how squalid the hospital seemed as I enquired my way to his bed. He was sitting up, minus a leg, with a faraway look in his eyes. I leant forward slightly to get myself in his eyeline.

'Tom! Tom! How are you? How are your teeth?' he said with immediate and astonishing recall.

'Oh, they're fine now, John, absolutely fine.'

'What are you up to?'

'I'm doing a Noël Coward story for the BBC. I have to learn to tap-dance.'

'That must be frightfully difficult.'

'Yes, it is. I think they may have to film somebody else's feet.'

'Somebody else's feet! That's very good.'

And later, sadly: 'We used to think we were the mainstream and youngsters like you were interesting diversions. But it's you and others like you who were the mainstream.'

After the pressure of rehearsals with all these old pros, the first night in Edinburgh came as something of a relief, if not a triumph. I could never have triumphed with those teeth. During the performance, as Ann Bell playing Nina told me, 'Don't cry, don't cry,' I held my hands over my face and heard a young voice in the audience whisper, 'He isn't crying.' The feeling that I had been cheating was alleviated by Cliff Michelmore who afterwards told me with a huge grin that I was very different and would go far. The production was well received in Edinburgh. Especially, for me, in *Punch*, my sixth-form Bible. There was a drawing of me by Ronald Searle, the original of which my agents bought for me. The reviewer Eric Keown said how intrigued Searle had been by my appearance. It's a very good drawing, though it doesn't look much like me. It's the sort of friendly personal remark that doesn't usually appear in reviews. I remember vividly something else that Keown said because he took a favourable view of one of my chief difficulties: 'He seems to have an engine too big for the rest of his body.' (Reviews used to stick to my brain. A couple of years later I stopped reading them for good after someone wrote 'He staggers about like an unlicked foal.') I often had great difficulty in controlling the emotion that I felt. My arms would fly all over the place and I could scarcely get the words out.

Some nights I had great difficulty with the scene between Constantin and his mother, when they quarrel. I often made a mess of it. The intensity of my feeling made me lose all control. Peter Barkworth, so influential at RADA, came to the Vic one night and from the look on his face I got nought out of ten. But the scene affected me hugely because it was about Constantin and his mother and it would have been unthinkable not to meet it head on.

What do I remember of when Mam and Dad came to London to see me at the Vic? Constantin, like me, is such a mother's boy that I wasn't aware of Dad. (He had his turn some years after Mother's death when he came to see *Hamlet*. 'Methinks I see my father' was very tricky.) Now it was the scene with Mamma. 'You've got magic hands. Just lately I've felt I loved you as tenderly as when I was a child.' That didn't come out easily. Mother had seen me on the stage at school, but that was the first and last time she saw me when I got paid for doing it. I don't think she knew quite what to make of it. She knew I wasn't too pleased with myself, and of course there were the teeth, intruders to both of us. I can see her in the corridor outside my dressing room in her new grey coat, quietly drinking it all in. People were very nice to her. Mam and Dad came to Highbury Crescent, and Vic Symonds was very sweet to them too. So after my being five years in London she finally got to see where I laid my head.

[13th October 1960]

Dear Tom

SAT BY THE FIRE

I've just been washing my hair. Two horrible women are singing on TV, your father is painting the doors, we are decorating, the fire has just been mended. Ann out at the pictures and I've got a towel round my head. It seems a long time since we heard from you. Why can't you ring? Is it because you have no exciting news to tell? You will be lucky if you have always good things to say. I hope your cold has not returned. I really did enjoy our weekend in London. It was marvellous although you seemed rather uneasy I thought but it did not spoil my weekend. I loved the play and then coming backstage and meeting interesting people and going to Soho, and your friend Vernon was very kind. It was worth having a headache for. I enjoyed coming to Highbury Crescent. Vic's very nice and clever too. Monday was a nice day then coming to the theatre again and the little pub next door and so on. We called in a pub before coming

to see you Monday and I paid 4/- for a chicken sandwich.
Hell!

The journey home wasn't too bad. But Hull and Longhill! It
seemed like the first time I had gone to Longhill. Was I depressed. I
couldn't bear to look through our windows and it rained and rained
and Aunt Al looked like she had looked for years and when I set
the table I felt like a boarding house keeper.

Wednesday. Seeing as your father was still on his holidays we
thought we would have a ride out to Dorries. Who would we
meet in town I wondered. It was Aunt Agnes! and she not
seeming very happy. We went for a coffee and she said 'I was
pleased about Tommy but Wilf didn't like what was in Hull and
Yorkshire Times about Jim Courtenay.' Your father agreed.
[Dad had little to do with his ex-Rugby-League-playing cousin.]
I found myself trying to explain things but got nowhere. Wilf
thought mentioning Jim Courtenay and not your father looked as
if your father was nobody. Why Jim Courtenay? Wilf was going
to see some reporter or other about it. I started feeling mad inside.
Your father said 'The next week the Times also mentioned how
Brian Rix [also from Hull] had got a big money contract. What
did it make us look like?' 'Like you're shooting a line' answered
Aunt Agnes. 'But Brian Rix comes from wealthy people and we
are poor' I said. I didn't know where the hell I was. Many a time I
haven't liked seeing Wilf Spav in the paper but I wouldn't tell him.
Suddenly I arent responsible. I shall never be forgiven for someone
taking advantage of me just talking to them. So it ended up we
argued the rest of the way to Dorries. Even Dorrie said Dan had
told her I had been opening my mouth. I could imagine Aunt
Agnes in London. With her fur coat on and white shoes and diamond jewellery. Well I just couldn't deck myself out for anyone. I
just try and be nice and understand and I like a little fun as well
when I know people.

Towel off my head, a cup of tea and the paint smells sickly. So – I
seem to spend so much time liking Longhill and so much time feeling very homesick, but I aren't supposed to mention this. But
Sunday came and strangely I started planning a new electric stove,

curtains and carpet and your father happily painted the bathroom. He is throwing himself wholly into decorating.

All for now. Love Mam Dad and Ann

There were those, including myself, who didn't think I was quite cutting the mustard, yet there were also those who were plenty interested in what I might have to offer. Much of the interest was coming from what might be termed the Royal Court direction. It was at the Royal Court that John Osborne's *Look Back in Anger* had been produced.

Penelope Gilliat, who reviewed *The Seagull* for *Queen* magazine, was at that time married to John Osborne. He was a partner in Woodfall Films with Tony Richardson, who had made the films of *Look Back in Anger* and *The Entertainer* and was about to make *A Taste of Honey*. They were also going to make Alan Sillitoe's *Saturday Night and Sunday Morning* into a film with Karel Reisz directing Albert Finney. Knowing that Tony intended to make a film of Sillitoe's *The Loneliness of the Long Distance Runner*, they told him about me. So during the week after we finished playing *The Seagull* I was summoned to see Tony at the Royal Court Theatre in Sloane Square, where he was directing *The Changeling*, with Mary Ure and Robert Shaw. I was even more excited to go for an interview at the Court than at the Vic. The Court was where it was at. I bet they wouldn't have wanted my front teeth removed. I wasn't with him for long and I can't remember whether he gave me a copy of the book or not. I told him that my teeth had been buggered about with and might well need more work. I wanted him to know he wasn't seeing the real me. I seemed to be looking up at him, though he wasn't that tall. All I can remember him saying to me, amazingly soon after I appeared before him, is: 'You'll be absolutely marvellous in the part.' As I left him I was both excited and bemused. At the Vic I was by then understudying Mercutio and more or less walking on. (I had the part of Abraham, a servant, who has the line, 'Do you bite your thumb at me, sir?') At the Royal Court I was being promised the leading part in a film by one of the leading lights in the most fashionable and influential group of people in our theatre. Was I coming or going? Backstage at the Vic I bumped into John Stride, who was terribly excited to be playing Romeo. Not wanting to feel left out of exciting developments and being only an understudy in the production, I asked him if he'd heard of a book called *The Loneliness of the Long Distance Runner*. He hadn't.

[7th November 1960]

Dear Tom

Its Sunday and I think the time for writing a letter. Ann is in bed your father is at work and I am writing with his fountain pen. He doesn't like us to use it although he played hell when we bought it because he thought it cost too much. It's a lovely bright day and I nearly feel I like being up here today, but when I don't hell it's terrible and I don't know what's the best thing to do. If we flit back up West Hull I might not feel any different. It's just knowing what to do if you know what I mean. Poor me I suffer like hell I certainly live. If I had known how I was going to feel at times, I would never have left the other house – I dare not have. The best part of Longhill is the fresh air and its clean. I am not the pioneering type like Alice. She invites all newcomers who have exchanged with some poor buggers who don't like Longhill to call on her. She met someone the other day who had lived up here 9 year and was going to move out if possible. How are you? Well I hope.

It is now nearly eight o clock at night. I have once again washed my hair and am sat near the fire with a blue towel around my head. I will try and recollect a few things that have happened since I last wrote.

As you might well understand, me feeling so unsettled causes lots of misunderstandings. The week before last my depression was so bad I neither baked nor cleaned up and I let your father know I wasn't kidding how I felt. He said he could have cried too. And he let me know that if it came to it we weren't tied to Longhill. That was just before you rang up saying how unsettled you was at the Old Vic. Anyhow we cleared the air as clear as Longhill air. But the following week I had to go and see the doctor. Ann came along. I hate going to any doctor. It was a Polish doctor. 'I'm strange here' I said as I walked in his room. What was my trouble, he asked. Hesitantly I said 'I think I'm run down.' 'How?' he said. 'I've been feeling depressed' I said. 'Why?' he said and his voice started on a low note and went higher. 'I get funny heads and I don't think I feel settled in this district.' 'It's a nice district and they are nice people aren't they' he sang. I thought 'what put shit in their dustbin.' I said 'The fresh air's good.' 'Haven't you any friends here?' he asked. 'Oh yes I've got a sister' I said, and he started going through my medical reports and I felt myself ready for battle, but he just kept glancing at me and talking on the phone at the same time. After telling him I'd been having pills for my blood and how old my bairns was I said 'I'm very nervous and sensitive but I can't help my nature.' That appealed to him and he looked at me and said slightly smiling 'I will give you something to help your nature and put some life in you and you will stay in this district and you will like it.' Hell! 'It's a nice place you've got here' I said as I squeezed out the door. I told Ann and she laughed and we walked back along the strange road under Anns umbrella.

Thursday Uncle Bernard his Marie and new baby was coming. I didn't feel like any work just sick and nervous. The woman next door has been very kind and come in to talk and invited me in her house for a cup of tea. She is a bit rough but kind and good natured and she doesn't worry me at all. Jean is her name or Mrs Sole (no one in her family has the initial R). She and Aunt Al helped put our carpet down and make it look very cosy for Uncle Bernard coming. I might add it didn't stay that way long. Uncle Bernard said he didn't think I'd settle up at Longhill and laughed when I told him 'You even miss people you don't like.'

My birthday and when you rang I was sat on the settee eating my dinner and looking out through the window. November 2nd and I had thought a few days before, my birthday buried among the smouldering heaps of bonfire nights, Armistice days and Hull Fairs. Your father bought me a frame for your photo (black sweater), some chocolates, a brass cup to stand the poker in and some fish.

Love Mam Dad and Ann

*

The Polish doctor seems off-hand, but he wasn't at all. He was placing a call on Mother's behalf, and another doctor came to see her a few days later. His diagnosis was that she was acutely depressed. She wasn't thought to have cancer because it was more than ten years since the previous outbreak had been successfully treated. So she was given anti-depressants.

From Dad

Dear Tom

The fact that it's a long way to work and back seems to give me less leisure time plus we have a lot of work yet to do in the house. I've got the bathroom, living room finished, next job the staircase. By the time you get home it will look good. Enough of me what about you. I hope you've got yourself an accountant. He can save you a lot of money. Your last letter gave me the impression of being dissatisfied. You'll have to be patient, Tom, you're doing very well. Perhaps better than expected. The ball is running right for you and you are sure to score. But you'll have to be patient. (Can you.)

Love Pop.

It was very good for me not to have a part in *Romeo and Juliet*, though I was not a little irked. It was the great hit of that Old Vic season. Franco Zeffirelli made his English directorial debut, and his wonderful settings were evocative of Renaissance Italy. John Stride and Judi Dench were the star-crossed lovers. The part of Tybalt had been up for grabs, but it went to Tom Kempinski, a contemporary at RADA. He was more Italian-looking than me by a long chalk – but never mind that, it was better I didn't have everything I wanted. As it was, I got something I tried not to get.

Michael Langham, who was based at the Stratford Ontario Theatre in Canada, came over to direct *A Midsummer Night's Dream*. Puck had yet to be cast. This caused great excitement among my colleagues in the top-floor dressing rooms, all of whom were walking on. I wasn't so fussed because I felt I might be whisked away from the Vic at any moment. Joe Losey wanted me for a film (which was never made), I was about to audition for Peter Hall who was then running Stratford, I was wanted for a yet-to-be-written television play, and the *Runner* was going to happen, though I didn't know when. Furthermore, when I read the part of Puck I didn't consider myself – how shall I put it without being politically incorrect? – I didn't consider myself enough of a fairy.

But audition I did for Michaels Langham and Benthall. I was the last of four to perform. The others had learnt a speech and did quite a bit of what they thought to be puckish prancing about. When my turn came I apologized and told Michael Langham that I had auditioned for Stratford the previous day (Michael Benthall knew – he had given me permission) and hadn't had time to learn anything. 'That's all right, just read some.' I started as follows:

> 'I am that merry wanderer of the night.
> I jest to Oberon, and make him smile
> When I a fat and bean-fed horse beguile,
> Neighing in likeness of a filly foal;
> And sometime lurk I in a gossip's bowl . . .'

I stopped quite suddenly. My heart wasn't in it. 'I'm sorry, Mr Langham, but I really don't think I can play this part,' I said, and I wasn't joking. Thinking to save the day, Michael Benthall chimed in. 'Why don't you do "How all occasions" for Mr Langham? You like doing that.' I didn't think it very suitable, but I had done it only the day before, for Peter Hall, so I concurred, was thanked, and the audition was over.

A couple of days later the cast list for *The Dream* was put up on the board. The part of Puck was to be played by yours truly. I was now sharing a dressing room at the top of the Old Vic with half a dozen actors, three of whom wanted to kill me.

[7th December 1960]

Dear Tom

I am sorry I have been so long in writing but you know how
unsettled I have been feeling. I am afraid to write when I'm feeling
so miserable in case it depresses you. I have just been making some
corn beef hash and it is nicely simmering in the oven but it will be
an hour before your father gets home so I thought I would write a
few lines. I have drawn the curtains. I am always glad to. The
weather here is very cold. I have been washing some sheets and
curtains this afternoon and Christmas is gradually creeping in on
us. I suppose it makes a change for everyone during the horrible
winter. Your father is up around six o'clock and off to work and he
doesn't get home till six at night. But as Alice would say 'You see
me.' Ann arrives home along with your father. I see quite a lot of
Mrs Sole, she is very stout but kind hearted. I have been glad of her
company. I am feeling a bit less depressed this afternoon and I think
'Don't let it get you down you can always move.' Anyhow it's much
too near Christmas for moving, people are making the best of
things. But after Christmas we will go all out for an exchange
Gypsyville or near Hessle area because I'll never feel at home in
Longhill. Your father said 'No because you don't want to.' We have
had more rows etc. lately than I can remember and tears and
misery. Alice said I may feel the same if I move. I have all my
friends up West Hull looking for a house. Your father said he isn't
in love with Longhill but he likes the house. Well Tom, I'm pleased
you're doing well and hope your health is good. It's our silver
wedding on the 21st but I don't want any celebration. Aunt Barbara
is patiently awaiting her baby and so am I. It will be nice to have a
baby in the family. It's about time you and Ann got married. Only
kidding.

Love Mam Dad and Ann

Aunt Barbara had a little boy, called Billy. Being very much the
youngest of the family, Barbara had been almost like a sister to Ann
before she got married. She was the shortest-lived of the Quests who

reached adulthood, dying before she was forty. Aunt Alice lived long after Jack Stathers' death, slipping away in contentment in 1999.

Tony Richardson was as good as his word, and a year or so after I met him at the Royal Court he shot *The Loneliness of the Long Distance Runner* with me playing the runner, Colin Smith, and I was well and truly discovered. I suppose it was inevitable that I would be, so much a child of my time was I.

That period in the British cinema was known as the 'New Wave'. Several films were made that were interesting and internationally admired, and shot, crucially, without recourse to American dollars. The New Wave, to me, is simply the product of writers of my generation who had benefited, unlike their parents, from the post-war Welfare State which gave them, through the eleven plus, the chance of being educated. Alan Sillitoe, Keith Waterhouse and Willis Hall, Shelagh Delaney, Arnold Wesker, David Storey . . .

It is hardly surprising that young actors such as Albert and myself should be the ones to benefit from the leading parts that suddenly appeared. With our lowly social backgrounds – especially mine, I have to say; Albert's Dad was a bookie and almost lower middle class – we were excellent casting for what was being written.

I had been only a few weeks out of RADA when Tony Richardson saw me. My instinct told me he would stick to his word. The down side was that I couldn't concentrate wholeheartedly on learning my trade, and, exciting as it was to be discovered and made a fuss of, I didn't feel I had earned the right to call myself an actor. I hadn't served my time. I hadn't paid my dues. The time whose child I was picked me up and rushed me along at its pace, not my own. That made me feel vulnerable, which along with my extremely youthful appearance made me even more in demand.

The good thing about my success coming so early, however, was that Mother had a chance to enjoy it.

THE OLD VIC
1961

For the whole of 1961 I have only one of Mother's letters. I know she wrote more because I can remember that when I was on television that spring, in *Private Potter*, she wrote 'three cheers for Hessle Road'. I don't have that letter now, but I don't think there were many more letters because she felt very low. And she wouldn't have written to me if she couldn't be lively.

While my friend James Maxwell was studying at the Old Vic School of Drama he became friends with Casper Wrede, who had come from Finland to study directing and was now working in television. James brought Casper to see me in *Shut Up and Sing*. I thought he was the deepest person I had ever met. He could see right through me and out the other side. His little nod of approval was more of a compliment than any of the extravagant things that were said to me at that time. Some months later Casper got in touch with me. He was working on a television script with Ronald Harwood about a private soldier who mucks things up by having a vision in the thick of the action. Would I mind going to meet Ronnie Harwood at the Savile Club?

The combination of the teeth and a gentleman's club proved too much for me and I felt horribly shy. Ronnie told me many years later that after my departure he had said to Casper, with some firmness, 'That boy is not an actor. I don't want him in my play.' And Casper had said, 'Fine, but in that case I don't want to direct your play.'

Michael Benthall gave me permission to appear in *Private Potter* while I was still at the Vic (it was recorded on a Sunday) and it was aired in the spring of 1961. It had a wonderful cast: Leo McKern, Brewster Mason, Ralph Michael (again), and my friends James Maxwell and Eric Thompson (Emma and Sophie's dad). It was inspiring to work with all these wonderful men. And lovely that Mother saw it. It was much more effective on television than when it was later filmed for the big screen: 'Three cheers for Hessle Road.'

Albert Finney was at this time enjoying a huge success at the Cambridge Theatre in *Billy Liar*, written by Keith Waterhouse and Willis Hall and directed by Lindsay Anderson. I had seen it twice and loved it. It was so easy for me to identify with Billy Fisher's daydreams – his longing to go to London and make something of himself. Albert was just marvellous. So commanding, so easy for him to do whatever he wanted to do, so funny. I can remember Thaw and me being awestruck (for a second time) when Albert sat near us in the Seven Stars Grill at the Lyon's Corner House, a much-favoured after-theatre spot. (A juicy cut of beef, well done, and a baked potato with a lot of butter didn't make that much inroad into my fifteen pounds a week. I never had any other dish there.) Lindsay had been brought by his Royal Court colleague Anthony Page to see me in *The Seagull*. Albert was going to leave *Billy* in June 1961, to play in John Osborne's *Luther*, and the show's success warranted that someone take his place. Quite a plum for some fortunate young actor. Lindsay asked me if I would audition for him and the writers. If successful I would have to ask to leave the Vic before my contract was up.

I got to the Cambridge Theatre early and loitered outside the front entrance. Huge photos of Albert, and a blow-up of a review from the *Evening Standard*. I gazed at it thoughtfully. 'Albert Finney gives the funniest performance in London.' I became aware, out of the corner of my eye, of someone watching me. I turned my head, and there was Lindsay, smiling at me. I think he thought my looking at the review before being auditioned made a nice little shot. I think he was right.

I didn't quite have the prescience about Billy that I had had about Constantin, but maybe it wasn't so necessary. I knew I had a good chance of success. I had been offered a range of small parts at Stratford, but Billy Fisher interested me far more. I had met Lindsay several times and had already got to like him. The audition went swimmingly. I was at home with the text and I could hear Keith and Willis chortling away. I got the part, and Michael Benthall generously allowed me to leave the Vic before the end of the season. Perhaps he felt guilty about my teeth.

While at the Vic, in addition to Puck, I got the part of Poins in *Henry IV, Part 1*, and Feste in *Twelfth Night*. Colin Graham, who mostly directed opera, had seen me in the musical at RADA. He saw Feste as a lost boy and with me that's what he got. I was far too distracted to apply myself properly, and the high heels didn't help. (Settings and costumes after Watteau.) It was a good production except for me. Alec McCowen was excellent as Malvolio, and Colin Graham's touch was deft. Perhaps his lost boy was a deliberate mistake. Eric Keown, of *Punch*, who had found me so promising in *The Seagull*, was forced to eat his words. One evening I started the closing number in the wrong key, and, not realizing my mistake, fought the band as they got louder and louder. Some wag stuck a newspaper cutting on my dressing room mirror one night. 'Feste is played by Tom Courtenay, surely the most overestimated young actor in the country.' Perhaps it was put there by one of those I had ousted as Puck, or all three of them in gleeful collusion. It was meant to wound but it failed. I thought there was some truth in it.

Henry IV was an unmitigated disaster but quite a bit of fun. The director and designer were from television, so we saw a lot of Michael Benthall as the opening approached. The whole event took place on a ramp made out of duckboards. It was meant to throw the play towards the audience, but if you got your foot or your sword caught in the spaces between the boards it threw you arse over tit. Or if you stood on the downstage end of a board that had worked loose it rose up and hit you. It was especially hazardous in the battle scenes at the end when the stage was covered in dry ice. By then I had finished my duties as Poins and had become some sort of guard. I had to tie up Nicholas Meredith and bring him on stage. He was playing Worcester, who was supposed to be a bad lot, though his wig made him look like Margaret Rutherford. His great delight was to hide in the wings till the last minute, so that I couldn't get my rope round him. In the exertions the capture now necessitated, I would either lose my guard's hat, or have to hold on to it, un-guard-like. At the outset Worcester, Douglas and other warring lords were required to wear huge battle helmets over their imitation chainmail balaclavas. All these helmets had enormous horns, some going sideways as well as upwards, some just sideways, which meant that if you wore one you took up an awful lot of room. A sudden turn to left or right made life on the duckboards very hazardous. There was much clashing of horns at the technical run-through, till someone cried out passionately, 'I am not wearing this fucking helmet a minute longer.' Michael Benthall came forward from the stalls, his arms raised to placate, and helmets were abandoned. For the rest of the season, whatever dressing room you visited, there would be a helmet gazing down forlornly from a shelf, its chance of glory gone. On the last night, however, one of them had its moment.

'I hate this fucking play,' must often have been sung by actors doing bits and bobs in Shakespeare companies. Geoffrey Bayldon told me that that's what he wailed at Stratford in *Julius Caesar* as he arrived breathless after his third change of costume to enter in procession behind John Gielgud. Added Gielgud, 'Oh, so do I! "Hail Caesar."' Whether Michael Meacham said it during his stint as Douglas, the war-like Scot, I cannot say. He certainly looked it backstage, quietly sipping his Guinness and sweating, completely obliterated by a huge red beard and much wiggery and armour. He was playing one of the lovers in *The Dream* and Hastings in *She Stoops* – much more his usual line of work. I can imagine Michael Benthall inveigling him into playing Douglas. 'It'll be a marvellous contrast for you.' Sure was. He suffered in silence, then came his revenge. It was simple and very effective. On the last night, without warning, he came on in his helmet, its horns in all directions. That's all it took. There was great mirth among the warriors present.

A couple of years on, when I first went to America, they described me as an 'Old Vic actor'. I never really was. I didn't give a good performance there, though I may have showed promise. But I had some fun and I learnt a bit. Alec McCowen was very helpful to me generally and in quite an unexpected way in particular. He played Oberon. We both, being fairies, had pixie-like extensions to our ears. I remember being surprised at how much these ear bits cost. I kept mine as a memento, and used to like to answer the door in them from time to time. (Only to friends, not to, say, the gas man.) Puck has to do quite a lot of listening to Oberon, as he is given his instructions, so my ears proved especially useful. Moreover, my own ears being bigger than Alec's, my ear extensions were more noticeable than his. I found that at the schools' matinees I could get a lot of mileage out of my listening acting. I wasn't discouraged at the outset by the impish Michael Langham, but as I grew in cheek I started overdoing it. Of course I wasn't listening to Oberon, I was pulling faces, moving my head about (therefore my ears), being daft and generally showing off to the girls in the audience, who I could hear giggling. And all during Oberon's beautiful speeches on which Alec had doubtless worked hard. I can remember sitting in the Vic canteen with Alec and being told gently but firmly that I was out of order. I didn't feel at all cowed, just suddenly wiser than before. He reminded me that one has to think about one's colleagues as well as oneself on the stage. He did it without hurting my feelings and I shall always be grateful to him.

Mother wrote that writing should be 'like music, running up and down and all over the place', which is my justification for including a story that Barbara Leigh Hunt, who played Helena in *The Dream*, told me recently about herself and Michael Langham. It seems that she had given him blood while performing in Canada, when he had been taken ill. Hers was the only blood in the company that matched his. He recovered sufficiently to be directing her in a show not long after her timely donation. He sounds to have been unmindful of her generosity because my namesake Maggie Courtney, no relation, found her sniffing quietly and quite upset. 'What's up, Bar?'

'It's that Michael Langham. Who does he think he is? He's made me feel so small.'

'Why don't you tell him you want your blood back?'

At the risk of being accused of blowing my own trumpet, I cannot leave *The Dream* behind without mentioning one extremely favourable review. R.B. Marriot in *The Stage* described me as being the finest Puck he had seen since Jean Forbes-Robertson.

My best friend in the company was the ubiquitous Vernon Dobtcheff. He wasn't ubiquitous then, being stuck at the Vic, but now he lives in both Paris and London, sees all the shows on both sides of the Channel and the Atlantic, appears in films in many a language, and sends first-night cards from all corners of the globe. It is said by some that there are four of him who live in the lions in Trafalgar Square. The one I knew had graduated from Cambridge where, though eminently successful, he had decided the academic life was not for him. He was very encouraging to me while I was at the Vic, and he found me Benedict Dewe-Mathews.

Dewy, as I liked to think of him, was a dentist who had the technique to remove my hated gnashers and replace them with something that looked like teeth and with which I could speak more easily. He rescued me from a horrible and unnecessary mess, and in time for me to take over from Albert.

Over the years I sent many friends to him. He was especially delighted to treat the occasional beautiful young actress. Thaw became a patient and we used to love to compare Dewy notes. He was proud of doing what he called 'decent, honest work – you follow?' 'You follow?' became a catchphrase of ours. Dewy would use it when slyly explaining that a small job, say a filling, could be a bit cheaper paid for in cash. 'You follow?' A lover of good wine and expensive cigarettes, he was a devout Roman Catholic. He was the best advertisement for a believer I have ever met – who knows, he might even have made an impression on Mother. One of the high points of his life was when his friend and patient, Basil Hume, was made Cardinal. On the day his elevation was announced the Cardinal Elect was being treated by Dewy. Quentin Stevenson, a family friend and like several of Dewy's sons a former pupil of Hume, was in the waiting room. Dewy could not contain himself and excitedly dragged him into the presence of the great man, who, sitting in the dentist's chair, his mouth frozen, agape and full of Dewy's finest cotton-wool wedges, graciously received his former pupil's congratulations.

I used to love it when the intensity, not to say ferocity, of Dewy's concentration gave way, as he downed tools, to the sweetest twinkly-eyed smile you could ever hope to see. He was one of the dearest men I have ever known, but had it not been for the Butcher of Wimpole Street I never would have met him. Two wrongs may not make a right, but I have sometimes noticed that one wrong does. As Mother used to write, 'Funny isn't it.'

What with *Potter*, *Twelfth Night*, long and arduous dental appointments, my other bits and pieces at the Vic, and rehearsals for *Billy*, I had no time to get home.

Mother wrote to wish me luck for the opening of *Billy*. We'd spoken on the phone, but it was weeks since I had seen her. She wasn't at all well.

9th June 1961

Dear Tom

Second attempt. Your father is fed up with me. Ann puts up with me and I'm fed up with me too.

It's been such a long week this week. It took me all my time to go to the wedding last Saturday morning.

Things came to a head last night. Ann had gone to Beverley with Ken [a shipping clerk, later to become my dear brother-in-law]. There was a film on TV called 'All this and Heaven too.' No. 1. I couldn't see where the title came from. No. 2 Charles Boyer acted bad and I didn't think much to Bette Davis and it was a terrible story about a governess who wormed her way into a posh household and won the affection of the husband (who was unhappily married) and his four children. Bette Davis never got angry once with the four children and not even one child clung to its mother but loved the father and governess best. I'm sure the father wouldn't have looked at the governess. He sent her a present in the middle of the night and put up with his bad wife (she'd four of his bairns). He was perfect. In the end he killed his wife and took poison to avoid the governess being blamed. She was so deep no words were needed to say they loved each other. Just long looks. It was all a big lie and made me raving mad.

Your father said lately I'm mad at everything. He started telling me what a fraud I am and I told him how I hate Longhill and I didn't think much of him getting drunk at the wedding. 'I was just tired' he said.

I don't think I can be bothered writing about the wedding. [Uncle Pat's daughter Cath.] I bought a new hat. Ann and me went in Hammonds. The hat I got I liked the colour, a dull shade of green (match my eyes). The shape is tallish and I said to Ann 'I'll have to get used to the shape.' Ann said 'Why should we have to get used to things.' It's a good subject for a discussion. I can't get used to Longhill.

It was a lovely day for the wedding. We took a bus from here and a taxi from town. Aunt Agnes, Uncle Wilf and Suzanne sat behind us. Aunt Marie and Ivy in front. It was a short service. We all stood. 'They don't bother much with mixed marriages' Aunt Agnes said. [Cath's husband, Alan, wasn't a Catholic.] Uncle Wilf gave me and your father a lift from Hessle Town Hall in their new red warm-inside car.

Uncle Dan was very quiet and I thought he could have cried. Everyone was given sherry and cake and photos were taken. A group of Cath's pals wore flowery hats. Speeches were short. Cath gave Yvonne [Aunt Dorrie's sister-in-law whose husband had died] her wedding flowers for Ken's grave and Yvonne started to cry and I tried very hard to bring her back and said how nice she looked and how nice it was to have a French girl with us and all sorts of things like that. What a life!

The part I liked best was when Dorrie said 'lets find a phone and ring Teresa and find out why she hasn't come to the wedding.' Dorrie cocked her hat on one side so she could use the phone. Poor Teresa had forgotten about the wedding. I told her Dorrie and me were drunk at Hessle Town Hall. (Teresa and Stan are having one of their quarrels and Stan had cleared out.) Poor Teresa just missed seeing Cath and her husband off on their honeymoon. Cath looked splendid and had made all the wedding clothes. My hat got knocked about four times at the reception. When we arrived at

Dorries I took it off. We had tea and sandwiches and all the men went to club to drink beer and they didn't know when it was time to come back and Aunt Ivy got fidgety and I said I couldn't be bothered about them. And about four times during the day I said 'I'm ever so pleased to see everyone' and I was. Uncle Bernard's Marie didn't turn up for some reason. Aunt Ivy had an idea why. I aren't making much of this wedding am I. I don't try.

Always at some time with Aunt Agnes do I feel like I'm doing the wrong thing. If you aren't with her and are following your own route or maybe somebody else's she knows.

Well Tom I promised to write and I have managed something. I am constantly thinking of you and hope you are well and that Billy Liar will be just fine. I am going to buy you a present when I can go for one, maybe next week. My head has been bothering me, my nerves aren't very good. Ring us after the show and reverse the charges. I've had a letter from Aunt Hilda. She wants to hug you.

Love Mam Dad and Ann

BILLY

My pocket diary for 1961 tells me I opened in *Billy Liar* on Monday, 12 June. It also says 'Taxi home 7/-' which I don't remember. I can remember the warmth of the audience as I entered down the hall stairs of the Fisher residence. *Billy Liar* is very funny, and it was wonderful to hear all that laughter. More than you got at the Vic.

BARBARA [Ann Beach]:	Oo, Billy, what a lovely cocktail cabinet!
BILLY:	I made it.
BARBARA:	How clever of you, sweet. I didn't know you could do woodwork.
BILLY:	Oh yes. I made all the furniture. And the garage.

I can remember the great sense of release the text gave me after my recent struggle to make sense of Feste. The rehearsal period was a mixture of delight in having a wonderful part that suited me and fear that I was taking it over from such a powerhouse. Everyone in the cast was very patient with me. Albert was the only one to leave, and though strictly speaking I was better casting for the part, being physically slighter and altogether more of a daydreamer, they must have missed the panache and confidence of his rendition. And the speed of it. By the time he left, Albert was going like an express. When I took over, George A. Cooper, playing Billy's dad, had to get a later train home.

I can remember Lindsay wanting me to do imaginative exercises during rehearsals as Albert had – making up scenes that happened at Billy's place of work (Shadrack & Duxbury, undertakers, not seen in the stage version). And he was very keen that I imagine Billy's fantasy world, Ambrosia. Albert had drawn a map of Ambrosia and stuck it on the inside of the sideboard door, downstage right. I couldn't have cared less about Ambrosia. I didn't need to imagine Billy's fantasy world. It was in every molecule of my body and I had been practising it since childhood. I had only three weeks, and it was a long part with a lot of Peter Barkworth stuff: buttering bread, pouring tea. Technique! Though definitely of the New Wave, I had something of the old school in me. I didn't like doing exercises. I liked to get my words off pat, then practise them. The better I knew them, the more I could make it seem that I was making them up. And my imagination responded to the security I derived from knowing the text. More the way a musician might approach a piece of music – learning it then not thinking about it, just doing it.

During the last week of my rehearsal period I was summoned to a photo session with Albert. I felt very edgy in his presence. I wish I had realized that it was perfectly natural in the circumstances. But I didn't and so I felt edgier still. He had such a shine to him. Alec Guinness got it very well: 'Albert was like an apple, a shiny English apple.' I felt very much in awe of him. It was a feeling that had built up since I had first been linked with him at UCL. He always gave the impression that he didn't give a bugger about anything. I worried about everything. Even more so when I thought I wasn't supposed to. Perhaps my being in awe of him was the reason for our not becoming friends in those days. That didn't happen till the eighties when we worked together. Then we got on great and laughed a lot. And have to this day.

On the Monday after Albert's departure I arrived at the Cambridge Theatre late morning to do a dress rehearsal, and, approaching along Earlham Street, was astonished to see my name in huge neon lettering. It was my name in lights, but everyone else in that play had performed it more than 200 times and knew things that I didn't. I have no recollection of the dress rehearsal, just of Lindsay attempting to give me notes after it, while I clutched my telegram from home. 'Thinking of you.' I found it very difficult to pay attention to Lindsay. I just wanted to get my first performance over with. (Albert's telegram said simply 'Cheers.')

I didn't have much press on my opening night, only Fergus Cashin of the *Daily Sketch*. I can remember what he wrote because it was painted low down on a space alongside the theatre entrance that had previously been decorated in praise of Albert. It said of me: 'The audience hugged him with their chuckles,' and, bless them, they did. After the performance I phoned Mother to say that all had gone well.

There was a speech in *Billy* that really caught me out. It comes after Billy's dad tells him he should be grateful. This is too much for Billy.

BILLY: Grateful for this, grateful for that. Grateful you let
               me go to the grammar school!
BILLY'S DAD: Well, it's a chance we never had!
BILLY: Yes, and don't we bloody well know it! I even had to
               be grateful for winning my own scholarship!'

And here's where I couldn't continue.

And what did you say when I came running home to tell you I'd won it? Don't think I've forgotten! I was eleven years old! I came belting out of those school gates and I ran all the way! Just to tell you! And what did you say? That you'd have to pay for the uniform and I'd have to be grateful!

That was very close to home.

I had been performing at the Cambridge for three or four weeks when Albert arrived with *Luther* at the Phoenix Theatre. They had a different matinée day from us. I went to see *Luther,* and Albert threatened to come and see me. Fortunately I didn't know when he was in, otherwise I might not have been capable of my best stuff. One evening, the week before, the company manager had told me very unwisely and ominously, 'There's somebody very, very important in front tonight.' Who was it? The Recording Angel? I was frozen to the marrow. It turned out to be Harold Hobson of the *Sunday Times*, who obviously didn't know I wasn't myself because he likened me not too unfavourably to Edwige Feullière, whom he thought the bee's knees. Had I not been so adversely affected by the company manager's warning, who knows what might have resulted? 'Skinny newcomer knocks doyenne of French theatre into cocked hat,' for example?

In the event the performance Albert saw of *Billy* was quite relaxed. We had tea afterwards round the corner. He raised only one point of interpretation. 'The grateful speech.' 'Oh yes?' 'You're having a bit of trouble with it. You don't seem to be able to finish it.' 'No, I don't,' I said meekly.

'You're going to have to do something about that,' said Albert, as practical then as he is now. But what I should do he didn't suggest, and what I did do I can't recall.

Shortly after I was installed in *Billy*, Mother was admitted to Castle Hill hospital in Cottingham not far from where Ann now lives. She was diagnosed as having a bad chest and depression. And her depression was treated directly and brutally.

Right alongside Castle Hill is De La Pole mental hospital. In Hull the way to say somebody isn't right in the head is to say they should be in De La Pole. Mother was taken there for electric shock treatment in an attempt to help her depression. She woke up from this treatment in a ward full of lunatics. She told me, when I went to see her one Sunday in Castle Hill, how terrified she had been by the poor creatures. 'Lunatics, Tommy, you know, jibbering, slavering, mad people.' A terrible way to treat her. And there was nothing I or Dad or Ann could do.

What the hospital staff seem not to have realized was that cancer was slowly tightening its grip on her. She also had jaundice, perhaps a tributary of the cancer, so she had two illnesses for which she wasn't given credit.

The hospital treatment must have done something to help her, however, because she was discharged after a few weeks. She didn't feel so depressed and had put on a bit of weight, so we thought that she was on the mend. She never felt strong enough to come to London to see *Billy*, but during the run I went home every other Sunday. It was quite a traipse. I wish now of course that I had gone home every weekend.

Taxi to King's Cross, after the two shows, one at five o'clock, the second at eight. (I have never liked back-to-back shows. I prefer a space in between. 'One show straight after another,' I once complained to my great director friend Michael Elliot. 'Better than both at the same time,' he said.) A curly sandwich at the station. Change trains in the middle of the night at Doncaster, and arrive in Hull around seven a.m. Taxi to Longhill. A long, tedious and tiring journey, but those Sundays were the last times I saw her when she was anything like well. I'd go straight to bed. She would wake me later with a cup of tea, but I would go back to sleep. I can hear her now calling me to get up (like in that essay 'King for a Day'), good-humouredly, but also anxious that bloody London would swallow me up again before she'd had time enough to hear all my news. I have never since felt at once so tired and at the same time that I shouldn't be.

Thankfully the news was pretty terrific. *The Runner* was to be filmed the second I finished in *Billy*. Not only that but the makers of the film of *Billy Liar*, Joe Janni and John Schlesinger, wanted me to be in that, too. I must have acted out the whole of *Billy* for Mother. She loved it, especially when I did Mona Washbourne, Billy's mum:

> He told me that young lad who works in the fruit shop had gassed himself and he knows I go in there every Tuesday. Grammar school! You'd think he'd been to the silly school. He shows me up. He got them suede shoes so he wouldn't have to clean them. He trod in some dog dirt on Tuesday and he walked it round this house for three days. I had to get a knife and scrape it off myself in the finish. Pooh! You could smell it all over the house.

That made her smile like she did when we had sung 'Mary Ellen at the church turned up'. She was so happy at the upturn in my fortunes. Though barely out of drama school, I was going to play the lead in two films. The most brilliant start to a career that could be imagined.

All her worry when I had been so unhappy at university; when I had failed my degree; all her concern about the wisdom of my chosen career – it all seemed groundless now. And the blame she suffered after her interview with the *Hull and Yorkshire Times*, when she said nothing but the truth, yet was thought to have been shooting her mouth off – of that she was now cleared. Her little ray of sunshine, who kept his pigeons in the back yard in Harrow Street and who used to love reading the lesson in assembly, seemed to have the world at his feet.

RUNNER

My first day filming *The Loneliness of the Long Distance Runner* was the longest of my life. February 1962. A Monday. Though I had finished playing Billy Fisher at the Cambridge Theatre on the previous Saturday, *Billy Liar* was about to set off on a tour of the provinces, and I had to play the first two dates: Streatham Hill and Golders Green, a week at each. So my first two weeks' filming were very tiring. But it is the first day that has stuck in my mind.

Around five thirty in the morning a large old Rolls-Royce arrived at Highbury Crescent to pick me up. Woodfall Films had acquired it and its driver cheap. It was roomy inside, but the beige felt hung loosely and had a musty air. Mother wouldn't have liked the smell of it, and neither did I. We set off on a tour of London, picking up actors. It took ages and made me feel sick. To my certain knowledge we picked up James Bolam, Avis Bunnage, Julia Foster and Topsy Jane, but who knows, there may have been one or two more. We eventually arrived at our nondescript destination in Acton, and my new playmates got out of the car. I stayed on board, hoping I would be forgotten about and the film would be made with someone else. I sat there for quite a while feeling nervous and miserable. A young man peered in at me. He was known as a second assistant, I was to learn, and he had a

275

sycophantic manner I didn't like. 'Would you care to join us, sir?'

'What for?' I asked him.

'For your first scene.'

I wasn't prepared for the throng of people gathered around the camera. I had done some work on the film – some shots of me running that were called 'tests', though they were used in the film. That way they didn't have to pay me. But there seemed to be far more people in attendance now. I didn't want anybody to be there, especially me. Then things took a turn for the better. 'I'm Otto. I'm your stand-in. Can I get you a bacon roll and some tea?' He certainly could, and did, and things didn't seem quite so bad. Otto was a gentle, caring soul who made sure I was never without sustenance.

The first shot required that I simply walk past the camera, I didn't have to come out of my shell all day, and in the late afternoon the musty Rolls carted me off, without my playmates, to the cavernous Theatre Royal, Streatham Hill.

Having changed into pyjamas and raincoat, I made my way to the stage. Our set looked lost plonked in the middle of the vast Streatham Hill stage. I just had time for a word with Mona Washbourne and George A. Cooper, Billy's Mam and Dad, before the curtain went up. I was very fond of them. Mona was in the film, later on, but not George, and I missed him. He was steady as rock, and very funny. He had a Saturday-night routine to celebrate his approaching day off that always made me laugh. Just behind the upstage entrance to the Fisher living room, he used to pretend he was having the most enormous shit. This mime (with some noises) involved him lowering his trousers and braces. The art was to get all done and dusted and trousers back up at the very last second before he went on stage. On a good night he could do it – trouser-hoisting, braces-lifting and walking on stage – in one flowing movement. Mona wasn't aware of this game, but I don't think she would have minded because it didn't affect his performance. Mona was a wonderful pro with excellent timing, and a great sense of fun, but on our first night at Streatham Hill she felt obliged to tell George and me off.

Amidst all the excitement and fatigue of this inordinately long day, it never occurred to me to check out the new stage. Billy enters from upstairs, down the hall steps, so I simply climbed up the rostrum, making sure I had my two-shilling piece, and entered on cue. But Streatham Hill's huge rake made the hall stairs of the Fisher residence twice as steep as usual and I fell down them.

Having arisen, I took the morning paper out of the letterbox, fixed my two-shilling piece in place to represent a monocle and entered the living room while reading the headlines. 'Morning, Mater, morning, Pater. Cabinet changes imminent,' I uttered, not failing to notice the enormous area of stage between me and the audience. 'And you'll be bloody imminent if you don't start getting up of a morning,' said George. I raised my eyebrows at this clumsy remark of Pater's, the coin fell from my eye as usual, hit the floor and set off downstage till lost from sight.

The Fisher wall decorations didn't like being in Streatham. The first one to fall was a gong-like thing and it came down with a clang. Not sure what to do with it, and being alone on stage at the time, I put it on a chair. After my day's exertions I was feeling accident-prone and light-headed but I held myself together. The oranges were the next thing.

Billy's girlfriend Barbara (Sheila Steafel by then) loved an orange, much to Billy's consternation when he tries to make up to her. So he takes the offending orange from her grasp and flings it away, crying, 'You and your bloody oranges.' I used to throw it into an armchair, but that night my aim wasn't good and suddenly the orange was speeding downstage towards the distant audience in search of the two-shilling piece.

Unbeknown to me George had been watching all this, which turned out to be the cause of our undoing, for George the rock was beginning to be undermined. Just as we started our scene in Act Two a flying duck, disappointed at no longer being in the West End, relinquished its hold on the wall. His strong, low baritone suddenly and uniquely became high and squeaky: 'She likes her food. She'll tek some keeping by bloody hell' doesn't sound right high and squeaky, so my voice followed his up the scale. This of course made it more difficult for George to bring his back down. The rock had crumbled and me with him.

When the curtain came down on Act Two, Mona approached the two naughty boys. 'What was all that? You were a disgrace. The first night in a new date is very important. You should be ashamed.' It helped us calm down in Act Three.

At the end of my exhausting week I phoned home to report on my exploits, only to learn that Mother was due to return to hospital the following day. Her chest was bad.

Ward 3, Castle Hill Hospital. Tuesday
Dear Tom,   [February 1962]

The flowers arrived yesterday just after I got here. It's a peculiar ward not as nice as 3A. I'm in a small cubicle with another woman who once lived at Longhill and hated it and left after 18 months. The flowers are lovely all colours and nicely scented, everyone keeps admiring them.

  The weather here is cold and its snowing. I hope it doesn't set, Dr Jones will be coming this morning. I feel strange. I hope you are much better and are able to cope with your play and film. My dressing gown has been very useful and is lovely and warm. Your Dad came last night and Ann will be coming tonight. What a trail for them. I won't write anymore but will wait until I feel more like it. Thanks for flowers and look after yourself. Will write again soon.

Lots of love, Mam xxx

Because she was in hospital, Mother didn't write 'Love Mam, Dad and Ann'.

Ward 3, Castle Hill Hospital. Sunday
Dear Tom,   [February 1962]

I've been wondering should I write. I can't write and never could. I don't seem to settle here. It's a square ward in pale yellow and blue walls and a large TV. I'm always in a lousy humour. There's five in this ward. One youngish woman who knits, the simplest things make her laugh. She likes Cheyenne and all those TV stars. Her friend is similar but reads more than knits. There's another woman so rough looking and within minutes she was telling us about her second husband who likes her being in hospital and won't come and see her. He drinks and likes a night out. Hell, I nearly found myself feeling interested. Then there's the one who came in with me. She likes to shout out quickly now and again, chuntering at people, it makes me laugh.

Ann and your Dad's been today. Your father always starts yawning, I told him. I suppose he's fed up and so am I. Ann does very well for us. Family – I haven't seen one this week. Our George has seen me once since last June. My God could I tell him a thing or two and Phyl. Gran will come, Aunt Al and Barbara, I reckon.

I was sorry if you tried to ring me, we had the phone for about 5 minutes and no one told me you rang. It's a funny ward, all little wards. The phones will be here on Wednesday, if you ring me make it after 4 o'clock. Ann said you wasn't liking the film and you wasn't keen on the production. Maybe one day you will be a producer. I'm sure you will do your best. You are clever and would like to have a say in things.

Maybe you can write to me on one of your sit down rests and tell about the cast and work, you know I would like to know the lot. I suppose really I'm a nosey bugger.

The grounds at Castle Hill are supposed to be lovely but I can't get the feeling yet. Trees I don't like in winter, they are I think ugly. I've been trying to like winter trees but can't. The copper beech tree outside Ward 3A when I was here before was really a beautiful tree, lovely red colour and the sensitive branches would dance up and down and touch the ground. And I thought before I go home I will cross over to the tree and touch it. I kept on thinking I would, but the day I went home it was raining like hell and I never went near enough to touch it. Bloody soft isn't it.

Your flowers were nice but I lost some in the week. I found out they had been moved to a ward the lord Mayor was visiting. I was mad. I can't get about and one feels helpless. I liked the sister in the other ward, she was strict and very clean – I liked it better than this ward. It's a bit slip shod here and the food isn't very good.

Well Tom I hope this letter doesn't bore you. One woman's knitting, one woman reading, two watching telly and me writing to Tom. I'll have to write more and maybe I'll relax myself. I still don't like winter trees. I would sooner watch the buses and cars moving by, or a chimney on fire and someone trying to put it out, or a man gardening. I will write again. As usual forgive bad writing and grammar.

Lots of Love. Mam xxxx

It was distressing enough for her to be in hospital once more, but after she had been there for two or three weeks a dreadful thing happened. Ann came to see her at visiting time without Dad. They sometimes took turns at visiting because Castle Hill was a long journey from Longhill Estate. To Ann's horror she saw that Mother's bed was empty. 'Where's my mother?' she demanded of the ward sister. 'I'm sorry, we couldn't get hold of you to let you know, but while she was having her chest X-rayed she tried to turn herself over and her leg broke. It was nothing we did to her, her leg just snapped under her own weight. She's been moved to the infirmary.'

We were filming just off the A3 at a disused building, Ruxley Towers, which served as the Borstal in the film, when Mother's leg broke. It's a white tower I still see atop some trees near Esher, on the left driving into London. Dad somehow managed to phone me on the set, in what was meant to be the Borstal canteen. I was utterly bemused by this latest development and wanted to go and see her. My old stand-in Otto recently assured me that the producers of the film wouldn't allow me any time off, and I was very upset about it. But neither they nor I knew she was dying. I was filming six days a week and maybe it wasn't possible to get trains to Hull and back on a Sunday. I can't say for sure.

She was moved to the broken limb department of the Hull Royal Infirmary. Pointlessly, as it turned out, for there was no way her leg would ever mend; but at least it was easier for Ann and Dad to get to see her. I wrote to her, and she wrote to me. I think these last four letters are heroic – she even managed a title. Perhaps the act of writing made her feel better. Or was it simply that she wanted to keep the worst from me? Ann and Dad were not so spared. She didn't shield them from her rage and her bitterness. 'I would like to see somebody, just one, in this bloody place who is worse off than me. But there isn't anybody.' It was only Ann and Dad whose visits really counted. They were in this with her. They had to share it with her. I had gone away. 'It was as though it was our privilege,' Ann told me. 'If we don't go,' she said to Dad, 'Mother hasn't got anybody she can row at.'

Dear Tom,

Houghton Ward, Royal Infirmary. Sunday [March 1962]

SCARLET QUILL

Thought I would try and write a few lines. It's Sunday and the weather is brighter. Visitors come 2.30–3.30. I hope you're well. Don't worry too much about Albert Finney coming to see you work. [Albert came to see Tony Richardson, not me. It made me edgy to see him on the set, and I kept away from him.] He may be a little jealous of you. He hasn't had three years at UCL.

We're all a lot of sufferers here. There's some people on this earth don't know they're bloody born. I don't know. I'm still as wheezy as hell and hope my Castle Hill doctor will be calling soon. My leg has been made comfortable for a while I hope. I haven't much appetite.

Thanks for the photos. I like having them. You said I'm a poet, well I suppose I am a bit that way but it's very hard and shouldn't be and I'm lazy. Do you remember all them story letters? Hell. I do know now things left out can be used other times. I've always been interested in writing. Sunday was always a day I wanted to write. I've got all my little poems I used to try and write in Harrow Street.

> I know a place near Arundel
> With crossroads and a pub perched high
> Its never dowley there   I wish we were there
> you and I

A road nearby leads to a beach
its private and a Lord lived there
I wish we were there
   You and I

   (Then surprise)
   I'm telling a lie   I've never been
   But I heard someone say perched high.
   Never mind it doesn't matter
   Cos we can't go there
      You and I

Good job I don't get the urge now. The last time I did was when you came home for Christmas with all the presents but I let it go and that was it. Its just something that makes a moment stay and you don't forget that time that's all.

Your father is still having trouble with his knee. I think he's done too much trailing about on it. All my fault we went to bloody Longhill.

Ann does well at home fitting in bits of cleaning up and cooking. She still goes out with Ken. Ann is 24 soon. Whether she'll marry him or not she doesn't say. I've got all your newspaper cuttings stuck in a scrap book. They are much tidier now. I hope you like it.

There's a piano three or four yards away from me. I really do like playing a piano and never once have gone off it. Well Tom all for now I think.

                         Love Mam

I'm glad I told her she was a poet. The idea of poetry meant so much to her. Poetry was the best part of life. Imagination, self-expression, excitement, fun. It was the happiness she felt when she wrote something that seemed true and to the point. 'They pick me out and I'm glued,' 'I'm your father's poetry,' 'Why do you act mean when you're not?' And, summing up her life in a sentence, 'I suppose my luck is You, Ann and Dad and more so if I could really write.'

You could, Ma, you could.

Houghton Ward, Royal Infirmary. Wednesday
Dear Tom   [March 1962]

Thanks for letter, write soon and often. I wish you could have got
home for a few hours. You seem to be enjoying filming.

It amuses me how you say Tony Richardson gets carried away. It
is so possible to get carried away and things get left out. They do
with me I'm sure. Well Tom I don't want to talk about me and
everything.

The weather is sunny. This is a very large ward. I get fed up. Its
visiting day. We've no TV. I don't think I'm bothered. I daren't ask
how long I've to be in. My leg is sort of strung up by hell.

Don't forget to send some photos will you.

Yesterday my visitors were Alice, Barbara, Dorrie, and Aunt
Jane. I like best your Dad and Ann to come. Granny fell a few
weeks ago and can't walk much. Don't I give your Dad and Ann a
lot of inconvenience? I aren't writing a very thoughtful letter today
but will sometime.

I can hear some children at play somewhere. It is Mill Street
Junior Catholic School and I can see the school outside the window.
Seems to ring a bell! But I aren't getting too thoughtful. I can soon
get going about things you know.

Well Tom I hope you are keeping well. (Temperature and tablet
time.)

I can imagine you liking the antics of the Borstal Boys. I can
imagine Sir Michael Redgrave in the film. His nervousness could
help him (maybe).

Well Tom, I won't write anymore now. Write soon and often. It
is very lonely here among such a lot of strangers. Excuse writing I
get worse.

Lots of love

Mam xxxx

I *was* enjoying filming by now. I had got used to the process, and my ego
enjoyed being at the centre of activities. Tony Richardson made it as
easy for me as possible. I scarcely remember a shot ever lasting more

than one or two takes. He gave me the impression that he was letting me do whatever I wanted, even sometimes asking me to *say* whatever I wanted. All very '*cinéma vérité*', and not so technically demanding as filming usually would have been before the New Wave. Tony made me feel very much the man of the moment. And I liked that. Though some nights I would hold one of Mother's sad little letters from hospital close to my chest and cry myself to sleep.

Houghton Ward, Royal Infirmary. Wednesday
Dear Tom   [March 1962]

Thanks for wonderful photos. They are all marvellous. I like the one with Topsy Jane. The one where you're weighing up the detective you look like Uncle George. They are all beautiful.

We've just had the doctor round but they don't say much to one. I get so fed up.

Yesterday visiting day I had Aunt Al, Aunt Marie and Peggy who was with me in Castle Hill. She looked fairly well. I found out sick as I felt I'm the one who does the entertaining. Peggy and me were talking about things that went on in Castle Hill. I've often noticed that if I'm not on entertaining terms things are dead. Funny isn't it.

Well Tom, I hope the film is going well. It certainly looks to me as if its going to be good. Your hair Tom is certainly like mine, unruly, especially now.

I've just been having a sleep. Sometimes its hard to realise I am here in this position. I'm hoping to see Ann and Dad tonight for half an hour. It isn't long is it.

Well Tom, I just wanted to let you know how much I liked the photos. The three you're on your own are smashing. You'll be getting all the girls after you.

Well cheerio for now   love   Mam xxx

Eventually shooting was finished and I went to see her in the broken limb department of the Hull Royal Infirmary.

The change in her was heart-rending. She was still there. Mother. My mother. Still so sweet. But terribly pathetic. They had taken her teeth out. She was sitting up on the bed with her broken leg lying impotently between two splints, its shin bone grotesquely twisted. I tried not to look at it. She had been proud of her legs. Mother and me the same: the top half a bit scrawny but a good pair of legs.

And she was so happy to see me. She was holding her hand over her toothless mouth, but her eyes were shining with love. That was the unbearable part. And I sobbed and sobbed.

I think those sobs, so utterly out of my control, were my goodbye to her.

'It's all right, it's all right. Don't worry. It's all right.' And she took my hand, and not for the first time she comforted me.

As I was leaving, a young nurse – with massive insensitivity, I thought – asked me to sign a photograph of me she had somehow acquired. I was so upset that I could barely see it. Mother watched with that oh-so-modest pride of hers, and I left her.

Dad saw me off at Paragon Station. He told me that Mother had no hope of recovery. This time he wept, and we held on to one another.

'Dad, if there's nothing they can do for her why doesn't she come home with you? I can give you the money while you're off work. I'm starting another film straight away. They have to pay me for this one. You'll just have to try and kid her about why she's coming home. Even if you can't, she'll be much better off with you. Ask them at work if you can have the time off. You don't have to worry about the money.'

On the train to London I travelled first class. Not so much because I could now afford to, but because I reckoned that way fewer people would see my tears.

Houghton Ward, Royal Infirmary. Friday morning.

Dear Tom   [April 1962]

Thanks for coming to see me. I hope you was able to sleep on the train. Its such a long journey in one day. I like the nightdress.

Ann and your Dad came last night. I had a better night. The night before my wheezing was horrible and kept me awake. The weather here looks brighter outside and I have a window near me, sometimes its awful warm in here. I haven't started my crossword yet and I've nearly finished my cardigan. Everything here is just the same.

I've been reading in the paper about Dora Bryan maybe winning an Oscar for her part in Taste of Honey (Tony Richardson director). The Daily Express are printing A Kind of Loving next week because they are so taken up with the story. I liked that book.

Well Tom, I'm wondering what you are doing today, meeting Agents, Accountants and directors etc. I bet sometimes you get fed up with them, but it is your job. I hope you are looking after yourself. I only hope you are O.K.

Ann still going out with Ken but she's in no hurry. Ann is 24 next month.

I asked that young nurse Diane if the autograph was alright and she said yes but her young man was a bit put out about it. Hell! Well Tom this is only a short letter hoping you arrived back safe and are well. Your Dad is not all that good and no wonder. I shall write again later on.

So lots of love

Mam xxxx

END

When thou dost ask me blessing I'll kneel down
And ask of thee forgiveness.

King Lear

Dad got the time off work and brought her home. She had a bed down-stairs in the living room.

It wasn't easy to kid her about what was happening. 'I'm no fool,' she used to write. Mother knew it was a trial for her brothers and sisters to visit her in her wretched condition. Uncle George, at a loss for something to say, tried 'By hell, I wish I was in that bed. It looks really comfortable.' Mother turned away from him. The Polish doctor called in unexpectedly one night, because he happened to have been called out close by. 'He was a lovely man,' Ann told me. 'As I saw him out he apologized for dropping in. He told me he was supposed to come the next day, but he found it so distressing to see Mother that he'd welcomed the chance to get his visit over and done with. "It's those eyes, those eyes. They know exactly what is happening, and I'm sorry, Ann, but it really disturbs me."'

Mother's reference, in her very last letter, to my having to meet 'Agents, Accountants and directors', fills me with sadness and, to this day, guilt. I used to make one or other the excuse for leaving her and going back to London. I would go to Hull most weekends, once I had finished my next job, the film version of *Private Potter*. We did some filming in Wales and I bought her a red woollen Welsh blanket, nice and colourful. I've still got it.

I was there when she died. I had missed the previous weekend's visit, when, Dad told me, she had been childlike and as lively as anything. But I had stayed away, lured by the Establishment, Peter Cook's nightclub. It was my hang-out. I was becoming more and more famous in good old London town. As Mother wrote, 'You'll be getting all the girls after you.' Those Slade girls wouldn't have been so indifferent now.

When I got to Duddon Grove I went in the back way and Dad was washing up. 'Your mother's bad. She had some halibut not so long since. She really enjoyed it. She was fine and then all of a sudden she just seemed to – I don't know – she just seemed to go.' He never forgot that last meal he had cooked for her.

Mother's bed was in the sitting room, and I went in to see her. She was propped up, with a blue cardigan over the pale nightie I had bought her. Her head was leaning slightly to one side, and she didn't move.

'It's Tommy, Ma. I've come to see you. Come to see you, Ma.'

But I got no response.

Dad looked at her sadly. 'What a shame you couldn't come last weekend, she was as lively as anything.'

She did wake up occasionally during the weekend, but she was never aware of my presence. Dad made her some tea at one point and put it beside her bed. 'Bread, bread,' she called it and he gave her a sip. I don't know whether it was on account of the guilt I felt about the previous weekend, but I thought her last hours were for him, and for Ann. I would have loved her to come to and speak. I would have liked her to see me one last time, but I felt she wouldn't. I had had my chance and spurned it.

At one time she called out to Dad, but not in agony. 'Tom, Tom.' I knew she meant Dad, not me. I was Tommy at home, only Tom in her letters, and I stayed where I was, on the sofa. He went over to her and sat on her bed. 'Yes, love?'

She spoke carefully, formally, as though it was something she had thought through. 'I'm going to die, Tom. You've been very good to me, Tom. Very good. Thank you, Tom. I'm going to die. I don't blame our Tommy. Thank you, Tom.'

She stopped breathing twenty-four hours later. She was propped up in her bed and it wasn't for several seconds that we could be sure that

that particular breath had been her last. When we were sure there would be no more breaths, the three of us, Dad, Ann and me, embraced in what was no longer a quartet but a trio, without speaking. Then Dad went over to Mother's bed, gently laid her body down, and finally closed her scarcely open eyes.

'No more, no more,' he said. I thought he meant no more suffering, not no more Annie Eliza. But he may have meant both.

DAD

A year or so after Mother's death Dad and I went to the Odsal Stadium, Bradford, on a coach trip organized by the Subway Street Club to see Hull play Oldham for the Rugby League Championship Play-off. Odsal I knew to be an awkward ground from which to get a good view when it was full. It was important to get there in good time. Our coach pulled in for refreshment, and its occupants, once settled in the bar, took some shifting. Second pints were bought, and by the time we got back on board I was, to quote Mother, 'raving mad'. Dad, watching me, and two pints to the good, smiled sweetly at my anger. 'Your mother will never be gone while you're here.' The thought seemed to be making him happy.

We always had our ritual phone call on her birthday, 2 November. 'I don't have to tell you what day it is, do I, Tom?' 'No, Dad, you don't.' And he never needed encouragement to tell of the last meal he gave her. 'Halibut. That was the last meal your dear mother had. With parsley sauce. Beautiful.'

He became desperately reliant on Ann. When she was first married he would go and see them every night of the week and reminisce about his perfect marriage. Ann's husband, Ken, had to ask him if he would mind not coming round every night – just some nights, please. Ann said he looked so disconsolate as he trudged home. 'I felt awful. But imagine how he'd have felt if Grandma Quest had come round every night.'

He eventually had a nervous breakdown. That's when he burnt Mother's old handbag, full of photos and letters. I was working, so missed the full force of it, but when I finally saw him his hair had gone grey and there was a disturbing light in his eye. I told Ann I could see this light and could imagine how he had been. 'I was there,' was all she needed to say.

He recovered and was able to moderate his visits, and he had Uncle Pat and Uncle Bernard who loved him and saw him regularly, and when Ann had her sons Peter and John he got a lot of pleasure from them. He used to like to lecture Ann on the bringing up of children, a subject he felt well versed in.

One nice thing that happened after Mother's death was that Uncle Pat got Dad back into the fold. He never told me about it, but one night I dropped Uncle Pat off in Hessle before running Dad home. 'See you Sunday morning, Tom,' said Uncle Pat. 'We'll have a pint after Mass.' I was glad to hear this, thinking it would be good for Dad, but he looked very sheepish in front of me. As though I had caught him doing something soft or, worse still, going behind Mother's back. 'Mebbe, mebbe,' he said shiftily.

Never, ever, could he resist checking up on my doings. Decades after my brilliance as a toddler, he found a friend who read the *Sunday Times*, so he would be shown the theatre reviews – mine and my contemporaries' (even worse). 'That so and so's had a good write-up, I see.' Christ, I used to think, and this is the man who scarcely knew what a theatre was. 'The only acting you'll ever do is acting the bloody goat.' 'I wish you'd mind your own business, Dad,' I would say to myself, though I didn't voice it.

When he came to London to see *The Norman Conquests*, in the seventies, my friend Mark Kingston told me that Dad had been slyly sounding him out about my golfing prowess. 'Has he really got a handicap?' he enquired. Mark assured him I had. And I hope he knocked a couple of strokes off it for good measure.

Were Dad here now, he would say to Ann, 'You know our Tom's got himself one of them computers. He's taught himself how to work it. Whatever he's wanted to do, our Tom, he did it.'

We always had our love of sport to help keep us close. There were several outings to make up for the Hull v. Wigan débâcle. Hull managed to beat Oldham, in spite of our late arrival. Our finest sporting hour was in 1966 at Stamford Bridge in the FA Cup when Hull City came from two down to draw with Chelsea, courtesy of two beautifully taken goals from our beloved Waggy, Ken Wagstaff. The magic of the occasion was intensified by the presence just behind us of the incomparable Len Hutton and his son Richard, who I had met with the Yorkshire side in Burbank, California, of all places. We were thus able to wave cheerily, one Yorkshire father and son duo to another, and Dad's chest swelled with pride.

When he came to see me in London I used to take him to restaurants, but he was never comfortable in them. He would hang on to his knife and fork for dear life throughout the meal, even when sipping his beer. He would lean on his elbow in mid-chew, his knife held aloft. I never said 'Put that bloody knife down, Dad,' but I did try and make him realize it would be better on his plate. 'I use my hands such a lot, Dad. That's why I put my knife and fork down when I'm having a meal. On the plate. Out of harm's way.' 'He just looked at me,' to quote Mother, 'and no wonder.' The penny never dropped, and his knife and fork stayed in the air. I can now scarcely believe that his table manners should have bothered me. The other side of that particular coin was that I felt for him when he was self-conscious in front of people he thought were his betters. He would try to speak more correctly than was natural for him. Aitches would fly all over the place and 'ing's would crop up when only 'in's were required. Then I would think to myself, 'You shouldn't have to bother, Dad, they're not better than you. They may not be as good as you.'

I was always relieved when he went back to Hull after his London trips. I felt unburdened, though he did leave the smell of his tobacco behind for a day or so. He had a little job as a storekeeper, but no longer on Fish Dock. (The last time I took him for a drive down Hessle Road he was quietly amazed. 'Antique shops!' He shook his head. 'Who would have imagined it, antique shops on Hessle Road.') 'I've got to get back,' he liked to joke. 'Got to keep the wheels of industry turning.' But as I saw him off at King's Cross we would smile and embrace, and my eyes would always moisten. 'It's been lovely spending time with you, Tom. Lovely.' And off he'd hobble.

He liked to be philosophical about life whenever possible. Of his aches and pains he would say, 'There's plenty in Division Road cemetery wish they had 'em.' But the old Dad, the one who had been so keen on my school reports, took a curtain call shortly before he died, aged seventy-five. He had a protracted fit, a brainstorm. Ann as usual was there and saw his rage. Again I just saw what was left of it, what was in his eyes still. Before I saw Dad I spoke with the hospital doctor. He seemed relieved I wasn't expecting a cure. 'We're not too busy, so we'll sedate him as little as possible. We might want him to go quietly, but he may not want to.'

'Who's this come to see you?' Ann asked Dad as I appeared in the ward before him. He took his time before committing himself, carefully weighing me up. Then he got it. 'It's Tom ... jockey Tom,' and the three of us laughed. Was that from when I used to ride on his boot? He explained to me that he had been feeling as though he had a pigeon on his shoulder. 'An eagle, more like,' said Ann after we had left him.

When I went to see him the following day he was more himself, though he looked baleful and self-absorbed. To help pass the time I told him what I was up to, though I couldn't tell whether he understood me. I told him that the film of *The Dresser* which I had made with Albert was being well received in America.

No reaction.

'It's been chosen for the Royal Command Performance.'

No reaction.

'I'll be working that night in Manchester. Columbia Pictures are going to ask the Royal Exchange Theatre if they'll release me for the night.'

No reaction.

'I don't mind either way. After all, the theatre has to come first.'

No reaction.

'Mind you, it would be nice to be presented to the Queen.'

'Will Albert be there?' he suddenly asked.

He had the previous day been out of his mind, and could still have been, for all I knew. I had no way of telling whether he realized what *The Dresser* was, who the Queen was, what America was. I had only been talking to fill the silence. But he had got the gist. He knew that something he thought advantageous was happening, that I might miss it, and that Albert, whom he took to be my rival, might put one over on me. That I might, in fact, come second out of two. Just as bad as in the fourth form when I was fourth out of thirty. You wicked old sod, I thought.

People used to ask me if I wanted to be a father. 'A father!' I'd say. 'I haven't got over being a son yet.'

He survived for twenty-odd years after Mother's death, but his life never quite made sense to him without her. A day or so before he died, sitting up in his hospital bed, he sang a little ditty I had never heard before:

> See you in my dreams tonight dear,
> See you in my dreams.
> You are my inspiration
> See you in my dreams.